河合塾 SERIES

採点基準

要点解説

新英語長文問題集
New Approach 4

700-800 words

読解のカギは単語力

瓜生 豊・早﨑スザンヌ・矢次隆之　共著

問題編

Vocabulary Building

Summary

Exercise

河合出版

河合塾
SERIES

採点基準
要点解説
語句リスト

新英語長文問題集

New Approach

4

700-800 words

読解のカギは単語力

瓜生 豊・早﨑スザンヌ・矢次隆之　共著

問題編

Vocabulary
Building
Summary
Exercise

河合出版

もくじ

本書の使い方

読解問題について

各回で目標解答時間を設定しているので，時間も意識しつつ取り組んでください。また，配点は全問題共通で50点満点としています。全設問を解き終わった後は，解答・解説編の**【解答】**と**【配点と採点基準】**を参照して，答え合わせ・採点をしてみてください。

《Vocabulary Building Exercise》について

空欄を含む例文と【　】内の英語で記された単語の意味を参照して，空欄に入る適切な単語を ***Ans.*** 内から選んで書く，計10問の穴埋め式の単語問題です。例文の文意と英英辞書をイメージして書かれた【　】内の意味を理解したうえで，適切な単語を選ぶ問題なので，語彙力・読解力ともに鍛えることができます。

《Summary》について

問題英文の要約文内にある１空欄を埋めるのに適切な単語を ***Ans.*** から選んで書く，計６問の穴埋め式の単語問題です。問題英文全体の趣旨を理解する，要約文でそれがどうまとめられているかを読み解く，その上で適切な単語を選ぶ，という工程を踏む必要があるので，しっかり時間をかけて取り組むことで読解力・語彙力の両方を鍛えることができます。

第1問 『相手の目を見て説得するのはよいことではない』

目標解答時間：35分　配点：50点

次の英文を読み，設問に答えなさい。

Most of us think that when we want to make a point, we should look the other person in the eye. Spouses, bosses, car salespeople, and politicians all use a direct gaze when they are trying to convince an audience of many or one that their position is the most (a) valid. Now it turns out that they should probably cast their glance in a different direction.

Julia Minson, a psychologist and assistant professor at Harvard's Kennedy School of Government who studies group decision making and negotiations, and her longtime collaborator, Frances Chen, a psychologist and assistant professor at the University of British Columbia, realized that no one had studied this piece of conventional wisdom — that staring at someone will make the person more likely to see your point. Until now, most of the academic work has focused on what Minson calls "lovey-dovey contexts," like mothers and babies gazing at each other (which strengthens their bond) and (b) potential mates meeting one another's gaze (also improving their connection). But when it comes to persuasion, academics have really only looked at interactions from the perspective of speakers, who almost always feel they are getting their point across if they are making eye contact.

In a new paper just published in the journal *Psychological Science*, Minson and Chen tested the (c) proposition that eye contact can win over people who disagree with the speaker. In two different studies (conducted by Chen at the University of Freiburg), their data show that people respond more favorably to opposing arguments when the speaker looks at an angle to the recipient or focuses his eyes on his counterpart's mouth instead of his eyes.

Minson says that she and Chen weren't totally surprised by their results. Those who study animal behavior have proved that many species, like dogs, control others by staring them down and then attacking. "(1) <u>The intuition that drove our research was that when someone disagrees with you and they look you in the eye in a prolonged, direct manner, it gives you the feeling of someone trying to dominate you</u>," says Minson. "Our reaction may be (d) <u>instinctive</u>."

To test their theory, Minson and Chen ran two studies. In the first one, they observed 20 students watching videos of people making arguments about controversial subjects like the percentage of women hired, assisted suicide, and a nuclear power phase-out. They tested various scenarios, including instances where the students had a tendency to agree with the speaker or to disagree. Through eye tracking, they measured whether the students were looking at the speakers in the eye. In some of the videos the speakers stared directly at the camera. In others, they gazed out at a 45-degree angle. What Minson and Chen found: In cases where the students disagreed with the speakers' positions at the (e) <u>outset</u>, direct eye contact made them less likely to change their minds. "In cases where participants made more eye contact, they were less persuaded," says Minson.

In a second study, they relied on a bigger sample of 42 students who watched eight videos made by four students who gazed straight at the camera, with their heads centered against a white background. Again the speakers discussed controversial subjects like hiring more women and farming practices. All of the listeners disagreed with the speakers' opinions. The professors directed them either to look directly at the speakers' eyes or at their mouths. Again Minson and Chen found that those who looked at the speakers' eyes, rather than their mouths, were less likely to change their opinions.

What does this mean for those of us who want to make a point? Minson observes that most people don't make consistent eye contact. "Your eyes naturally go back and forth between the eyes and the mouth," she notes. "There's also some time when your eyes just wander around." Don't force yourself to look into the other person's eyes more than you naturally would, she advises.

I had one big question about the study: Is a video interaction really the same as in-person communication? No, says Minson. (2) When people are face-to-face, there are lots of other things going on, like body language where a speaker might lean in or respond in other ways to an attractive or unattractive recipient. At least the video interaction isolates eye contact.

Next time I want to make a point, I think I'll let my eyes wander.

問1．次のA～Dの質問に対する答えとして最も適切なものを，後の①～④からそれぞれ1つずつ選びなさい。

A　How is the research of Julia Minson and Frances Chen different from previous research?

① It focused on the point of view of the listener.

② It focused on the mouths of listeners.

③ It studied "lovey-dovey contexts".

④ It focused on the speakers' feelings of success or failure.

B　According to the second study, which listeners were more likely to have their opinions changed by the speakers?

① listeners who stared directly into the speakers' eyes

② listeners who switched between the speakers' eyes and mouth

③ listeners who could not see the speakers at all

④ listeners who stared solely at the speakers' mouth

C According to Minson, what was one reason to use video rather than a live interaction?

① Using video meant that listeners and speakers could be in different places.

② Using video allowed the research study to focus on eye contact.

③ Using video allowed the researchers to include various forms of body language.

④ Using video prevented listeners from being attacked by the speakers.

D Which statement is true according to the passage?

① To be convincing it is important to maintain constant eye contact.

② Most people's eyes naturally move from place to place.

③ Speakers feel less convincing when they are making eye contact.

④ People in emotional situations respond similarly to eye contact.

問２． 下線部(a)〜(e)に最も意味が近いものを，次の①〜④からそれぞれ１つずつ選びなさい。

	①	②	③	④
(a)	fun	violent	friendly	correct
(b)	possible	concerned	tragic	extended
(c)	process	idea	emotion	passion
(d)	emotional	intentional	natural	rational
(e)	text	conclusion	plot	beginning

問３． 下線部(1)を日本語に訳しなさい。

問４． 下線部(2)を日本語に訳しなさい。

《 Vocabulary Building Exercise 》

次の例文中の空欄に入るものとして最も適切な単語を，後の ***Ans.*** から１つずつ選んで書きなさい。なお，【　】内は各空欄に入る適切な単語の意味を英語で説明したものです。

1. You, or your [　　　], must be at least 60 to participate.
【a husband or wife】

2. Each party had its own quite [　　　] reasons for its policies.
【based on what is logical or true】

3. Rents are agreed by [　　　].
【formal discussion between people who are trying to reach an agreement】

4. We are aware of the [　　　] problems and have taken every precaution.
【that can develop into something or be developed in the future】

5. Trust that develops through social [　　　] between individuals can often be very important.
【the way that people communicate with each other】

6. I'd like to put a business [　　　] to you.
【an idea or a plan of action that is suggested】

7. To make a decision quickly, people have to rely on their [　　　].
【the ability to know something by using your feelings rather than considering the facts】

8. Horses have a well-developed [ ] for fear.
【a natural quality that makes people and animals tend to behave in a particular way using the abilities that they were born with】

9. From the [ ] he had put his trust in me, the son of his old friend.
【the beginning of something】

10. One weakness of the research was that interviewers were not [ ] in the way they asked questions.
【always behaving in the same way, or having the same opinions or standards】

Ans.

negotiation	intuition	valid	instinct	potential
outset	spouse	proposition	consistent	interaction

《 Summary 》

次の英文は問題英文の要約である。空欄(a)~(f)に入るものとして最も適切な単語を後の ***Ans.*** から1つずつ選んで書きなさい。

It is commonly believed that we should look someone in the eye when we want to make a point. However, recent studies have shown that this is not actually effective. Instead, we should look in a different direction if we really want to [(a)] someone that we are correct about something. Until now, researchers tended to focus on how direct gazes strengthened intimate bonds. Otherwise, they studied whether speakers felt like they were able to persuade others. But nobody had studied how the listeners felt. A new paper has tested the [(b)] that making direct eye [(c)] is effective in changing the minds of people that disagree with you. The study used video [(d)] to avoid the influence of other factors like body language. It found that people [(e)] more favorably if the speaker looks down at the mouth of his [(f)] instead of looking directly into his eyes. (149 words)

Ans.

respond	request	convince	interaction
contact	proposition	persist	opposite
permission	convey	counterpart	interference

第2問 『英国で第二次世界大戦中に起こったペットの大量殺処分』

目標解答時間：40分　配点：50点

次の英文を読み，設問に答えなさい。

In early September 1939, the citizens of London set about killing their pets. During the first four days of World War Ⅱ, over 400,000 dogs and cats — some 26 percent of London's pets — were put to death, a number six times greater than the number of civilian deaths in the UK from bombing during the entire war. It was a calm and orderly *massacre. One animal shelter had a line stretching almost a kilometer long with people waiting to turn their animals over to be *euthanized. Animal welfare societies ran out of *chloroform, and shelters ran out of burial grounds. One local hospital offered a field, where half a million pets' bodies were buried.

None of (1) <u>this</u> was done out of any real necessity. Food supplies were not yet scarce. The German **blitzkrieg* had not yet started, and wouldn't fully begin until September of the following year. (2) <u>Nor did the British government issue instructions telling its citizens to kill their pets for the greater good of *the Empire. Rather, it was a mass action that arose, apparently voluntarily, by a population terrified by the new reality of war.</u>

Almost immediately, people realized what a mistake they had made. By November, the *Times* newspaper was complaining that "there is daily evidence that large numbers of pet dogs are still being destroyed (3) <u>for no better reason than that it is inconvenient to keep them alive</u>." The BBC's Christopher Stone likewise argued against the massacre on his popular radio program that same month, saying that "to destroy a faithful friend when there is no need to do so, is yet another way of letting the war creep into your home." By then, the mass killing of pets had lessened, and many of the animals that survived those first four days would last through the war. But the damage had already been done.

The killings had a great deal to do with the changing relationship of humans to dogs and cats in the early 20th century. Like pigs, chickens, and cattle, humans learned to keep dogs and cats around because they were useful to us: we kept dogs for security and hunting, and cats for *pest control. Their status as companion animals was initially just a side benefit, but with urbanization that began to change: people living in cities had less and less need for their dogs and cats to do useful jobs about the house, but we kept them around anyway. No longer useful in the traditional sense, dogs and cats became simply part of the family, and (4) <u>we started to ask not what pets could do for us, but what we could do for them</u>.

These attitudes were all well and good in peacetime, but during World War I a significant portion of the British population felt uneasy about the thought of pets getting better treatment than some humans. The *Times* ran images from a London cat show in 1916, showing pets on silk pillows, noting that "several were fat." This comment no doubt was made because it was a time when many were going hungry, and the widespread opinion seemed to be that pets were luxury items competing with human beings for food.

In many ways, it was the memory of World War I that determined the fate of animals in World War Ⅱ. Many remembered starving cats and dogs wandering the streets of London. However, despite the attention it received at the time, the pet massacre has since been all but (5) <u>written out of</u> British history. (6) <u>A researcher who asked the Royal Society for the Prevention of Cruelty to Animals (RSPCA) for information about the killings</u>, was told that "there is no evidence in our surviving records of any 'massacre' of pets at the start of World War Ⅱ," despite the fact that the RSPCA's magazine *Animal World* had reported in October 1939 that "the work of destroying animals continued, day and night, during the first week of the war."

It makes sense, of course, that Londoners would not want to remember such an unhappy chapter in their history, one (7) <u>(a / deep-rooted / reveals / tendency / that)</u> toward needless panic. The British pride themselves to this day on their self-control in the face of war, a legacy captured in the phrase: "Keep Calm and Carry On." This odd but significant moment of panic weakens this self-image, suggesting the terror and lack of reason beneath *"the stiff upper lip."

This article was originally published in the Los Angeles Review of Books (www.lareviewofbooks.org).

注）massacre: 大量虐殺　euthanize: 安楽死させる
chloroform: クロロホルム　*blitzkrieg*: 電撃戦（大空爆）
the Empire: 大英帝国　pest control: 有害生物駆除
"the stiff upper lip": 我慢強さ

問1. 下線部(1)は何を指しているか。30〜40字の日本語で記述しなさい。

問2. 下線部(2)を日本語に訳しなさい。

問3. 下線部(3)の意味に最も近いものを，次の①〜④から1つ選びなさい。

① only because the British government told their owners to kill them

② only because their owners think it is troublesome to keep them

③ only because their owners think they are wild and dangerous

④ only because there is not enough food and water

問4. 下線部(4)の意味に最も近いものを，次の①〜④から1つ選びなさい。

① Although we never expected our pets to do things they couldn't, we forced them to do too much.

② Although we started to ask what our pets could do for us, we never found a good answer.

③ Although we used to keep dogs and cats because of their usefulness, we began to treat them as companions.

④ Although we wanted dogs and cats to do useful jobs, they could not do what we wanted.

問5．下線部(5)の意味に最も近いものを，次の①～④から１つ選びなさい。

① criticized by　　② discussed by

③ forgotten by　　④ remembered by

問6．下線部(6)の researcher に対する RSPCA の回答の説明として最も適切なものを，次の①～④から１つ選びなさい。

① The RSPCA gave an accurate answer because it was their duty to do so.

② The RSPCA gave an accurate answer because they needed more cooperation from Londoners during World War Ⅱ.

③ The RSPCA's answer was inaccurate because everybody in London knows what happened to pets during World War Ⅱ.

④ The RSPCA's answer was inaccurate because they had indeed reported on the work of destroying animals in their magazine.

問7．下線部(7)の（　　）の中の単語を適切に並べ替えなさい。

問8．本文の内容と一致するものを，次の①～⑦から２つ選びなさい。

① At the start of World War Ⅱ, Londoners killed their pets because Germany had suddenly attacked the United Kingdom.

② Londoners still think that they did a good thing by killing their pets at the start of World War Ⅱ.

③ The number of pets killed in London continued to increase during World War Ⅱ.

④ While the *Times* newspaper was opposed to the work of killing pets at the start of World War Ⅱ, the BBC's Christopher

Stone thought their killing necessary.

⑤ During World War Ⅰ, a fairly large number of British people felt troubled when they found out that there were pets better provided for than some humans.

⑥ While pets and animals were abandoned during World War Ⅰ, they became more important to British people during World War Ⅱ.

⑦ Londoners would not want to remember the killing of their pets at the start of World War Ⅱ, because it does not agree with their proud self-image.

《 Vocabulary Building Exercise 》

次の例文中の空欄に入るものとして最も適切な単語を，後の ***Ans.*** から 1 つずつ選んで書きなさい。なお，【 】内は各空欄に入る適切な単語の意味を英語で説明したものです。

1. The share of [ ] casualties in armed conflict has increased.
【connected with people who are not members of the armed forces or the police】

2. They are seeking an [ ] and peaceful resolution to the crisis.
【arranged or organized in a neat, careful and logical way】

3. The squirrels started to [ ] nuts and seeds in the ground.
【to place something in the ground, especially a dead body in a grave】

4. Skilled workers were becoming increasingly [ ].
【there being not enough of something and it is only available in small quantities】

5. Refugees have not [ ] chosen to leave their country of origin.
【willingly; without being forced】

6. More people have been infected than was [ ] thought.
【at the beginning】

7. All animals [ ] with other members of their species.
【to try to be more successful than others】

8. The new job doesn't pay as much, but we won't [ ].
【to suffer or die because you do not have enough food to eat; to make somebody suffer or die in this way】

9. The collapse of the USSR ended one [ ] of human history.
【a period of time in history or a person's life; a separate section of a book, usually with a number or title】

10. These photos [ ] the spirit of those times.
【to succeed in accurately expressing a feeling, an atmosphere, etc. in a picture, piece of writing, film, etc.】

Ans.

orderly	compete	capture	starve	bury
scarce	voluntarily	civilian	initially	chapter

《 Summary 》

次の英文は問題英文の要約である。空欄(a)〜(f)に入るものとして最も適切な単語を後の ***Ans.*** から1つずつ選んで書きなさい。

During the first few days of World War Ⅱ, over 400,000 dogs and cats were put to death. This was done even though food supplies were not [(a)] yet. People may have done it because they were terrified by the beginning of a new war or they may have remembered seeing [(b)] dogs and cats during World War Ⅰ. Almost immediately, people regretted the mistake. Reporters argued that it was wrong to destroy [(c)] friends. In part, the reason it happened was that people's relationships with the animals around us changed due to [(d)]. People living in cities did not need dogs and cats to be useful. They simply became part of the family. But some people became [(e)] during the war because pets seemed like an unnecessary luxury. Despite reports of the [(f)] in magazines at the time, it has been written out of British history. This is probably because British people don't want to admit that they panicked at the beginning of the war. (166 words)

Ans.

urbanization	victory	scared	faithful
immigration	scarce	guilty	massacre
dangerous	uneasy	cruel	starving

第3問 『スポーツ心理学の意義』

目標解答時間：35分　配点：50点

次の英文を読み，設問に答えなさい。

My grandparents' bathroom, unlike many others, didn't have a wide selection of magazines to flip through to pass the time. Other than a slightly odd framed sketch of a man selling apples, there was only one other object that warranted my attention: a paperback entitled *The Yogi Book*. A crazed Yankee fan as a kid, I loved flipping through a quote book of one of the greatest Yankees of all time, Yogi Berra. I must have read that short book one hundred times over. Of the many Yogi-isms I read, a few stuck with me to this day. "When you come to a *fork in the road, take it;" "Nobody comes here anymore, it's too crowded;" and, most famously, "It ain't over 'til it's over." But there's another saying that stood out to me.

"Baseball is 90% mental, and the other half is physical."

While the numbers don't add up and few people attempt to unpack the philosophy of Berra, there is an obvious point he makes. Mentality is important to baseball. Berra suggests it's even more important than the physical part — which may seem to be a crazy concept. (1) <u>This mathematically erroneous phrase</u> retains its value across sports. Today, the idea that mental strength has a role in sports is common knowledge and finds its way into many of sports' most popular clichés, like "Get your head in the game!" and "You have to want it more!" It's a universally accepted truth that there is more to sports than pure ((2)). Sports psychology, the broad study of how the mind affects performance and participation in sports, started gaining attention in the early twentieth century, but it would be silly to assume that people considered the mind and the athletic body separate before then. There was just no way to scientifically test the link between the two, an obstacle that still gives researchers trouble even with our current technological innovation.

Despite the absence of methods to test the theory, the distinction between mind and body in athletic competition can be traced back to the time of the ancient Greek Olympic Games. Soon after the first ever Olympics were held in Greece nearly 2,500 years ago, Aesop wrote his famous fables. The only one of Aesop's stories I remember is "The Tortoise and the Hare." The moral of that story is clear: slow and steady wins the race. We've heard it thousands of times. The distinction Aesop makes is a simple one, and its message still holds true today. No matter how much more physically equipped and skilled one side is, the mental approach of the team can enhance its chances at winning. Mentality can level the playing field and affect the result regardless of physical skill.

If Berra is right, it's remarkable how little we understand about the mind of an athlete. What does it mean to have the mental strength to thrive at the top levels of sport? And why, in an era of exploding statistics, analysis, and data, do we understand so little about the mental side of the game?

We know that mentality is vital in everything we do. Saying the mind is not utilized in sports is ridiculous, but since Aesop's time, we have taken this concept for granted. We know the mental aspect is important, but we don't know why, and because of this, we cast mentality aside. The implications and intricacies are forgotten, and we take this dogma (3) <u>at face value</u>. The sports world, including fans, does not fully understand the significance of mentality. It isn't seen as a (4) <u>make-or-break</u> factor for an athlete, whereas physical skill and athleticism are defining features. An athlete is an athlete because he consistently bats around .300 or because she can drive a golf ball over two hundred yards, not because of how he or she performs under pressure; mentality is undermined constantly by physical skill and physical appearance. (5) We need to offer alternatives to the biases surrounding mentality in sports and shed light on many overlooked concepts that are rarely investigated because of how commonsense they seemingly are.

Luca Romeo, Mind Over Data, New Degree Press

注）fork: 分かれ道

問１. 下線部(1)で mathematically erroneous とはどういうことを指して言っているのか，日本語で説明しなさい。

問２. 空所（ (2) ）を補うのに最も適切なものを，次の①～④から１つ選びなさい。

① health benefits　　② mental power

③ physical talent　　④ smashing victory

問３. 下線部(3)の意味に最も近いものを，次の①～④から１つ選びなさい。

① as it seems without questioning

② based on sound advice

③ by looking at the deeper meaning

④ through discussion with others

問４. 下線部(4)の意味に最も近いものを，次の①～④から１つ選びなさい。

① confusing　　② futile

③ vital　　④ unnecessary

問５. 下線部(5)を日本語に訳しなさい。

問６. 次の(a)～(e)の空所を補った場合に本文の内容と一致しないものを，次の①～④からそれぞれ１つずつ選びなさい。

(a) Yogi Berra (　　).

① fascinated the author in his childhood with his quirky quotes

② was a professional sports psychologist

③ was not very well understood in his views

④ wrote about his thoughts on life and sports

(b) Aesop's fables ( ).

① argued for the importance of physical training

② contain some messages that are taken for granted despite their wisdom

③ had deep messages that are still relevant today

④ were written not long after the first Olympics

(c) The mental side of sports ( ).

① has been accepted for a long time as a prerequisite for success

② has been researched extensively despite the lack of data

③ is a part of many clichés in modern sporting circles

④ is not really understood regarding its significance

(d) The author ( ).

① criticizes Berra for his unusual philosophies

② does not remember most of Aesop's fables

③ often read in his grandparents' bathroom

④ was an avid baseball fan as a child

(e) Sports psychology ( ).

① examines the role of the mental side of sports

② has still not been able to understand the complexities of the mind

③ uses science to explore the link between mental and physical aspects

④ was the first attempt to separate mind and body

《 Vocabulary Building Exercise 》

次の例文中の空欄に入るものとして最も適切な単語を，後の ***Ans.*** から１つずつ選んで書きなさい。なお，【　】内は各空欄に入る適切な単語の意味を英語で説明したものです。

1. This ______ is well known to children around the world.
【a story which teaches a moral lesson】

2. It was certain that the condition did not ______ antibiotic therapy.
【to make something necessary or appropriate in a particular situation; justify something】

3. A simple comparison between species can lead to ______ conclusions.
【not correct; based on wrong information】

4. Until recently, this additive was widely used to ______ engine performance.
【to increase or further improve the good quality, value or status of somebody/something】

5. Today his company continues to ______.
【to become, and continue to be, successful, strong or healthy】

6. The ______ show that the number of complaints has declined in recent years.
【a collection of information shown in numbers】

7. Sound engineers ______ a range of techniques to enhance the quality of the recordings.
【to use something, especially for a practical purpose】

8. It's [ ] to suggest that she was involved in anything illegal.
【not at all sensible or reasonable】

9. We do not allow the teaching of religious [ ] in our schools.
【a belief or set of beliefs held by a group or organization that others are expected to accept without argument】

10. Offering advice on each and every problem will [ ] her feeling of being an adult.
【to make something gradually weaker or less effective】

Ans.

utilize	fable	ridiculous	thrive	erroneous
enhance	warrant	dogma	statistics	undermine

《 Summary 》

次の英文は問題英文の要約である。空欄(a)～(f)に入るものとして最も適切な単語を後の ***Ans.*** から１つずつ選んで書きなさい。

The baseball player Yogi Berra is known for saying strange things like, "Baseball is 90% mental, and the other half is physical." Obviously, this is mathematically [(a)], but he makes an important point: Mental strength plays a vital role in sports. However, in spite of our current technological [(b)], it is still too difficult to scientifically test the link between mind and body in athletes. Even so, the importance of a strong mental approach to sports was understood by the ancient Greeks. The [(c)] of Aesop's story "The Tortoise and the Hare" is that a good mental strategy can [(d)] an athlete's chance of winning. It is [(e)] to say that athletes don't use their minds, but we tend to ignore the [(f)] and intricacies of the mental side of sports and believe that physical skill and athleticism are the most important factors. We need to re-examine this attitude. (149 words)

Ans.

ridiculous	intervention	error	erroneous
enhance	mortal	possible	innovation
detract	moral	implications	impatience

第 4 問 『異文化の中で母語を次世代へ継承することの難しさ』

目標解答時間：35分　配点：50点

次の英文を読み，設問に答えなさい。

"You understand Grandmother when she talks to you, don't you, darling?" The girl nods. We met her — and her Danish mother and English father — at the airport, *en route to Denmark. The parents were eager to discuss their experience of bringing up their daughter bilingually in London. It isn't easy. The husband does not speak Danish, so the child hears the language only from her mother, who has come to accept that she will reply in English.

This can be painful. Not sharing your first language with loved ones is hard. Not passing it on to your own child can be especially tough. Many *expat and immigrant parents feel a sense of failure. They wring their hands and share stories on parenting forums and social media, hoping to find the secret to nurturing bilingual children successfully.

(1) Children are linguistic sponges, but this doesn't mean that *cursory exposure is enough. They must hear a language quite a bit to understand it — and use it often to be able to speak it comfortably. This is mental work, and a child who doesn't have a motive to speak a language — either a need or a strong desire — will often avoid it. Children's brains are already busy enough.

So languages often wither and die when parents move abroad. Consider America. The foreign-born share of the population is 13.7%, and has never been lower than 4.7% (in 1970). And yet foreign-language speakers don't (a) accumulate. Today just 25% of the population speaks another language. That's because, typically, the first generation born in America is bilingual, and the second is monolingual — in English, the children often struggling to speak easily with their immigrant grandparents.

In the past, governments discouraged immigrant families from keeping their languages. Teddy Roosevelt worried that America would become a "*polyglot boarding-house." These days, officials tend to be less *interventionist. Some even see a valuable resource in immigrants' language abilities. Yet many factors (b) conspire to ensure that children still lose their parents' languages, or never learn them.

A big one is (2) institutional pressure. A child's time spent with a second language is time not spent on their first. So teachers often discourage parents from speaking their languages to their children. This is especially true if the second language lacks prestige. Parents often reluctantly (c) comply, worried about their offspring's education. This is a shame; children really can master two languages or even more. Research does indeed suggest their vocabulary in each language may be somewhat smaller for a while. But other studies hint at (3) cognitive advantages among bilinguals. They may be more skillful at complex tasks, better at maintaining attention, and (at the other end of life) suffer the onset of *dementia later.

(4) Even without those side-effects, though, a bilingual child's connection to relatives and another culture is a good thing in itself. How to bring it about? When both parents share the heritage language, the strategy is often to speak that at home, and the national language outside. But when they have different languages, perhaps the most common approach is "one parent, one language." François Grosjean, a linguist at the University of Neuchâtel in Switzerland, emphasizes necessity. He recommends reserving occasions on which the only language that may be spoken is (5) the one that needs support.

Sabine Little, a German linguist at the University of Sheffield, puts the emphasis elsewhere. Making the heritage language yet another task (d) imposed by parents can lead to rejection, she argues. She recommends letting the child make their own emotional connection to the language. Her son gave up on German for several years before returning to it. She let him determine when they would speak it together. He decided on the pair's trips in her car to after-school activities, during which his father, who doesn't speak German, would not be excluded. They joke about his *Anglo-German mash-ups and incorporate them into their *lexicon. Like many youngsters, his time on YouTube is (e) restricted — but he is allowed more if he watches in German. Ms. Little suggests learning through apps and entertainment made for native speakers. The educational type is too much like homework, she thinks.

Languages are an intimate part of identity. It is painful to try and fail to pass them on to a child. Success may be a question of remembering that they are not just another thing to be drilled into a young mind, but a matter of the heart.

注）en route: 途中で　expat: 国外移住した　cursory: いい加減な
polyglot boarding-house: 多くの言語集団から成る下宿屋
interventionist: 干渉主義の　dementia: 認知症
Anglo-German mash-ups: 英語とドイツ語のごちゃ混ぜ
lexicon: 語彙

問 1．下線部(1)が意味していることを最も的確に示すものを，次の①～④から１つ選びなさい。

① Children can flexibly create their own languages
② Children naturally resist using language
③ Children communicate freely without language
④ Children absorb languages very easily

問2．下線部(2)が意味していることを最も的確に示すものを，次の①～④から1つ選びなさい。

① children's need to please their parents and grandparents
② the difficulty of learning different vocabulary and grammatical systems
③ the priority placed by schools on one language
④ teachers' efforts to encourage students to be bilingual

問3．下線部(3)に該当する3つの具体的な項目を，日本語で簡潔に記述しなさい。

問4．下線部(4)を日本語に訳しなさい。

問5．下線部(5)が意味していることを最も的確に示すものを，次の①～④から1つ選びなさい。

① the language less frequently encountered
② the language previously spoken in the region
③ the language spoken at the child's school
④ the language spoken as an official language

問6．下線部(a)～(e)の意味に最も近いものを，次の①～④からそれぞれ1つずつ選びなさい。

(a) ① communicate ② deposit
③ increase ④ trust

(b) ① decrease in number ② disturb each other
③ struggle separately ④ work together

(c) ① challenge ② interrupt
③ obey ④ protest

(d) ① approved ② encouraged
③ excluded ④ required

(e) ① extended ② limited
③ permitted ④ wasted

問7．本文の内容に一致するものを，次の①～⑥から2つ選びなさい。

① Many immigrant parents are struggling to find ways to have their children succeed in learning the official language of the place where they currently live.

② As many as a quarter of the American people speak another language, as a result of the government's policy to promote foreign languages.

③ Immigrants' children born in America are often bilingual, while their grandchildren are mostly monolingual and cannot speak their heritage language.

④ As views on the desirability of multilingualism have changed, the majority of immigrant children now acquire their heritage language.

⑤ If a child has two parents who speak different languages, it is better to speak one at home, and one in the car, while if the child lives in a single-parent household, it is best to focus on learning one language.

⑥ Sabine Little recommends children's learning the second language through their favorite activities in a relaxing atmosphere, since she believes in the importance of emotional connection with the language.

《 Vocabulary Building Exercise 》

次の例文中の空欄に入るものとして最も適切な単語を，後の ***Ans.*** から1つずつ選んで書きなさい。なお，【　】内は各空欄に入る適切な単語の意味を英語で説明したものです。

1. Parents want to know the best way to ＿＿＿＿ their child to adulthood.

【to care for and protect somebody/something while they are growing and developing】

2. The report recommends that people avoid prolonged ______ to sunlight.
【the state of being in a place or situation where there is no protection from something】

3. Dust and dirt soon ______ if a house is not cleaned regularly.
【to gradually increase in number or quantity over a period of time】

4. High interest rates will ______ investment.
【to make somebody feel less confident or enthusiastic about doing something】

5. They will never ______ to overthrow the government.
【to secretly plan with other people to do something illegal or harmful】

6. Some companies failed to ______ with environmental regulations.
【to obey a rule, an order, etc.】

7. Among those surviving ______, 15 were females.
【the young of an animal or plant; someone's child/children】

8. Even minor head injuries can cause ______ impairments.
【connected with the mental processes of understanding】

9. These laws ______ additional financial burdens on many people.
【to force somebody/something to deal with something that is difficult or unpleasant】

10. We ______ the number of students per class to ten.
【to limit or control the size, amount or range of something】

Ans.

accumulate	discourage	restrict	cognitive	exposure
nurture	comply	impose	conspire	offspring

《 Summary 》

次の英文は問題英文の要約である。空欄(a)〜(f)に入るものとして最も適切な単語を後の ***Ans.*** から1つずつ選んで書きなさい。

In families where the parents speak different languages, it can be difficult to raise a bilingual child. Even when parents make every effort to [(a)] children who speak two languages, their children will avoid learning a second language unless they have a strong [(b)] to speak it. That is why foreign-language speakers haven't accumulated in America, even though over 10% of the population was born in a different country. One factor that may [(c)] to ensure that children in the U.S. only learn English is that teachers often discourage parents from speaking their native languages to their children. Parents often [(d)], even though mastering two languages can give bilinguals [(e)] advantages. But when parents do try to pass on their language, their children may reject it if it is [(f)] on them like homework. It may be best to allow children to find their own ways to make an emotional connection with a second language. (155 words)

Ans.

imposed	nurture	excluded	conflict
conspire	cognitive	avoid	conclude
comply	motive	reluctantly	discuss

第５問 『極地探検と英雄たちの悲劇』

目標解答時間：35分　配点：50点

次の英文を読み，設問に答えなさい。

The twentieth century opened with a piece of unfinished business from the nineteenth century: polar exploration. The Arctic and Antarctic continents were the last regions on earth to (a) defy Europe's explorers, scientists and adventurers, and as late as the 1850s the old dream of the *Northwest Passage remained still a lure to commercial and imperial ambitions. The disappearance of the expedition led by Sir John Franklin in the Canadian Arctic in 1846 became a famous case in Britain, and initiated a dozen rescue expeditions in as many years before the truth was discovered. That truth was (b) disturbing: that every Englishman had died, some on the ice-bound ships, but most while trekking overland to seek aid, succumbing helplessly to an environment where the Innuit people were able to dwell permanently and to flourish. Franklin's widow proclaimed that the 130 men of the expedition had laid down their lives in the service of their country as truly as if they had (c) perished in battle. Yet the commercial and naval importance claimed for the Northwest Passage had been a myth, and the real motive was national pride, the European drive to (d) appropriate — psychologically if not politically — even such remote regions.

The same was still more true of the Poles themselves, two unique but featureless geographical points on the planet, whose inaccessibility attracted generations of explorers. (1) There was no reason to go there, except to test the limits of human endurance, to declare that mankind was master of the planet, and to establish which nation was really the best at this kind of thing. The North Pole was reached first in 1909 by the American naval officer Robert

Peary, but a decade earlier the Norwegian, Fridtjof Nansen, had survived probably the most extraordinary of polar journeys, locked in his ship in the ice for three years as it (e) drifted almost two thousand miles, thus demonstrating that the Arctic was not a land-mass but a moving ice cap. Nansen's (f) narrative of this wilderness experience in *Farthest North* is remarkably sane, good-tempered and humorous, as he sees himself transformed into a filthy savage living on bear meat and *walrus fat.

The South Pole generally produced literature of a bleaker but more *exalted kind, where the traveller is brought face to face with intense physical suffering, and with the philosophical question, Why am I here? Robert Scott's own diary of his last fatal expedition of 1912 was found with his body, and the entries are mostly short and factual as he attempts to rationalise the fate he now knows he cannot escape: 'We are showing that Englishmen can still die with a bold spirit.' But there is a sharper *poignancy about those entries when his officer-trained mask slips away and he confronts the fact that he has been brought here solely by his own choice, perhaps by his own (g) vanity: 'All the day-dreams must go ... Great God, this is an awful place.'

His fate (2) (all / made / more / the / unbearable / was) to him by his sense of failure, knowing he had been beaten by Roald Amundsen in the race to be first to the Pole, and he must have been additionally tormented by the question whether ordinary people, including their own families, would sympathise, and understand what had driven them on: 'Surely a great rich country like ours will see that those who are dependent upon us are provided for.' And the final entry seems to ache with a sense of personal guilt for his family: 'For God's sake look after our people.' (3) Scott need not have feared, for failure and death made him a hero perhaps even more securely than success could have, or rather his story forced people to re-examine what success and failure mean, for he had pursued his vision to the ultimate end, and given his life for an idea. This form of idealism was seen as essential to the process of nation-building, and still more of empire-building. The sacrifice of the individual self in a noble cause: this was what Scott came to symbolise, and surely there could be no higher destiny than that. Scott became part of the mythology of Britishness, and the ideal of sacrifice was one which millions were called upon to consider, to embrace or to reject, in *the Great War.

Travel: A Literary History, Peter Whitfield, THE CHANCELLOR, MASTERS AND SCHOLARS OF THE UNIVERSITY OF OXFORD, for its Bodleian Library, at the Clarendon Building, Broad Street, Oxford, OX 1 3 BG, England.

注）Northwest Passage: 北西航路（北大西洋と北太平洋の間の航路）
walrus: セイウチ　exalted: 気高い　poignancy: 痛恨の思い
the Great War: 第一次世界大戦

問１．下線部(1)を，‘there’ が指す場所を明示して日本語に訳しなさい。

問２．下線部(2)の（　　）の中の単語を適切に並べ替えなさい。

問３．下線部(3)を日本語に訳しなさい。

問４．下線部(a)～(g)の意味に最も近いものを，次の①～④からそれぞれ１つずつ選びなさい。

(a) ① accept　② attract　③ record　④ resist

(b) ① distressing　② exciting　③ misleading　④ uninteresting

(c) ① died　② expected　③ fought　④ participated

(d) ① adapt　② be fitted　③ devote　④ take over

(e) ① directed　② floated　③ intended　④ piled

(f) ① account　② destiny　③ ignorance　④ reputation

(g) ① bravery　② conceit　③ failure　④ glory

問５．本文の内容と一致しないものを，次の①～④から１つ選びなさい。

① A Norwegian, Fridjof Nansen's narrative of his extraordinary adventures in the Arctic is marked for its soundness and good humour.

② After his death, Scott came to embody the British ideal of sacrificing oneself for a noble cause.

③ It was national pride rather than commercial and naval importance that drove European people to explore the Northwest Passage.

④ Scott's diary entries are all very short and keep to facts, never referring to his doubts or anxieties about his failed expedition.

《 Vocabulary Building Exercise 》

次の例文中の空欄に入るものとして最も適切な単語を，後の ***Ans.*** から１つずつ選んで書きなさい。なお，【　】内は各空欄に入る適切な単語の意味を英語で説明したものです。

1. This was the first time that I dared to [   ] my father.
【to refuse to obey somebody/something】

2. Few can resist the [   ] of adventure.
【something that you find attractive】

3. He said his country would never [   ] to pressure.
【to be unable to fight an attack, a temptation, etc.】

4. Most of the butterflies [   ] in the first frosts of autumn.
【to die, especially in a sudden violent way; to be lost or destroyed】

5. This book offers no coherent [ ] of the American Civil War.
【a story or an account of a series of events】

6. Why are the streets so [ ] in this part of the city?
【very dirty; very unpleasant and disgusting】

7. He fails to distinguish [ ] information from opinion.
【based on or containing facts】

8. No doubt the idea appealed to his [ ].
【the fact of being too proud of your own appearance, abilities or achievements】

9. At times the memories returned to [ ] her.
【to cause somebody extreme mental suffering】

10. He dedicated his life to fighting for the [ ] of animal rights.
【an organization or idea that people support or fight for】

Ans.

vanity	factual	cause	perish	torment
filthy	narrative	lure	succumb	defy

《 Summary 》

次の英文は問題英文の要約である。空欄(a)〜(f)に入るものとして最も適切な単語を後の ***Ans.*** から１つずつ選んで書きなさい。

At the beginning of the 20th century, the Arctic and Antarctic ((a)) were the last places remaining for Europeans to explore. A British expedition to the Canadian Arctic in 1846 became famous when it was learned that every Englishman had ((b)) to the harsh environment. In the end, it turned out that the commercial and naval importance of the Northwest Passage which the group had been searching for was a myth. However, explorers were still attracted to the remotest regions of the ((c)), like the North and South Pole, for psychological reasons. They wanted to prove which nation was best at ((d)). Fridtjof Nansen wrote about his experience of being trapped on a ship surrounded by polar ice for three years in a surprisingly sane and humorous way. ((e)) about the South Pole are often bleak, but philosophical. In Robert Scott's diary of his fatal ((f)), he confronts the fact that his own choices led him to the fate he cannot escape. In the end, Scott became a hero who symbolised the ideal of self-sacrifice for a noble cause. (179 words)

Ans.

narratives	exportation	conferences	exploration
myths	expiration	continents	expedition
survived	planet	civilization	succumbed

第6問 『狩猟採集民の生活の方が人類には適していた』

目標解答時間：35分　配点：50点

次の英文を読み，設問に答えなさい。

The United Nations estimates that by 2050, 66% of human beings will live in cities. Such a high percentage may suggest that it is usual for humans to live in this way. However, (1) the growth of cities is a comparatively recent development in human history. Modern humans (that is, humans we would recognize as anatomically similar to us) have been around for about 200,000 years. For the vast majority of that time, they have had a hunter-gatherer existence.

The development of cities only began following the agricultural revolution, which took place in different parts of the world from about 12,000 years ago. The fundamental change involved in this was that rather than wandering from place to place in search of food (following animal migrations and the fertility patterns of plants), humans started to grow crops and breed animals in a particular location. Gradually, humans began living in separate families, rather than together in large tribal groups.

12,000 years is not a long time for humans to adapt to a new way of life. (2) Our feelings and instincts are suited to a hunter-gatherer lifestyle, rather than a more settled agricultural-industrial one. There are many material advantages to living in a city, such as a ready supply of food and water, safety from wild animals, access to a large range of medical services, and convenient transport systems. But urban conditions produce emotional problems that our hunter-gatherer ancestors were less likely to have, problems such as depression, loneliness, and the stress that comes from living in an overcrowded environment. Humans are social animals, so when we don't have regular contact with close friends or family — because of working long hours, for instance — we become *dejected. Most of us may live in cities, but are we really happy there?

To judge this, in his 2014 book *Sapiens*, the Israeli author Yuval Noah Harari compares the life of a hunter-gatherer in the past with the life of a city-dweller today. Harari describes how hunter-gatherers were free to move around. They decided when to work (to find food), and who to work with (their friends and family). They had no household chores to do, like washing dishes or ironing clothes; nor did they have to pay bills, go to the bank, or listen to a boss scolding them. There were no problems like pollution, traffic accidents or *mugging to worry about. The hunter-gatherer ate a varied diet, and infectious disease was less common, since people were not living in crowded conditions. Hunter-gatherers were skilled in many different ways, since they had to make, rather than buy, everything they needed, and they were very physically fit, given that they had no transport other than their legs. They also knew their environment extremely well. Imagine if you were stranded 100 kilometers from home today, with no phone, money, transport, food or water: would you panic? Could you survive? A situation that we might consider an emergency today was ((3)) our hunter-gatherer ancestors.

Most present-day humans work to gain money they can exchange for food, rather than finding or producing food themselves. In *Sapiens*, Harari relates how a worker in a city today might leave home early in the morning — walking the same route every day to take a subway train, on which nobody talks — and then sit in one place in a factory at a machine, performing the same process hour after hour. The worker is told when he or she can eat and drink, and when work is finished. Arriving home in the evening, perhaps twelve hours after leaving in the morning, the worker then has to cook (maybe eating the same kind of food for the third time that day), and then clean, wash clothes, and try to sleep peacefully in a noisy and bright apartment.

((4)) there were disadvantages to the hunter-gatherer lifestyle: there would be periods when food was in short supply; infant mortality was high; and medical care was not highly developed. But hunter-gatherers experienced good mental health, high 'job' satisfaction, and very little jealousy, since no one had more than anyone else. Members of a hunter-gatherer tribe knew each other very closely, because their life and death depended on other members of the group. That's a difficult feeling to achieve for a present-day human working in an office with strangers. Our hunter-gatherer ancestors may have been materially poorer than us, (5) <u>but in other ways, they may have been richer than we can ever be.</u>

注）dejected: 意気消沈した　　mugging: 路上強盗

問１． 下線部(1)の根拠を，第１・２パラグラフの内容に基づいて60～80字の日本語で説明しなさい。

問２． 下線部(2)を日本語に訳しなさい。

問３． 空所（ (3) ）を補うのに最も適切なものを，次の①～④から１つ選びなさい。

① a daily reality for　　② also an impossible burden for

③ an advantage of　　④ beyond the imagination of

問４． 空所（ (4) ）を補うのに最も適切なものを，次の①～④から１つ選びなさい。

① As a result　　② Furthermore

③ Of course　　④ Likewise

問５． 下線部(5)の理由として最も適切なものを，次の①～④から１つ選びなさい。

① In big cities, it was not difficult for hunter-gatherers to find well-paid work.

② Our hunter-gatherer ancestors had little stress in their life.

③ The hunter-gatherer lifestyle was the most efficient way of collecting food.

④ The hunter-gatherer lifestyle was very productive because the tribal members knew each other very well.

問６．本文の内容と一致するものを，次の①～⑦から３つ選びなさい。

① A hunter-gatherer way of life resulted from the development of cities.

② Because everyone had the same level of wealth, hunter-gatherers did not envy each other much.

③ For most of their history, human beings preferred living in a fixed area to a nomadic existence.

④ Harari gives a vivid picture of a factory worker whose daily schedule is very restricted.

⑤ Our hunter-gatherer ancestors were materially better off than we are now.

⑥ The author contrasts an agricultural lifestyle in the countryside with an industrial lifestyle in cities.

⑦ The examples taken from Harari's book tend to emphasize the favorable side of a hunter-gatherer lifestyle.

《 Vocabulary Building Exercise 》

次の例文中の空欄に入るものとして最も適切な単語を，後の ***Ans.*** から１つずつ選んで書きなさい。なお，【　】内は各空欄に入る適切な単語の意味を英語で説明したものです。

１．Often it is not possible to [　　　　] the probability of a catastrophe.
【to approximately calculate or judge the value, number, quantity or extent of something】

2. The company is a [ ] newcomer to the software market.
【measured or judged by how similar or different something is to something else】

3. There are some minute [ ] differences between these insects.
【relating to the structure of the bodies of people and animals】

4. Those policies resulted in massive internal rural-to-urban [ ].
【the movement of large numbers of people or animals from one place to another】

5. This curriculum is especially [ ] to middle-grade students.
【right or appropriate for a particular purpose or a particular job】

6. The extra money should be spent on improving public [ ].
【a system for taking people or goods from one place to another】

7. Shopping is a real [ ] for me.
【a task that you do regularly; an unpleasant or boring task】

8. [ ] diseases are a major global threat.
【that can be passed easily from one person or animal to another】

9. She tries to keep [ ] by jogging every day.
【in good physical or mental condition】

10. Reduced [ ] among newborns led to an increase in life expectancy.
【the number of deaths in a particular situation or period of time】

Ans.

comparative	chore	migration	anatomical	infectious
transport	fit	estimate	mortality	suited

《 Summary 》

次の英文は問題英文の要約である。空欄(a)~(f)に入るものとして最も適切な単語を後の ***Ans.*** から１つずつ選んで書きなさい。

By 2050, 66% of human beings will live in cities. Given the fact that modern humans have existed for about 200,000 years, living in cities is a very recent change for us. For most of human history, we have been hunter-gatherers. Although we have not changed [(a)], we have completely changed our way of life. Most of us no longer live in [(b)] groups, wandering from place to place to find food. Now we have convenient [(c)] systems and ready access to medical services, along with basic necessities like food and water. However, our feelings and [(d)] are still suited to a hunter-gatherer lifestyle, not an [(e)] one. We have lost a lot of our freedom and our close ties to others. In many ways, our hunter-gatherer [(f)] might have been richer than we are. (135 words)

Ans.

instincts	urgent	mentally	ancestors
institutions	anatomically	temporary	rivals
transport	urban	transfer	tribal

第7問 『顔の表情は単に感情が表に出たものではない』

目標解答時間：35分　配点：50点

次の英文を読み，設問に答えなさい。

While conducting research on emotions and facial expressions in Papua New Guinea in 2015, psychologist Carlos Crivelli discovered something startling. He showed *Trobriand Islanders photographs of the standard Western face of fear — wide-eyed, mouth wide open — and asked them to (a) what they saw. The Trobrianders didn't see a frightened face. Instead, they saw an indication of threat and aggression. In other words, what we think of as a universal expression of fear isn't universal at all. But if Trobrianders have a different interpretation of facial expressions, what does that mean? One emerging — and increasingly supported — theory is that facial expressions don't reflect our feelings. Instead of reliable displays of our emotional states, they show our [(1)] .

The face acts "like a road sign to affect the traffic that's going past it," says Alain Fridlund, a psychology professor who wrote a recent study with Crivelli. "Our faces are ways we direct the course of a social interaction." That's not to say that we actively try to manipulate others with our facial expressions. Our smiles and frowns may well be unconscious. But (2) our expressions are less a mirror of what's going on inside than a signal we're sending about what we want to happen next. Your best 'disgusted' face, for example, might show that you're not happy with the way the conversation is going — and that you want it to take a different course.

While it may seem sensible, this theory has been a long time coming. The idea that emotions are fundamental, instinctive, and expressed in our faces is deeply fixed in Western culture. But (3) this viewpoint has always been criticized. New research is challenging two of the main points of basic emotion theory. First is the idea that some emotions are universally shared and recognized. Second is the belief that facial expressions are reliable reflections of those emotions.

That new research includes recent work by Crivelli. He has spent months living with the Trobrianders of Papua New Guinea as well as *the Mwani of Mozambique. With both native groups, he found that study participants did not (b) emotions to faces in the same way Westerners do. It was not just the face of fear, either. Shown a smiling face, only a small percentage of Trobrianders declared that the face was happy. About half of those who were asked to describe it in their own words called it "laughing": a word that deals with action, not feeling. In other words, Crivelli found no evidence that what is behind a facial expression is universally understood.

Making matters more complicated, even when our facial expressions are interpreted by others as exhibiting a certain feeling, those people might (a) an emotion we're not actually experiencing. In a 2017 analysis of about 50 studies, researchers found that only a minority of people's faces reflected their actual feelings.

If our expressions don't actually reflect our feelings, there are enormous consequences. One is in the field of artificial intelligence (AI), specifically robotics. "A good number of people are training their artificial intelligence and their social robots using example faces from psychological textbooks," says Fridlund. But if someone who frowns at a robot is signalling something other than simple unhappiness, the AI may (c) to them incorrectly.

For most of us, though, the new research may have most of an effect on how we interpret social interactions. (4) It turns out that we might communicate better if we saw faces not as mirroring hidden emotions — but rather as actively trying to speak to us. People should read faces "kind of like a road sign," says Fridlund. "It's like a switch on a railroad track: do we go here or do we go there in the conversation?" That frown on your friend's face may not be actual anger; maybe she just wants you to agree with her point of view.

Take laughter, says Bridget Waller: "when you laugh and how you laugh within a social interaction is absolutely crucial." A poorly-timed laugh might not (d) your inner joy at what's going on — but it might show that you're not paying close attention to the conversation, or may even signal hostility.

For Crivelli, our faces may even be more calculating than that. (5) He compares us to *puppeteers, with our expressions like "invisible wires or ropes that you are trying to use to manipulate the other." And, of course, that other person is manipulating us right back. We're social creatures, after all.

Talya Rachel Meyers, Why our facial expressions don't reflect our feelings, BBC

注）Trobriand Islanders: トロブリアンド諸島の住民
the Mwani of Mozambique: モザンビークのムワニ民族
puppeteers：操り人形師

問1． 空欄 (1) に入れる語句として最も適切なものを，次の①～④から1つ選びなさい。

① beliefs and moral values
② intentions and social goals
③ likes and dislikes
④ opinions and level of intelligence

問2． 下線部(2)を日本語に訳しなさい。

問3． 下線部(3)の具体的な内容を日本語で説明しなさい。

問4． 下線部(4)を日本語に訳しなさい。

問5． 下線部(5)を日本語に訳しなさい。

問６．空所（ a ）～（ d ）を補うのに最も適切なものを，次の①～⑥からそれぞれ１つずつ選びなさい（aは２箇所ある）。ただし，同じものを２度以上選ぶことはできません。

① attribute　② examine　③ explain
④ identify　⑤ respond　⑥ reveal

《 Vocabulary Building Exercise 》

次の例文中の空欄に入るものとして最も適切な単語を，後の ***Ans.*** から１つずつ選んで書きなさい。なお，【 】内は各空欄に入る適切な単語の意味を英語で説明したものです。

1．Did you ＿＿＿＿ all those species correctly?
【to recognize somebody/something and be able to say who or what they are】

2．While apes sometimes ＿＿＿＿ staring as friendly, as humans do, most monkeys find staring threatening.
【to decide that something has a particular meaning and to understand it in this way】

3．You should ＿＿＿＿ your attention to the next task.
【to aim something at a particular goal or person, or in a particular direction】

4．I'm ＿＿＿＿ with the way that he was treated.
【feeling a strong sense of dislike and disapproval at something】

5．Given the difficult situation, their approach seems ＿＿＿＿ and appropriate.
【done or chosen with good judgment based on reason and experience rather than emotion】

6. They [ ] the belief that obesity represents wealth.
【to question whether something is right, legal or true; to refuse to accept or believe something】

7. They [ ] magical properties to the stones.
【to regard a quality or feature as belonging to somebody/something】

8. The [ ] between performers and their audience is very interesting.
【the way that people communicate with each other】

9. A thorough search failed to [ ] the murder weapon.
【to show something that previously could not be seen】

10. As a politician, he knows how to [ ] public opinion.
【to control or influence somebody/something, often in a dishonest way so that they do not realize it】

Ans.

identify	sensible	challenge	manipulate	attribute
interpret	interaction	disgusted	reveal	direct

《 Summary 》

次の英文は問題英文の要約である。空欄(a)〜(f)に入るものとして最も適切な単語を後の ***Ans.*** から1つずつ選んで書きなさい。

Recent research supports the [(a)] theory that facial expressions don't reflect our feelings. Instead, they show what our [(b)] or social goals are. The idea that we express our emotions instinctively on our faces and that these emotions are universally shared and recognized is fixed in Western culture. But new research is [(c)] these points. In places like Papua New Guinea and Mozambique, the native people did not recognize emotions on faces in the same way that Westerners do. This proved that facial expressions are not universally understood. This may have enormous [(d)] in fields like the AI used in social robots. It may also help people to [(e)] social interactions. If we think of expressions as social signals instead of instinctive [(f)] of our real emotions, we may be able to communicate better with others. (136 words)

Ans.

mistaking	interchange	emergency	challenging
intentions	instincts	emerging	consequences
interpret	reactions	reflections	considerations

第8問 『知性とは注意力を配分する能力だ』

目標解答時間：40分　配点：50点

次の英文を読み，設問に答えなさい。

In the late 1960s, the psychologist Walter Mischel began a simple experiment with four-year-old children. He invited the kids into a tiny room containing a desk and a chair and asked them to pick a treat from a tray of marshmallows, cookies, and pretzel sticks. Mischel then made the four-year-olds an offer: They could either eat one treat right away or, if they were willing to wait while he stepped out for a few minutes, they could have two treats when he returned. Not surprisingly, nearly every kid chose to wait.

At the time, psychologists assumed that the ability to delay gratification in order to get that second marshmallow or cookie depended on willpower. Some people simply had more willpower than others, which allowed them to resist tempting sweets and save money for retirement. However, after watching hundreds of kids participate (A) the marshmallow experiment, Mischel concluded that this standard model was wrong. He came to realize that willpower was (a) <u>inherently</u> weak and that children who tried to postpone the treat — gritting their teeth in the face of temptation — soon (1) <u>lost the battle</u>, often within thirty seconds.

Instead, Mischel discovered something interesting when he studied the tiny percentage of kids who could successfully wait for the second treat. Without exception, these "high delayers" all relied on the same mental strategy: (2) <u>These kids found a way to keep themselves from thinking about the treat, directing their gaze away from the delicious marshmallow.</u> Some covered their eyes or played hide-and-seek underneath the desks. Others sang songs from *Sesame Street*, or repeatedly tied their shoelaces, or pretended to take a nap. Their desire wasn't defeated, it was merely forgotten.

Mischel refers to this skill as the "strategic (b) allocation of attention," and he argues that it's the skill underlying self-control. Too often, we assume that willpower is about having strong *moral fiber. But that's wrong. Willpower is really about properly directing the spotlight of attention, learning how to control that short list of thoughts in *working memory. It's about realizing that if we're thinking about the marshmallow, we're going to eat it, which is why we need to look away.

What's interesting is that this cognitive skill isn't just useful for dieters. It seems to be a core part of success in the real world. For instance, when Mischel followed (B) the initial subjects thirteen years later — they were now high school seniors — he realized that their performance on the marshmallow task had been highly predictive on a vast range of *metrics. Those kids who had struggled to wait at the age of four were also more likely to have behavioral problems, both in school and at home. They struggled in stressful situations, often had trouble paying attention, and found it difficult to maintain friendships. Most impressive, perhaps, were the academic numbers: The kids who could wait fifteen minutes for a marshmallow had an *SAT score that was, on average, 210 points higher than that of the kids who could wait only thirty seconds.

(3) These correlations demonstrate the importance of learning to strategically allocate our attention. When we properly control the spotlight, we can resist negative thoughts and dangerous temptations. We can walk away from fights and improve our odds (C) addiction. Our decisions are driven by the facts and feelings bouncing around the brain — the allocation of attention allows us to direct this *haphazard process, as we consciously select the thoughts we want to think about.

Furthermore, this mental skill is getting more valuable. (4) We live, after all, in the age of information, which makes the ability to focus on the important information incredibly important. (Herbert Simon said it best: “A wealth of information creates a poverty of attention.”) The brain is a bounded machine, and the world is a confusing place, full of data and distractions. Intelligence is the ability to (c) parse the data so that it makes just a little bit more sense. Like willpower, this ability requires the strategic allocation of attention.

One final thought: In recent decades, psychology and neuroscience have severely (d) eroded classical notions of free will. The unconscious mind, it turns out, is most of the mind. And yet, we can (D) control the spotlight of attention, focusing on those ideas that will help us succeed. In the end, this may be the only thing we can control. We don’t have to look at the marshmallow.

Jonah Lehrer, Control The Spotlight, Wired

注）moral fiber: 道徳心　　working memory: 作業メモリ
metrics: 測定基準　　SAT: 大学進学適性試験
haphazard：偶然性の強い

問１．下線部(1)はどのようなことを意味しているか，日本語で説明しなさい。

問２．下線部(2)を日本語に訳しなさい。

問３．下線部(3)の例として適切なものを，次の①～④から１つ選びなさい。

① The harder students try to concentrate on their targets all the time, the higher chance they have of academic success in their school life.

② Students who achieved high scores on the SAT were those who had earlier ended up eating a marshmallow within fifteen minutes.

③ If children are allowed to have as many marshmallows as they can eat, they are likely to find it difficult to maintain friendships with other kids.

④ Children who were able to divert their attention to something other than what they wanted performed better academically in their later years.

問4．下線部(4)を日本語に訳しなさい。

問5．空所（ A ）～（ D ）を補うのに最も適切なものを，次の①～④から１つずつ選びなさい。

A ① in ② of ③ over ④ to

B ① away from ② on from
③ through with ④ up with

C ① against ② for ③ of ④ to

D ① also ② never ③ still ④ thus

問6．下線部(a)～(d)の意味に最も近いものを，次の①～④から１つずつ選びなさい。

(a) ① extremely ② innately
③ occasionally ④ simultaneously

(b) ① assignment ② definition
③ enlightenment ④ protection

(c) ① analyze ② contradict
③ protect ④ prove

(d) ① built up ② put away
③ set up ④ worn away

問7．本文の内容に一致するものを，次の①～④から１つ選びなさい。

① A series of psychological experiments by Walter Mischel found that human willpower is essentially strong enough to resist various temptations in daily life.

② Scientists used to believe that strong determination plays a vital role in sacrificing one's immediate desire for future benefits.

③ Desire to put yourself in the spotlight is important for achieving success in your career.

④ Walter Mischel's discovery was that self-control has little to do with your ability to manage your attention properly.

《 Vocabulary Building Exercise 》

次の例文中の空欄に入るものとして最も適切な単語を，後の ***Ans.*** から1つずつ選んで書きなさい。なお，【　】内は各空欄に入る適切な単語の意味を英語で説明したものです。

1. It is a misconception to ______ that the two continents are similar.
【to think or accept that something is true without having proof of it】

2. A feed will usually provide instant ______ to a crying baby.
【the state of feeling pleasure when something goes well for you or when your desires are satisfied】

3. He believed there was no ______ contradiction between religion and science.
【that is a permanent, basic or typical feature of somebody/something】

4. I couldn't resist the ______ to open the door.
【the desire to do or have something that you know is bad or wrong】

5. We should ______ more money for famine relief.
【to give something officially to somebody/something for a particular purpose】

6. The housing market continues to ______.
【to try very hard to do something when it is difficult or when there are a lot of problems】

7. There is a direct [ ] between exposure to sun and skin cancer.
【a connection between two things in which one thing changes as the other does】

8. He is now fighting his [ ] to alcohol.
【the condition of being unable to stop using or doing something as a habit, especially something harmful】

9. Television is a [ ] when we are reading.
【a thing that takes your attention away from what you are doing or thinking about】

10. Repeated failures began to [ ] her confidence in herself.
【to gradually destroy the surface of something through the action of wind, rain, etc; to gradually destroy something or make it weaker over a period of time】

Ans.

gratification	allocate	struggle	assume	correlation
distraction	erode	temptation	addiction	inherent

《 Summary 》

次の英文は問題英文の要約である。空欄(a)~(f)に入るものとして最も適切な単語を後の ***Ans.*** から1つずつ選んで書きなさい。

Psychologists used to believe that the ability to delay [(a)] depended on each individual's willpower. However, an experiment in which children were told they could get another marshmallow or cookie if they could wait for a few minutes made it clear that this [(b)] model was wrong. After watching hundreds of kids participate in the experiment, a researcher realized that all children have weak willpower, but those who successfully resisted [(c)] used the same mental [(d)] : They didn't look at the marshmallow. They realized that if they were thinking about the marshmallow, they would eat it, so they thought about something else. This experiment turned out to be highly [(e)] . The children who waited the longest got much higher scores on tests thirteen years later. This demonstrates the importance of [(f)] our attention, which is a very valuable skill now that we live in an age of information. With so much information around us, we need to be able to focus on things that are important and not become distracted by everything else. (173 words)

Ans.

gratification	strategy	predictive	development
temptation	spreading	experimental	allocating
testing	standard	success	potential

第 9 問 『職場の友情は過去のものなのか』

目標解答時間：35分　配点：50点

次の英文を読み，設問に答えなさい。

Decades ago, work was a major source of friendships in America. We took our families to company picnics and invited our colleagues to our houses for dinner. Now, work has become more of a place to do business. We go to the office to be efficient, not to form friendships. We have plenty of productive conversations but fewer meaningful relationships.

In 1985, about half of Americans said that they had a close friend at work; by 2004, this was true for only 30 percent. In several national surveys of graduating American high school students, the proportion who said it was very important to find a job where they could make friends dropped from 54 percent in 1976 to 41 percent in 2006. We may start companies with our friends, but we don't become friends with our co-workers. Americans may increasingly focus their efforts on forming friendships outside of work, but this is not the norm around the world. For example, Americans recently reported inviting only 32 percent of their closest colleagues to their homes, whereas people in Poland reported 66 percent and those in India reported 71 percent.

Why are Americans so determined to (　a　) business today?

The economic explanation is that long-term or lifetime employment has largely disappeared. Instead of spending our careers with one company, Americans expect to move on every few years. Since we don't expect to be in one place forever, we don't take the time or make the effort to form friendships. We view co-workers as a temporary presence in our lives, greeting them politely, but keeping them at arm's-length distance. We reserve our real friendships for outside of work. Often, we treat colleagues the way we would treat strangers we might sit next to and have a conversation with on an airplane or a long-distance train: (1) they become "single-serving friends."

Some observers blame the rise of flexible working hours and working from home. When more people are working remotely, we have fewer chances for the face-to-face encounters that are so critical to friendships. But a recent study found that as long as people were in the office at least two and one half days per week, "*telecommuting had no generally negative effects on the quality of workplace relationships." Still, technology affects relationships. When we're constantly (b) old friends on social media — and we can visit them anytime — why bother making new ones? Being connected to the Internet round the clock, we face a growing shortage of time, where the pressure to get work done (c) the desire to socialize: we become slaves to our 24-hour schedules.

The sociologist Max Weber argued that *the Protestant Reformation had a peculiar effect on American work. Leaders of that Reformation believed that hard work in any job was a duty demanded by God. (2) Some went even further, arguing that people should avoid socializing while working, as attention to relationships and emotions would distract them productively doing God's will. Over time, these ideas influenced Protestants, who came to view work as a place in which productivity was more important than relationships. Protestant men in particular were taught that work was a serious activity not to be mixed with socializing. For much of the 20th century, American workplaces were largely designed by Protestant men. Yet in recent years, America has become noticeably less Protestant, falling from about 70 percent in the 1950s to 37 percent in 2014. The number of Protestant CEOs has fallen, too. Racial and gender diversity at work is now more common and even

(d). Business culture has changed. Why, then, does the Protestant work ethic persist?

Regardless of our gender, race, or religion, generational shift has reinforced the idea that the workplace is mainly a place to conduct business. The value placed on leisure time has increased steadily. In a recent survey, 31 percent of *millennials said they highly valued more than two weeks of vacation time. (3) When we see our jobs primarily as a means to leisure, it is easy to convince ourselves that efficiency and productivity are most important so that we have time for friendships outside work.

But we may be underestimating the impact of workplace friendships on our happiness — and our effectiveness. Jobs are more satisfying when they provide opportunities to form friendships. When friends work together, they're more trusting and committed to one another's success. Companies like Google and Facebook now provide opportunities and facilities for employees to share games, exercise, and meals — and research suggests that playing and eating together are good ways to promote workplace cooperation.

注）telecommuting: 在宅勤務
the Protestant Reformation: プロテスタントによる宗教改革
millennials: ここでは「1982年～2000年に生まれた世代」を意味する。

問 1．下線部(1)が示唆することとして適切でないものを，次の①～④から1つ選びなさい。

① We only share part of our lives with them.

② We talk with them for a specific purpose.

③ We tend to ignore them to avoid trouble.

④ We don't allow the friendship to deepen.

問 2．下線部(2)を日本語に訳しなさい。

問３．下線部(3)を日本語に訳しなさい。

問４．空所（　a　）～（　d　）を補うのに最も適切なものを，次の①～④から１つずつ選びなさい。

a　①　get down to　②　go out of
　③　make friends in　④　put up with

b　①　behind the backs of　②　in touch with
　③　on the phone to　④　without benefit of

c　①　characterizes　②　equals
　③　includes　④　outweighs

d　①　actively disapproved of　②　considered out of date
　③　disliked by men　④　taken for granted

問５．筆者の意見に一致するものを，次の①～④から１つ選びなさい。

① Participating in activities with colleagues in the company can nurture better workplace relationships.

② Although it is regrettable that fewer American workers form friendships at work, it cannot be helped.

③ Younger workers tend to put more effort into making friends at work than workers from the older generation do.

④ Younger workers should adopt a more respectful attitude toward workers from the older generation

問６．本文のタイトルとして最も適切なものを，次の①～④から１つ選びなさい。

① Friends at Work: How and Why American Attitudes Have Changed

② Positive Views of Socializing in the Workplace: The Religious Origins

③ How Changes in Employment Policy Have Influenced Young Workers

④ Why American Business Should Discourage Social Interaction at Work

《 Vocabulary Building Exercise 》

次の例文中の空欄に入るものとして最も適切な単語を，後の ***Ans.*** から1つずつ選んで書きなさい。なお，【　】内は各空欄に入る適切な単語の意味を英語で説明したものです。

1. Over the past decades, it has become the accepted [　　　] for women to be in employment.
【a situation or a pattern of behaviour that is usual or typical】

2. The opposition to her plan made her more [　　　] than ever.
【having made a definite decision to do something and not letting anyone prevent you】

3. I didn't [　　　] trying to explain my feelings.
【to spend time and/or energy doing something】

4. The costs of such decisions are likely to far [　　　] their benefits.
【to be greater or more important than something】

5. The problem is by no means [　　　] to America.
【belonging or relating to one particular place, situation, person, etc., and not to others】

6. If symptoms [　　　], surgery may be required.
【to continue to exist】

7. They fear that those reforms would only [　　　] the power of the larger countries.
【to make a feeling, idea, habit or tendency stronger】

8. Don't [　　　] what she is capable of.
【to think or guess that the amount, cost, size or importance of something is smaller or less than it really is】

9. He said the government remained [ ] to peace.
【willing to work hard and give your time and energy to something】

10. My time spent in the library was very [ ].
【doing or achieving a lot】

Ans.

outweigh	productive	determined	norm	reinforce
bother	peculiar	underestimate	commited	persist

《 Summary 》

次の英文は問題英文の要約である。空欄(a)~(f)に入るものとして最も適切な単語を後の ***Ans.*** から1つずつ選んで書きなさい。

The workplace is no longer a major [(a)] of friendships. Decades ago, about half of Americans said they had a close friend at work, but by 2004 only 30% did. While in other countries, the majority of people said they invited work [(b)] to their homes, only 32% of Americans did. This may be partly due to the fact that lifetime and long-term employment are disappearing, and so people view their co-workers as a [(c)] presence in their lives. Or it may because the rise of [(d)] working hours and working from home means that co-workers rarely see each other face-to-face. Additionally, social media platforms make it easier to keep in touch with old friends, so we don't need to make new ones. The sociologist Max Weber argued that the Protestant work [(e)] has made especially Protestant men avoid socializing at work, but in spite of the racial and [(f)] diversity in the workplace today, the younger generation still does not place importance on forming friendships at work. Instead, they see work simply as a means to leisure and put emphasis on efficiency and productivity. (185 words)

Ans.

source	critic	extended	colleagues
gender	clients	flexible	ethic
laws	general	permanent	temporary

第10問 『アメリカにおける民族多様性社会の実情』

目標解答時間：35分　配点：50点

次の英文を読み，設問に答えなさい。

The civil rights movement benefited not only African Americans, but all minorities in the United States — Native Americans, Hispanics, and Asians. Racial discrimination in employment and housing was forbidden by law. The civil rights laws also advanced the rights of women, and these laws have reinforced the ideal of equality of opportunity for all Americans.

However, there is a paradox. (1) Though the amount of diversity in the United States continues to grow with each census, the 2000 census revealed that segregation according to race and ethnicity has persisted to a much larger degree than many Americans had realized. On the one hand, most young Americans say they would have no problem being friends with or even marrying someone of a different race or ethnic background. Polls show that the vast majority of Americans believe that segregation is a bad thing. On the other hand, races and ethnic groups still tend to live in segregated communities. This has been a trend in the cities, and as minority groups have moved into the suburbs the trend has continued. (a) However, these neighborhoods are the exception, rather than the rule.

Sociology professor John Logan has studied this phenomenon and reports that the 2000 census found the United States as segregated a nation as it has ever been. "The majority of Americans," Logan found, "are living in neighborhoods that continue to separate whites from blacks, Latinos, and people of Asian descent. (b) In those areas, people of color tend to *congregate in neighborhoods and housing developments apart from whites." Moreover, Logan sees this trend continuing into the future.

Is it a bad thing if groups of people choose to live in communities with others of their race or ethnic background? (c) Ethnic communities often provide valuable support to new immigrants, with their native-language newspapers and ethnic restaurants and grocery stores. Most white Americans, particularly those in and near cities, enjoy international food and many participate in cultural festivals from all over the world. They see this diversity as enriching their lives.

But there is a negative side to this picture. (d) Although African Americans represent about 12 percent of the population, they are still grossly under-represented in Congress, and the same is true of Hispanics. The median income of a married black or Hispanic man working full-time is still significantly less than that of a married white man. Segregation and discrimination are against the law, but residential patterns create largely segregated neighborhood schools, particularly in many urban areas. Whites are more likely than blacks and Hispanics to live in the suburbs, where the neighborhood schools are usually in better condition and offer a better education. Many blacks and other ethnic minorities in the inner city are trapped in cycles of poverty, unemployment, violence, and despair. Blacks are the most frequent victims of violent crime, and as many as one in five young males may have a criminal record. More black and Hispanic children than white children live in poverty and may have only one parent at home.

(2) <u>On the other hand, Americans continue to believe strongly in the ideal of equality of opportunity and to search for ways to give everyone an equal chance at success.</u> The American Dream still attracts immigrants and inspires people of all races and ethnic backgrounds. In reality, some immigrant groups have more success than others. As one would expect, history shows that immigrants

who come with financial resources, a good educational background, and the necessary work skills are likely to do the best. For example, immigrants from the Middle East tend to have a higher socioeconomic level than the average white American. (　e　) However, those who come without financial resources and a strong educational background do not do as well. Immigrants from the same country may have a different experience of the United States. For example, the Vietnamese who came in the mid-1970s were the educated elite, and they had better success than the Vietnamese farmers and fishermen who came later. The Cubans who came in the early 1960s had more wealth and education than many of the poorer Cubans who arrived later. Again, the educated elite have had greater success than those who came from poorer backgrounds.

注）congregate: 集まる

問１．下線部⑴を日本語に訳しなさい。

問２．下線部⑵を日本語に訳しなさい。

問３．空所（　a　）～（　e　）を補うのに最も適切なものを，次の①～⑥からそれぞれ１つずつ選びなさい。ただし，同じものを２度以上選ぶことはできません。

① So do Asians, as a group.

② The bad news is that there is still a gulf between different racial and ethnic groups.

③ In the future, the legal system will no longer accept immigrants into American society.

④ Shouldn't individuals have the freedom to live wherever and near whomever they want?

⑤ Of course, ethnically diverse neighborhoods do exist and are certainly chosen by a number of Americans.

⑥ In fact, the same color barrier that has dominated urban communities for decades has now spread to our fast-growing suburbs.

《 Vocabulary Building Exercise 》

次の例文中の空欄に入るものとして最も適切な単語を，後の ***Ans.*** から１つずつ選んで書きなさい。なお，【　】内は各空欄に入る適切な単語の意味を英語で説明したものです。

1. He was ＿＿＿＿ in an unhappy marriage.
【being kept in a bad situation that you want to get out of but cannot】

2. There is a seeming ＿＿＿＿ that people often feel advertising is untruthful, yet find it a useful source of information.
【a thing, situation or person that has two opposite features and therefore seems strange】

3. The 2000 ＿＿＿＿ data show a ratio of 118 males to 100 females.
【the process of officially counting something, especially a country's population, and recording various facts】

4. In retailing, a few large organizations tend to ＿＿＿＿ the market.
【to control or have a lot of influence over something/somebody】

5. Most European languages have a common ＿＿＿＿.
【a person's family background】

6. For many Americans today, weekend work has become the ＿＿＿＿ rather than the exception.
【the normal state of things; what is true in most cases】

7. He was a ＿＿＿＿ of racial prejudice.
【a person who has been attacked, injured or killed as the result of a crime, disease, accident, unpleasant circumstance, etc.】

8. At that time, the sea level was [ ] higher than it is today.
【in a way that is large or important enough to be noticed】

9. They intend to bring a swift end to racial [ ].
【the act or policy of separating people from different groups, for example people of different races, religions or sexes, and treating them in a different way】

10. We encourage students to [ ] fully in the running of the college.
【to take part in or become involved in an activity】

Ans.

paradox	census	victim	descent	significantly
rule	segregation	trapped	dominate	participate

《 Summary 》

次の英文は問題英文の要約である。空欄(a)~(f)に入るものとして最も適切な単語を後の ***Ans.*** から１つずつ選んで書きなさい。

While it is true that the civil rights movement benefited minorities and also women, there is a [(a)]. Even though most young Americans say they have no problem being friends with or marrying someone of a different race or ethnic background, Americans still tend to live in [(b)] communities. There are benefits to living in a community with members of your own race or ethnic background, such as the support new [(c)] receive and international food and festivals that enrich all Americans' lives. But there is also a negative side. Married black and Hispanic men's [(d)] incomes are still significantly lower than those of married white men. Blacks are the most frequent victims of violent crime, and black and Hispanic children are more likely to live in [(e)] than white children. Americans believe in the ideal of equal opoortunity, but in reality, people from a higher [(f)] level who have a better educational background are more likely to achieve success in America. (162 words)

Ans.

solution	paradox	poor	median
segregated	sociology	medical	supported
socioeconomic	employees	poverty	immigrants

第11問 『匂いを使った植物のコミュニケーション』

目標解答時間：40分　配点：50点

次の英文を読み，設問に答えなさい。

According to the dictionary definition, language is what people use when we talk to each other. Looked at this way, we are the only beings who can use language, because the concept is limited to our species. But wouldn't it be interesting to know whether trees can also talk to each other? But how? They definitely don't produce sounds, so there's nothing we can hear. Branches creak as they rub against one another and leaves rustle, but these sounds are caused by the wind and the tree has no control over them. Trees, it turns out, have a completely different way of communicating: they use scent.

Scent as a means of communication? The concept is not totally unfamiliar (a) us. Why else would we use deodorants and perfumes? And even when we're not using these products, our own smell says something to other people, both consciously and subconsciously. There are some people who seem to have no smell at all; we are strongly attracted to others because of their aroma. Scientists believe pheromones in sweat are a decisive factor when we choose our partners. So (1) <u>(we / it / that / to / possess / say / seems / fair)</u> a secret language of scent, and trees have demonstrated that they do as well.

For example, four decades ago, scientists noticed something on the African savannah. The giraffes there were feeding (b) *umbrella thorn acacias, and the trees didn't like this one bit. It took the acacias mere minutes to start pumping toxic substances into their leaves to rid themselves (c) the animals. The giraffes got the message and moved on to other trees in the area. But did they move on to trees close by? No, for the time being, they walked right by a few trees and resumed their meal only when they had moved about 100 yards away.

The reason for (2) this behavior is astonishing. The acacia trees that were being eaten gave off a warning gas that signaled to neighboring trees of the same species that a crisis was at hand. Right away, all the forewarned trees also pumped toxic substances into their leaves to prepare themselves. The giraffes were wise to this game and therefore moved farther away to a part of the savannah where they could find trees (3) (of / on / was / were / going / unaware / that / what). Or else they moved upwind. For the scent messages are carried to nearby trees on the breeze, and if the animals walked upwind, they could find acacias close by that had no idea the giraffes were there.

Similar processes are (d) work in our forests here at home. *Beeches, *spruce, and *oaks all register pain as soon as some creature starts eating them. When a *caterpillar takes a hearty bite out of a leaf, the tissue around the site of the damage changes. In addition, the leaf tissue sends out electrical signals, just as human tissue does when it is hurt. However, the signal is not transmitted (e) milliseconds, as human signals are; instead, the plant signal travels at the slow speed of a third of an inch per minute. Accordingly, it takes an hour or so before defensive compounds reach the leaves to spoil the pest's meal. Trees live their lives in the really slow lane, even when they are in danger. But this doesn't mean that a tree is not on top of what is happening in different parts of its structure. (4) If the roots find themselves in trouble, this information is broadcast throughout the tree, which can trigger the leaves to release scent compounds. And not just any old scent compounds, but compounds that are specifically formulated for the task at hand.

This ability to produce different compounds is another feature that helps trees avoid attack for a while. When it comes to some species of insects, trees can accurately identify which bad guys they are up against. The *saliva of each species is different, and trees can match the saliva to the insect. Indeed, (5) the match can be so precise that trees can release pheromones that summon specific beneficial predators. The beneficial predators help trees by eagerly eating up the insects that are bothering them. For example, *elms and pines call on small parasitic *wasps that lay their eggs inside leaf-eating caterpillars. As the wasp *larvae develop, they eat up the larger caterpillars bit by bit (　f　) the inside out. Not a nice way to die. The result, however, is that the trees are saved from bothersome pests and can keep growing with no further damage. The fact trees can recognize saliva is, incidentally, evidence (　g　) yet another skill they must have. For if they can identify saliva, they must also have a sense of taste.

The Hidden Life of Trees: What They Feel, How They Communicate --Discoveries from a Secret World by Peter Wohlleben, reprinted with permission from Greystone Books Ltd.

注）umbrella thorn acacia: アンブレラ・ソーン・アカシア，サバンナ・アカシア
beech: ブナ　spruce: トウヒ　oak: オーク　caterpillar: イモムシ
saliva: 唾液　elm: ニレ　wasp: スズメバチ
larvae: 幼虫（larva の複数形）

問１．下線部(1)の（　　）内の単語を適切に並べ替えなさい。

問２．下線部(2)は何がどのような行動をとることか，日本語で説明しなさい。

問３．下線部(3)の（　　）内の単語を適切に並べ替えなさい。

問４．下線部(4)を日本語に訳しなさい。

問５．下線部(5)の具体的な内容を日本語で説明しなさい。

問６．空所（　a　）～（　g　）を補うのに最も適切なものを，次の①～⑦から１つずつ選びなさい。ただし，同じものを２度以上選ぶことはで

きません。

① at　② for　③ from　④ in　⑤ of　⑥ on
⑦ to

問7．本文の主題として適切でないものを，次の①～④から１つ選びなさい。

① How insects and animals damage trees.
② How scent is used by trees for communication.
③ How trees communicate with each other.
④ How trees defend themselves from insects and animals.

《 Vocabulary Building Exercise 》

次の例文中の空欄に入るものとして最も適切な単語を，後の ***Ans.*** から１つずつ選んで書きなさい。なお，【　】内は各空欄に入る適切な単語の意味を英語で説明したものです。

1．There is no general agreement on a standard [　　　] of intelligence.
【a statement of the exact meaning of a word or phrase, especially in a dictionary】

2．There was a [　　　] of paper as people turned the pages.
【a light dry sound like leaves or pieces of paper moving or rubbing against each other】

3．The air was filled with the [　　　] of wild flowers.
【the pleasant smell that something has】

4．They didn't take into consideration the cost of cleaning up [　　　] waste.
【containing poison; poisonous】

5．It will take at least 6 weeks before they are able to [　　　] normal activities.
【to begin an activity again after an interruption】

6. Computers [ ] the data in digital form.
【to send an electronic signal, radio or television broadcast, etc.】

7. Water is a [ ] of hydrogen and oxygen.
【a substance formed from two or more elements】

8. Our boss would often [ ] us to his office.
【to order somebody to come to you】

9. I [ ] remember sending the letter.
【without doubt】

10. This is an example of the infection caused by a [ ].
【a small animal or plant that lives on or inside another animal or plant and gets its food from it; a person who always relies on or benefits from other people and gives nothing back】

Ans.

rustle	compound	scent	definition	resume
parasite	summon	toxic	definitely	transmit

《 Summary 》

次の英文は問題英文の要約である。空欄(a)〜(f)に入るものとして最も適切な単語を後の ***Ans.*** から1つずつ選んで書きなさい。

Have you ever wondered if trees could communicate with each other? Of course, they can't talk using sound. But it turns out that they can use [(a)] as a means of communication. Humans are affected by the way other people smell, both consciously and subconsciously. In fact, scientists believe that pheromones in [(b)] have a strong influence on how we choose partners. About 40 years ago, scientists discovered that acacia trees in Africa gave off a warning gas to signal to neighboring trees when their leaves were being eaten by giraffes. The [(c)] trees then pumped toxic substances into their leaves to keep the giraffes from eating them. Leaf tissue sends out electrical signals like human tissue does when it is hurt. However, the [(d)] is very slow. It takes an hour or so before [(e)] compounds reach the leaves to protect the tree. The types of compounds trees produce can be very specific. For example, some trees can identify the saliva of insects and release pheromones that summon specific beneficial [(f)] to get rid of the bothersome pests for them. (181 words)

Ans.

artificial	touch	scent	forewarned
adaptations	sweat	sweets	transmission
predators	defensive	foremost	translation

第12問 『ツーリズムが抱える課題』

目標解答時間：40分　配点：50点

次の英文を読み，設問に答えなさい。

In May 2015, a single Chinese company sent 6,400 of its employees to France for a four-day group vacation. The visit required private viewings of *the Louvre, bookings of 140 hotels in Paris, and more than 4,700 rooms in Cannes and Monaco. But how much further can we take this kind of tourism? Today we hear increasing complaints from cities as famous as Barcelona, Florence, and Venice, which are all overwhelmed with tourists. Furthermore, tourists are slowly destroying many fragile but beautiful natural sites, from coral reefs to rainforests. Either tourism must change, or it must begin to have restrictions placed upon it.

Restraining tourism is first and foremost our duty to the global environment. The Galapagos Islands are a perfect illustration. Famous as the remote location which helped Darwin develop his views on evolution, today they are visited by tens of thousands of tourists. However, the cruise ships (1) <u>(about / but / bring / help / cannot)</u> much pollution: oil and plastics, human and food waste, and non-native species carried from distant shores. Of course, this is an extreme example. Yet wherever they go, tourists put strains on the environment. They create pollution, excess traffic, and overcrowding on beaches and in parks.

Tourism to historical sites might seem immune to these dangers. The tourists are coming to experience cultural differences via an appreciation of heritage. All too often, however, such tourism fails to promote any meaningful cultural exchange. Take Florence, for example. The 11 million tourists it attracts each year (2) <u>often experience tourism itself as much as local culture</u>. They endure long queues, only to receive brief explanations and a very limited time at each attraction. An hour waiting in line for a two-minute viewing of a Botticelli hardly seems worthwhile. Indeed, many tourist magnets promise an "authentic cultural experience", but are ultimately obliged to sell fakes. Mass tourist destinations can often seem false: they fail to show the local culture accurately, but instead (3) (no / fantasy / better / offer / is / which / a) than a trip to Disneyland.

Promoters of tourism often cite its economic advantages. However, its local benefits can be exaggerated. The kinds of jobs which tourism creates are often low-paid service-sector jobs in housekeeping, retail, and transport. These jobs hold little attraction for the local youth, and many hotels instead turn to cheap immigrant labor to do the work. (　(4)　), much tourism is seasonal: towns and resorts may suffer off-season, due to the slowdown in income. Worse still, tourism can bring an increase in crime. Some destinations cater for young people, with bars and strip clubs, not museums and cultural attractions. (5) Unsurprisingly, then, the locals get more than the economic boom they had hoped for — social disturbances which can affect family life and the safety of children.

Desire for profit has driven the rapid growth of tourism. Tourism has become the world's largest and fastest-growing industry. In 1950, around 25 million people travelled abroad. However, according to the UN World Tourism Organization (UNWTO), international tourist arrivals by 2015 had reached close to 1.2 billion, generating $1.5 trillion in export earnings. By 2030, the UNWTO forecasts international tourist arrivals to reach 1.8 billion.

Nevertheless, the profits of tourism are often a mere illusion. Much of the money earned simply returns abroad. For example, researchers found that (6) less than half of the income from safari and beach tourism in Kenya remains in Kenya, mainly because of package tours arranged by foreign companies, which rely on foreign-owned airlines and hotels. Even worse, most tourists do not ((7)) the services they access: added tourists put excessive strain on existing water supplies, transport systems, parking, and on other public services, such as police and ambulance, which are paid for by local taxpayers. A popular tourist destination may also see housing prices increase, as visitors buy up houses, reducing the supply of accommodation for locals.

Eco-tourism, with its emphasis on sustainability and small-scale operations, is often portrayed as the answer to these issues. But even if it could help, the problem of scale would remain. ((8)) An abundance of eco-tourist ventures — mass eco-tourism — is necessarily a contradiction in terms. In order to weaken tourist demand we need to address tourism's external costs — its social and environmental damage — and employ some version of a tourism tax worldwide, in order to generate funds to repair the damage we are causing.

Does all of this affect how we should view travel? ((9)) All the evidence suggests we need to change our travel habits. In the age of the Internet we can all become, as Isak Dinesen put it, "travelers in our minds". We can explore remote corners of the globe without leaving our living rooms. Quite clearly, most travelers today are neither scientists nor explorers. Most modern travel is just tourism — a form of *escapist entertainment which, like most types of leisure, is best in moderation.

Binan Dunnit, Avoiding the Tourist Trap, 慶應義塾大学

注）the Louvre: ルーブル美術館　　escapist: 現実逃避の

問１. 下線部(1)の（　　）内の単語を適切に並び替えなさい。

問２. 下線部(2)の意味に最も近いものを，次の①～④から１つ選びなさい。

① (They) are often as experienced at tourism itself as at local culture.

② (They) often learn more by local culture than by their tourism experience.

③ (They) often learn about tourism itself as opposed to local attractions.

④ (They) usually experience the local culture itself through tourism.

問3．下線部(3)の（　　）内の単語を適切に並び替えなさい。

問4．空所（ (4) ）を補うのに最も適切なものを，次の①～④から1つ選びなさい。

① By contrast　　② However

③ Moreover　　④ For instance

問5．下線部(5)を日本語に訳しなさい。

問6．下線部(6)を日本語に訳しなさい。

問7．空所（ (7) ）を補うのに最も適切なものを，次の①～④から1つ選びなさい。

① express gratitude for　　② make enough use of

③ patiently put up with　　④ pay fully for

問8．空所（ (8) ）を補うのに最も適切なものを，次の①～④から1つ選びなさい。

① Creating a vast network of eco-resorts would clearly be sustainable.

② Even eco-tourist ventures have negative environmental impacts.

③ Financial burdens would go far beyond the environmental effects.

④ Little or no environmental damage is created by eco-resorts.

問9．空所（ (9) ）を補うのに最も適切なものを，次の①～④から1つ選びなさい。

① Actually, no.　　② I think it is unlikely.

③ Who could doubt it?　　④ Why should it?

《 Vocabulary Building Exercise 》

次の例文中の空欄に入るものとして最も適切な単語を，後の ***Ans.*** から 1 つずつ選んで書きなさい。なお，【　】内は各空欄に入る適切な単語の意味を英語で説明したものです。

1. Seats go quickly, so it is essential to [ ] in advance.
【to arrange to have or use something on a particular date in the future; to buy a ticket in advance】

2. Be careful not to drop it; it's very [ ].
【easily broken or damaged】

3. John managed to [ ] his anger.
【to stop something that is growing or increasing from becoming too large】

4. Many people are [ ] to this disease.
【able to resist catching or being affected by a particular disease or illness; not affected by something】

5. He tends to [ ] the significance of his job.
【to make something seem larger, better, worse or more important than it really is】

6. During the [ ] which followed, three college students were hurt.
【a situation in which people behave violently in a public place】

7. It is difficult to [ ] when the next earthquake will happen.
【to say what you expect to happen in the future, based on information that is available now】

8. The housing was to be used to provide temporary [　　　] for the homeless.
【a place to live, work or stay】

9. His public speeches are in direct [　　　] to his personal lifestyle.
【a lack of agreement between facts, opinions or actions】

10. Patients are commonly advised to drink alcohol in [　　　] and to avoid overeating.
【the quality of being reasonable and not extreme】

Ans.

disturbance	book	moderation	immune	accommodation
exaggerate	fragile	forecast	restrain	contradiction

《 Summary 》

次の英文は問題英文の要約である。空欄(a)~(f)に入るものとして最も適切な単語を後の ***Ans.*** から1つずつ選んで書きなさい。

Tourism has grown so much in recent years that it is starting to destroy many [(a)] but beautiful natural sites and put stress on famous cities such as Florence and Venice, which are [(b)] with tourists. When too many tourists visit remote locations like The Galapagos Islands, they put [(c)] on the environment. Even historical sites which people supposedly visit to appreciate cultural heritage fail to offer an authentic experience because places are too crowded and people spend more time standing in [(d)] than viewing art. Tourism does not really help local people economically because it only creates low-paid service-sector jobs. Instead, they have to deal with social [(e)] and pay high taxes for public services, such as police and ambulance. Eco-tourism places emphasis on [(f)], but this is impossible when the scale becomes too large. In the end, it may be best for us and the environment to stay home and become “travelers in our minds,” using the Internet. (160 words)

Ans.

queues	strains	sustainability	exchange
fraction	disturbances	overwhelmed	emphasis
cooperating	interactions	fragile	profits

第13問 『最優先すべき問題は貧困ではなく不平等だ』

目標解答時間：40分　配点：50点

次の英文を読み，設問に答えなさい。

Monkeys were taught in an experiment to hand over small stones in exchange for cucumber slices. They were happy with this deal.

Then the researcher randomly offered one monkey — within sight of a second monkey — an even better deal: a grape for a stone. Monkeys love grapes, so this fellow was thrilled.

The researcher then returned to the second monkey, but presented just some cucumber for the pebble. Now, this offer was insulting. Some monkeys would throw the cucumber back at the researcher in anger and disgust.

In other words, the monkeys cared deeply about fairness. What mattered to them was not just what they received but also what others got.

It is not only monkeys that are offended by inequality. For example, two scholars examined data from millions of flights to identify what factors resulted in "air rage" incidents, in which passengers become angry or even violent. One huge factor: a first-class cabin.

An incident in an economy section was four times as likely if the plane also had a first-class cabin; a first-class section increased the risk of a disturbance as much as a nine-hour delay did. (（1）)

Keith Payne, a professor of psychology at the University of North Carolina at Chapel Hill, tells of this research in a brilliant new book, *The Broken Ladder*, about how inequality destabilizes societies. It's an important, fascinating work arguing that inequality creates a public-health crisis in America.

The data on inequality reveals the shocking truth. The top 1 percent in America owns more than the bottom 90 percent. The annual Wall Street bonus pool alone is more than the annual year-round earnings of all Americans working full time at the minimum wage of $7.25 an hour, according to the Institute for Policy Studies. And what's becoming clearer is the weakening of the ties that hold society together.

Payne challenges a common perception that the real problem isn't inequality but poverty, and he's persuasive that societies are shaped not just by disadvantage at the bottom but also by inequality across the spectrum. Addressing inequality must be a priority, for we humans are social creatures, so society begins to break down when we see some receiving grapes and others cucumbers.

The breakdown affects not only those at the bottom, but also the lucky ones at the top. Consider baseball: Some team owners pay players a much wider range of salaries than others do, and one might think that pay inequality creates incentives for better performance and more wins.

In fact, economists have analyzed the data and ((2)). Teams with greater equality did much better, perhaps because the players felt a closer bond with each other.

What's more, it turned out that even the stars did better when they were on teams with flatter pay. "(3) Higher inequality seemed to have a negative effect on the superstar players it was meant to motivate, which is what you would expect if you believed that the chief effect of pay inequality was to reduce cooperation and team unity," Payne notes.

Something similar emerges in national statistics. Countries with the widest gaps in income, including the United States, generally have worse health, more killings, and a greater range of social problems.

People seem to understand this truth instinctively, for they want much less inequality than we have. In a study of people in 40 countries, liberals said company presidents should be paid four times as much as the average worker, while conservatives said five times. In fact, the average president at the largest American public companies earns about 350 times as much as the average worker.

(4) Presented with unlabeled charts depicting income distributions of two countries, 92 percent of Americans said they would prefer to live with the modest inequality that exists in Sweden. Republicans and Democrats, rich and poor alike, all chose Sweden by similar margins.

"When the level of inequality becomes too large to ignore, everyone starts acting strange," Payne notes. "Inequality affects our actions and our feelings in the same systematic, predictable fashion again and again."

"It makes us believe odd things, superstitiously clinging to the world as we want it to be (5) (so / is / it / rather / the / than / way), " he says. "Inequality divides us, splitting us into camps not only of income but also of ideology and race, eating away at our trust in one another. It generates stress and makes us all less healthy and less happy."

Think of those words in the context of politics today: Don't the terms "stress," "division," and "unhappiness" sound familiar?

So much of the national conversation gets focused on individuals such as Donald Trump — for understandable reasons. But I suspect that such people are a symptom as well as a cause, and that to uncover the root of these problems we must go deeper than politics, deeper than poverty, deeper than race, and confront the inequality that is America today.

問１．空所（ (1) ）に次の(a)～(c)の文を並べて補う場合の順序として最も適切なものを，後の①～⑥から１つ選びなさい。

(a) However, in some flights, they get on in the middle of the plane.

(b) Looking at those two scenarios, the researchers found that an air-rage incident in economy was three times as likely when economy passengers had to walk through first class compared with when they bypassed it.

(c) When there is a first-class section, it is at the front of the plane, and economy passengers typically walk through it to reach their seats.

① (a)→(b)→(c)　② (a)→(c)→(b)　③ (b)→(a)→(c)
④ (b)→(c)→(a)　⑤ (c)→(a)→(b)　⑥ (c)→(b)→(a)

問２．空所（ (2) ）を補うのに最も適切なものを，次の①～④から１つ選びなさい。

① discovered that the owners were right
② found that the opposite was true
③ revealed that this helped to raise wages
④ saw little value in their findings

問３．下線部(3)を日本語に訳しなさい。

問４．下線部(4)を日本語に訳しなさい。

問５．下線部(5)の（　　）内の単語を適切に並べ替えなさい。ただし，使用しない単語が１語ある。

問６．次のＡ～Ｃの内容を本文の内容に一致させるために空所を補うのに最も適切なものを，次の①～④からそれぞれ１つずつ選びなさい。

A The monkeys that threw slices of cucumber back at the researcher（　　）.

① disliked the type of cucumbers they were being given.
② failed to understand the importance of fairness.
③ felt upset that other monkeys were getting better treatment.

④ had no more stones they could throw at the researcher.

B Keith Payne suggests that we are mistaken to think that ( ).

① data regarding matters of inequality accurately reflects the true situation.

② earning the minimum wage will strengthen family relationships.

③ humans can best be described as social creatures

④ poverty is the reason for the weakening of social ties.

C The writer concludes that dealing with the problems he describes requires us to ( ).

① distinguish between the causes and symptoms of unhappiness.

② focus on how unequal American society has become.

③ increase the income of those at the bottom of society.

④ understand the importance of racial tension in the U.S.

《 Vocabulary Building Exercise 》

次の例文中の空欄に入るものとして最も適切な単語を，後の ***Ans.*** から 1 つずつ選んで書きなさい。なお，【 】内は各空欄に入る適切な単語の意味を英語で説明したものです。

1. After extended discussion, the ______ was made.
【an agreement, especially in business, on particular conditions for buying or doing something】

2. I find it ______ to be spoken to in that way.
【causing or intending to cause somebody to feel offended】

3. His decision can only be understood in ______.
【the situation or set of circumstances in which something happens and that helps you to understand it】

4. Neil did not mean to [ ] anybody with his joke.
【to make somebody feel upset because of something you say or do that is rude or embarrassing】

5. The messages were [ ] enough to encourage hundreds of people to join.
【able to persuade somebody to do or believe something】

6. The policy fails to [ ] the needs of the poor.
【to think about a problem or a situation and decide how you are going to deal with it】

7. This programme has provided a great [ ] for students to continue their studies.
【something that encourages you to do something】

8. These films [ ] life in Tokyo in 1960s.
【to show or describe something; to show an image of somebody/something in a picture】

9. She beat the other runners by a [ ] of ten seconds.
【the difference between two amounts】

10. I think this is just one [ ] of the poor state of the economy.
【a change in your body or mind that shows that you are not healthy; a sign that something has been caused by something else】

Ans.

context	incentive	offend	margin	insulting
address	symptom	depict	deal	persuasive

《 Summary 》

次の英文は問題英文の要約である。空欄(a)～(f)に入るものとして最も適切な単語を後の ***Ans.*** から 1 つずつ選んで書きなさい。

An experiment showed that monkeys care about fairness. When some monkeys saw other monkeys offered grapes instead of cucumbers in exchange for stones, they reacted with anger and [(a)]. Humans also care deeply about fairness. When scholars examined data from "air rage" [(b)], they discovered that a feeling of inequality was as likely to increase the risk of a disturbance as a long delay. In other words, inequality [(c)] societies. Keith Payne [(d)] the idea that poverty is the real problem. He claims that society begins to break down when some people are paid much more than others. Even professional baseball teams perform worse if superstars are paid much higher salaries than the other players because bonds between teammates are weaker. National statistics show that countries with large wealth gaps have a greater range of social problems. People seem to understand this [(e)]. Inequality affects our actions and feelings in a [(f)] fashion. It divides us into separate groups and makes us stressed, unhealthy and unhappy. (166 words)

Ans.

disease	strengthens	incentives	predictable
challenges	destabilizes	instinctively	incidents
disgust	improves	random	unwillingly

第14問 『大学における一般教養教育の重要性と学生へのアドバイス』

目標解答時間：35分　配点：50点

次の英文を読み，設問に答えなさい。

In a recent Skype call with a Dutch friend, we discussed her kids and their college experience in the Netherlands. Apparently, there had been protests on campus about costs and payments. "How much are they paying now?" I asked, gritting my teeth (a) preparation for the answer. "Well," she said, "it's now about 1,800 euro a year."

(1) Wow.

My friend's kids are going to some of the best universities in the world and, in the end, that education will cost them less than $8,000. Compare that to the U.S., where the average cost of a higher education is more than $128,000 at a private school, $96,000 for out-of-state residents attending public universities and about $40,000 for in-state residents at those same public universities.

These numbers were key data points I held in my mind as I addressed a group of parents and students last week in a talk titled "The Value of a *Liberal Arts Education." While liberal arts is defined to include some of the sciences, sometimes the term is used to contrast an education focusing on the arts and *humanities (English, history, philosophy, etc.) (b) one focusing on technical subjects such as engineering.

In spite of being a scientist, I strongly believe an education that fails to place a heavy emphasis on the humanities is a missed opportunity. (2) Without a base in humanities, both the students and the democratic society these students must enter as informed citizens are denied a full view of the heritage and critical habits of mind that make civilization worth the effort.

There is, of course, another way to view the question of whether a liberal arts education has value. It is to question whether college should instead be seen as some kind of higher vocational training: a place to go to for a specific certification for a specific job.

Here, too, I would push back strongly.

For those of us who go to college, the four years spent there are often the sole chance we give ourselves to think deeply and broadly about our place in the world. To turn college (c) nothing more than job training (emphasizing only those jobs that pay well), represents another missed opportunity for students and the society that needs them.

So, these are my traditional answers to the traditional questions about the value of humanities and arts education vs. science and engineering. From my standpoint as a scholar, I'll stand by them and defend what they represent to the last breath.

But the world has changed and, I believe, (3) these answers are no longer enough.

It's not just the high cost of college that alters the equation. It's also vast changes that have swept through society with the advent of a world run on information (i.e., on data). So, with that in mind, here is my updated — beyond the traditional — response to the value of the humanities in education: (4) The key is balance.

It is no longer enough for students to focus on *either* science/engineering or the humanities/arts. During the course of their lives, students today can expect to move through multiple career phases requiring a wide range of skills. A kid who wants to write screenplays may find she must learn how to build Web content for a movie-related app. That effort is likely to include getting her hands dirty with the technology of protocols and system architecture. Likewise, a kid who started up in programming may find himself working for a video game company that puts a high value (d) storytelling. Doing his job well may require him to understand more deeply how *Norse mythologies represented the relationship between human and animal realms.

These changes, combined with the ever-spiraling price of college, mean that students — and their parents — must strive for clarity and honesty as they make their choices. They should not fall into the easy traps of educational consumerism — thinking that only a "status" school will give students the opportunities they hope (e) to grow. There are many, many excellent schools out there. Students should be very careful about getting into debt and be clear about what the expected outcomes will be for their choices. If you long to become a poet or study Roman history, then, (f) all means, pursue those passions. But be realistic about what will happen when you graduate. Be prepared. And if the cost of education is an issue, make choices about those costs — and which school is right for you — wisely.

This means students must find a balance between the real pressure to find a job and the understanding that they will not get this chance to grow intellectually, morally and spiritually again. In dealing with (5) <u>this dilemma</u>, I would argue that everyone should have a second plan. One path toward a viable alternative plan is a double *major (or at least a *minor) that spans the divide between what C.P. Snow called the "Two Cultures."

What Is The Value Of An Education in The Humanities? by Adam Frank.

出題の都合上，原文の一部に変更を加えている。

注）Liberal Arts Education: 一般教養教育　　humanities: 人文系科目
Norse mythology: 北欧神話　　major: 専攻科目　　minor: 副専攻科目

問１．下線部(1)は何に対する驚きを表しているか，20～30字の日本語で説明しなさい。

問２．下線部(2)を日本語に訳しなさい。

問３．下線部(3)の内容として最も適切なものを，次の①～⑥から２つ選びなさい。

① 人文学の教育を軽視すべきではない。

② 大学を職業訓練の場とみなすべきではない。

③ 将来の夢を実現するのに適した大学を選ぶべきである。

④ 理科系の学生は文系科目の学問を副専攻とすべきである。

⑤ 大学における一般教養教育は専門教育への橋渡しとなるべきである。

⑥ 大学教育において，理科系科目よりも文系科目の割合を増やすべきである。

問４．下線部(4)の "balance" の内容として最も適切なものを，次の①～④から１つ選びなさい。

① a balance between the school's prestige and career preparation

② a balance between the university's status and the opportunities it gives to the student

③ a balance between the speed of information flow and the development of a liberal arts education

④ a balance between knowledge and skills gained in science/engineering and those gained in humanities/arts

問５．下線部(5)の具体的な内容を日本語で説明しなさい。

問６．空所（ a ）～（ f ）を補うのに最も適切なものを，次の①～⑧から１つずつ選びなさい。ただし，同じものを２度以上選ぶことはできません。

① at ② by ③ for ④ in

⑤ into ⑥ on ⑦ with ⑧ without

《 Vocabulary Building Exercise 》

次の例文中の空欄に入るものとして最も適切な単語を，後の ***Ans.*** から1つずつ選んで書きなさい。なお，【　】内は各空欄に入る適切な単語の意味を英語で説明したものです。

1. The use of animals in experiments has for long been the focus of political ______ .
【the act of saying or showing publicly that you object to something】

2. He is due to ______ a conference on human rights next week.
【to make a formal speech to a group of people】

3. Many countries want to develop stronger forms of ______ education.
【connected with the skills, knowledge, etc. that you need to have in order to do a particular job】

4. They didn't ______ the safety of those foods.
【to state officially, especially in writing, that something is true; to give somebody an official document proving that they are qualified to work in a particular profession】

5. The leap forward in communication was made possible by the ______ of the mobile phone.
【the coming of an important event, person, invention, etc.】

6. By the end of that conflict, Europe was entering a new ______ of historical development.
【a stage in a process of change or development】

7. Questions of consciousness lie outside the ______ of physics.
【an area of activity, interest or knowledge】

8. Her parents [　　　] hard to keep themselves very fit.
【to try very hard to achieve something】

9. It is not clear whether the television debates actually influenced the [　　　] of the elections.
【the result or effect of an action or event】

10. If there was any delay, then the rescue plan would cease to be [　　　].
【that can be done; that will be successful】

Ans.

certify	outcome	viable	phase	address
protest	advent	realm	strive	vocational

《 Summary 》

次の英文は問題英文の要約である。空欄(a)～(f)に入るものとして最も適切な単語を後の ***Ans.*** から１つずつ選んで書きなさい。

Unlike Europe, where the cost of a university education may be less than $8,000, higher education in America is extremely expensive. This means that students have to think carefully about whether to study (a) arts. Some people say that students should focus on technical subjects, such as engineering, in order to get a high-paying job. But the writer doesn't think that college should be a kind of (b) training for a specific job. Instead, he strongly believes that it is important to have a base in the (c) to have a full view of our heritage and critical ways of thinking. College is often students' (d) chance to think deeply and broadly about things. As a (e) , he defends the value of a traditional education, but he realizes that the world has changed. He believes students need a balance between technical skills and skills like storytelling. Students and their parents must think realistically about the expected (f) of their choices. They must consider the importance of finding a job, but also find ways to grow intellectually, morally and spiritually. (179 words)

Ans.

outcomes	scholar	sole	literature
answers	vocational	scholastic	vocabulary
humane	liberal	humanities	solid

第15問 『芸術への資金提供は政府の責務だ』

目標解答時間：40分　配点：50点

次の英文を読み，設問に答えなさい。

Long-established government organizations fund the arts in many nations, for example, the Arts Council England and the National Endowment for the Arts (NEA) in the US. Both support not only a variety of arts including painting, sculpture, music, dance, and folk arts, but also cultural institutions such as libraries, theaters, and museums. In addition, these organizations fund an array of programs to encourage people to enjoy the arts and cultural events. This support is critical, especially during economic recessions. (a) withdrawing state money, we need to protect and even increase government funding for the arts.

To begin with, (1) art and culture enrich public life. As Sandy Nairne, a former director of the National Portrait Gallery in London said, "Culture and art are a necessity for people both as individuals and as part of communities. Whether enjoying a visit to a museum or art gallery, singing in a choir, listening to extraordinary musicians, reading poetry or sharing in the excitement of street performance, this is a part of what makes life worthwhile." Furthermore, in an age of migration and social change, the arts serve an important role in bringing people together, helping to give citizens common experiences, and finding ways to accommodate their differences.

Art and culture represent the heritage in which a people's history and identity are firmly rooted. This heritage is preserved in the various cultural institutions of a nation. According to novelist Michael Rosen, "The wonder of libraries, museums, and archives is that we can relate ourselves with others — often stretching back hundreds or thousands of years. This is one of the ways in which we can discover the history and shape of humanity and where or how we fit into it." (b). It is, therefore, our duty to preserve, support, and encourage them.

Nevertheless, some fields of art cannot sustain themselves independently and require constant governmental funding to continue. In contrast to commercially successful grand theaters in big cities such as London and New York, local theaters in smaller cities and towns usually lack stability because ticket sales are necessarily limited. Also, (2) <u>since museums and libraries are non-profit cultural organizations, it is difficult for them to maintain their facilities and offer a high quality of services without support from government grants</u>. Moreover, such funding is required for artistic innovation because it enables artists to take risks and experiment for the sake of art itself.

Some may argue that, wherever possible, private donations can and should replace government grants. Whereas in the US, private support for art and culture is relatively secure, donations to the arts cannot be taken for granted in many other countries. Today, when extremely wealthy individuals and corporations are dominating the global economy, more can clearly be asked of them. However, charitable giving by the private sector will (3) <u>only go so far</u>. It would be unwise to make our arts *overly* dependent on the political or economic demands of private enterprise. During times of economic difficulty, private funding would constantly be at risk.

By contrast, stable government funding enables as many people as possible to enjoy art and culture. A government grant ensures *everyone's* affordable access to art and culture, and thus makes them an integral part of daily life. It allows (c). Moreover, gallery tours and cultural programs bring the arts to the poor and to children, not only to well-to-do adults. Through these programs, people can gain an understanding of the importance of art and the need to protect cultural heritage for future generations.

Government funding of the arts and cultural activities brings economic benefits by attracting tourists. (4) This, in turn, can promote the redevelopment of suburbs and encourage tourism-related services to grow. In the 1980s, politicians in the UK recognized art and culture as valuable resources that could play a part in the renewal of post-industrial cities in the country. At that time, a British politician Chris Smith took up the idea of the arts as one of the "creative industries." (5) Subsequently, an art policy was developed to widen public access to art and culture and to help drive urban rebirth and fight social exclusion. This change has been important. Today, the Arts Council of England estimates that the nation benefits by over $ 4 for every $ 1 of investment in art funding.

The arts are vital for a better quality of life; the Arts Council England makes this point clearly on their website, declaring that "great art and culture inspires us, brings us together and teaches us about ourselves and the world around us." However much individuals might contribute, providing art for citizens is always the responsibility of government. That is why continued (d) support of the arts is critical and must be ensured.

Sue Portagig, The Arts: Why State Funding is Critical, 慶應義塾大学

問 1. 下線部(1)に関して，第 2 段落に言及がないものを，次の①～④から 1 つ選びなさい。

① concerts　② exhibitions　③ films　④ literature

問 2. 下線部(2)を日本語に訳しなさい。

問 3. 下線部(3)の意味に最も近いものを，次の①～④から 1 つ選びなさい。

① have limitations　② go unchecked

③ never come true　④ remain unchanged

問4． 下線部(4)の具体的な内容を日本語で説明しなさい。

問5． 下線部(5)を日本語に訳しなさい。

問6． 空所（ a ）～（ d ）を補うのに最も適切なものを，次の①～④から 1 つずつ選びなさい。

a ① Except for ② Far from ③ In addition to
④ Thanks to

b ① Clearly, many writers are busy creating content for our heritage
② Indeed, museums are at the very heart of this heritage-related industry
③ Obviously, heritage is firmly connected to a sense of national pride
④ Ultimately, a sense of nationalism is essential for most modern nations

c ① all citizens to find common ground despite income inequalities
② governments to resolve income inequality through arts funding
③ minorities to feel unwelcome through funding their arts
④ only wealthier citizens to appreciate art

d ① financial ② mutual ③ private ④ state

《 Vocabulary Building Exercise 》

次の例文中の空欄に入るものとして最も適切な単語を，後の ***Ans.*** から 1 つずつ選んで書きなさい。なお，【　】内は各空欄に入る適切な単語の意味を英語で説明したものです。また，設問の都合上，***Ans.*** 内の語は全て小文字で表記している。

1. Drug companies and the government will jointly [　　　] the necessary medical research.
【to provide money for something, usually something official】

2. He has been singing in his church [　　　] since he was six.
【a group of people who sing together, for example in a church or school】

3. These were measures intended to pull the economy out of [　　　].
【a difficult time for the economy of a country, lasting months or years, during which trade and industrial activity are reduced, and more people are unemployed】

4. She decided to [　　　] her resignation.
【to no longer provide or offer something; to stop taking part in something】

5. She modified her views so as to [　　　] the objections of American feminists.
【to consider something such as somebody's opinion or a fact and be influenced by it when you are deciding what to do or explaining something】

6. The study was supported by a [　　　] from the government.
【a sum of money given by a government or other organization for a particular purpose】

7. The project is funded by public [　　　].
【something that is given to a person or an organization such as a charity, in order to help them; the act of giving something in this way】

8. We offer quality products at [　　　] prices.
【cheap enough that people can buy it】

9. Music is an [　　　] part of the school's curriculum.
【being an essential part of something】

10. [　　　], new guidelines were issued to all employees.
【afterwards; after something else has happened】

Ans.

fund	affordable	subsequently	choir	recession
grant	accommodate	donation	withdraw	integral

《 Summary 》

次の英文は問題英文の要約である。空欄(a)~(f)に入るものとして最も適切な単語を後の ***Ans.*** から１つずつ選んで書きなさい。

It is important for government organizations to fund the arts, especially during times of economic recessions. Art and culture enrich public life and help citizens find common experiences in age of [(a)] and social change. Each people's history and identity are firmly rooted in its art and culture. This heritage is preserved in cultural institutions like libraries, museums and [(b)], which allow us to relate to people who lived hundreds or thousands of years ago. These institutions need governmental [(c)] to continue, especially in small cities and towns. Extremely wealthy individuals and corporations can provide private [(d)], but the freedom of artists to take [(e)] and experiment would be lost if artists had to depend on the demands of private [(f)]. Government funding ensures that all people can enjoy art and culture. It brings economic benefits by attracting tourists. Since the arts are vital for a better quality of life, continued state support of the arts is critical. (158 words)

Ans.

archives	sector	risks	funding
imitation	architects	debates	enterprise
migration	advantages	donations	experts

第16問 『仕事にかかる時間についての見込みの甘さ』

目標解答時間：40分　配点：50点

次の英文を読み，設問に答えなさい。

I remain hopelessly optimistic about how much work I can accomplish. The time frame doesn't matter — I have optimistic predictions for how much I will finish today, this week, this academic term, and really in my life. (1) I've been known to bring home ridiculous amounts of work for weekends — more student essays than I can possibly read. I make what I think are reasonable estimates for when I will finish a project. Much, much later, I discover that my estimate was wildly optimistic and that it took me three times as long to actually finish the work.

I remember some advice I received once on how to make appropriate predictions of the amount of time a project would require. First, make your best estimate, then double that, and finally increase your unit of measurement. If your estimate is one hour, then make it ((2)a), and finally ((2)b). Why are we so poor at making estimates?

This failure is so well known that it has a name — (3) the planning fallacy. These sorts of planning failures can also be incredibly troublesome and expensive. The really cool thing is that we all know that we have been wrong in the past. I know how little work I accomplished last weekend, yet I nonetheless will bring home too much this weekend. (4) I know how long all of my articles have taken me to write, but I make what turn out to be silly predictions of my future writing time. I can remember the past, but I am doomed to repeat it anyway.

My favorite research on the planning fallacy is a set of studies by Beuhler, Griffins, and Ross (1994). They asked college students about their plans for finishing a large and important task — their *graduation thesis. The students gave their best estimate of when they would finish and then gave a pessimistic estimate (one assuming that everything that could go wrong would go wrong). The students' best estimates were that they would finish in 34 days on average and their pessimistic estimates averaged 48 days. In reality, the students finished in 56 days. (A) I guess everything that could go wrong went wrong and then a few more things went wrong as well.

The researchers replicated this on a shorter time period, asking students to estimate when they would finish both academic tasks (writing essays and doing assignments) and personal tasks (cleaning apartments and fixing bikes). The students were asked to choose things that they thought they would finish within one week. When the researchers called back the next week, they couldn't finish the study because the students hadn't actually finished about half the tasks. (B) Wildly optimistic estimates.

In other research, the researchers asked people to estimate when they would finish and submit documents regarding their taxes. For some people, this would be a good thing to finish because they anticipated getting refunds! People who anticipated refunds estimated that they would finish before people who didn't anticipate refunds. (No kidding, why do it if you have to pay?) But of course those expecting refunds did not finish any sooner. (C)

Why are people so optimistic about finishing tasks? The problem depends on what information people use to make the judgment. People typically focus on the future. They think about their plans: how much work there is, the various parts of the work, when they have time to work, and how important the work is. People rarely think about future problems. (D) So the first problem is that they may know they haven't finished on time before, but not use that information in making a new estimate.

But even if people do think about the past, they may dismiss their previous failures to meet goals. Yes, something went wrong last time, but that won't happen again. A college student may know that he didn't work last weekend because he went to John's party, but he also knows that John won't have a party this weekend (of course, Jim might have a party, but that doesn't come to mind). I know that my previous manuscript writing was disrupted by other demands. But I also know that those demands were one-time things and won't happen again. Of course, other one-time demands are bound to occur, but I don't realize that connection. We see past failures as unusual and unrelated to the current prediction. To some extent we are right. (　E　) Our failure is not realizing that a different problem is bound to happen.

So I want to use this as an opportunity to apologize to all my co-authors for all the times I've failed to meet my own estimates of when I would finish. (　F　)

Ira Hyman, Sorry I'm Late, Again, Psychology Today

注）graduation thesis: 卒業論文

問1．下線部(1)を日本語に訳しなさい。

問2．空所（　(2)a　），（　(2)b　）を補うのに最も適切なものを，次の①～⑤から 1 つずつ選びなさい。ただし，同じものを 2 度以上選ぶことはできません。

① one minute　② two hours　③ four hours
④ two days　⑤ four days

問3．下線部(3)は具体的にどのようなことを意味しているか，日本語で説明しなさい。

問4．下線部(4)を日本語に訳しなさい。

問5．空所（　A　）～（　F　）を補うのに最も適切なものを，次の①～⑥からそれぞれ 1 つずつ選びなさい。ただし，同じものを 2 度以上選ぶことはできません。

① The same problem is unlikely to occur again.

② Even the pessimistic estimates were optimistic!

③ I am completely sure that this time, my prediction is much better.

④ They think about past failures to meet deadlines even less frequently.

⑤ They were hopelessly optimistic even when money was sitting on the table.

⑥ On average they thought they would finish the tasks within five days and ended up taking 10 days.

《 Vocabulary Building Exercise 》

次の例文中の空欄に入るものとして最も適切な単語を，後の ***Ans.*** から1つずつ選んで書きなさい。なお，【 】内は各空欄に入る適切な単語の意味を英語で説明したものです。

1. The report expresses an [ ] view about reducing US dependence on foreign oil.
【expecting good things to happen or something to be successful; showing this feeling】

2. Not everyone is so [ ] about the future as you are.
【expecting bad things to happen or something not to be successful】

3. Mothers [ ] worry about their children.
【in a way that shows the usual qualities or features of a particular type of person, thing or group】

4. You've done so much work—you're [ ] to pass the exam.
【certain or likely to happen, or to do or be something】

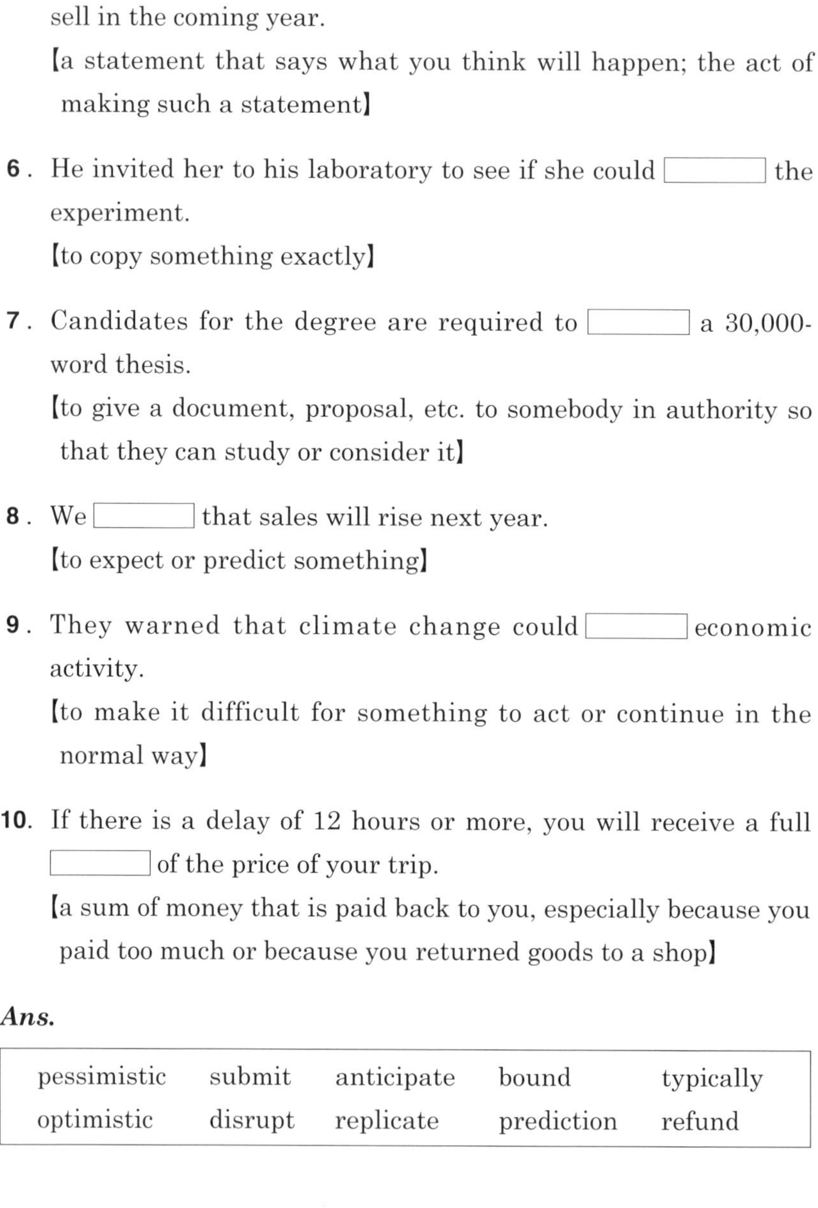

5. She was unwilling to make a ______ about which books would sell in the coming year.
【a statement that says what you think will happen; the act of making such a statement】

6. He invited her to his laboratory to see if she could ______ the experiment.
【to copy something exactly】

7. Candidates for the degree are required to ______ a 30,000-word thesis.
【to give a document, proposal, etc. to somebody in authority so that they can study or consider it】

8. We ______ that sales will rise next year.
【to expect or predict something】

9. They warned that climate change could ______ economic activity.
【to make it difficult for something to act or continue in the normal way】

10. If there is a delay of 12 hours or more, you will receive a full ______ of the price of your trip.
【a sum of money that is paid back to you, especially because you paid too much or because you returned goods to a shop】

Ans.

pessimistic	submit	anticipate	bound	typically
optimistic	disrupt	replicate	prediction	refund

《 Summary 》

次の英文は問題英文の要約である。空欄(a)〜(f)に入るものとして最も適切な単語を後の ***Ans.*** から1つずつ選んで書きなさい。

The author says that he is hopelessly [(a)] about how much work he can accomplish. He always makes unreasonable estimates, so he cannot make appropriate [(b)]. He explains that this failure is called "the planning [(c)]." A set of studies about this asked college students to estimate how much time they thought they would need to finish their graduation thesis. Everyone took even longer to finish them than their most [(d)] estimates. Researchers [(e)] these results using tasks that took less time. Even when people [(f)] getting tax refunds, they took longer than they expected to submit their tax documents. Why does this happen? People tend to believe that nothing will go wrong, even though delays are bound to occur. We think that past failures are unusual and this time everything will go smoothly. But that is almost never the case. (141 words)

Ans.

optical	optimistic	fallacy	challenged
replicated	denied	anticipated	pessimistic
accurate	presentations	fantasy	predictions

23X20

KP
KAWAI PUBLISHING

河合塾
SERIES

採点基準
要点解説
語句リスト

新英語長文問題集

New Approach

4

700-800 words

読解のカギは単語力

瓜生 豊・早﨑スザンヌ・矢次隆之　共著

Vocabulary
Building
Summary
Exercise

河合出版

はじめに

近年の大学入試では，そのレベルを問わず800語，場合によってはそれ以上の超長文を読み解く必要があります。このような分量の多さに慣れつつ，多岐に渡る文章のテーマにも幅広く対応するべく，既刊の①（400-500 words）・②（500-600words）・③（600-700words）に引き続く形で，以下４点に重点を置いて作成しました。

①　厳選された最新の良問を通じて，読解力の向上を実現する

既刊の他３冊と同様に，本書中のすべての問題は，予備校講師として数多くの授業と模試作成に携わった経験をもとに，“最新の入試問題から厳選した良問”です。質の高い問題を教材に用いることで，“正しく内容を理解する力（＝読解力）”を効率的かつ確実に鍛えることができます。

②　今まさに必要な語彙をフォローし，強化できる

解説編の**【設問別解説】**や**【語句】**，巻末の**【語句一覧】**などを通じて，今このタイミングで，“どの単語・語句を覚えておかなければならないのかを明確化し”，不足しているものがあればフォローできるようにしました。

加えて，《**Vocabulary building exercise**》や《**Summary**》といった設問解答とは別角度からの語彙力強化のための問題を用意することで，見て覚えるだけでなく“問題に答える形”でも知識をより確実にすることができるようになっています。

③　幅広いテーマの文章を通じて，多様な知識を広く身につける

引き続き〈社会問題〉・〈歴史にまつわる話題〉・〈心理学〉・〈健康科学〉・〈日常的話題〉といった今の大学入試で頻出かつ面白いテーマをできる限り多く取り扱っていますので，一通りの学習を終えれば“様々なテーマについての基礎知識を広く身につける”ことができ，読解力をより一層強固なものにできます。

④　問題英文の音声を聴くことで，より深く【英語】を理解できる

本書の問題英文はすべて音声として聴くことができます(詳細は次ページ参照)。しっかりと読んだ英文の音声で聴くことで“語句のまとまりや文意の流れ”をとらえることができるようになります。リスニング力の強化に役立つことは言うまでもなく，英文読解力・英作文力の向上のために本書を使った学習の不可欠の一部として，音声を聴くことを習慣づけてください。

本書の問題英文は，パソコンやスマートフォンから下記のURLにアクセスして聴く（ストリーミング）ことができます。

http://www.kawai-publishing.jp/onsei/01/index.html

また，以下からもアクセスできます。

※ファイル形式はMP 4形式になります。再生する際は，最新版のOSをご利用ください。

また，パソコンから下記URLにアクセスしていただくことで，音声データのダウンロードも可能です。

※ホームページより直接スマートフォンへのダウンロードはできません。一度パソコンにダウンロードしていただいた上で，スマートフォンへお取り込みください。

http://www.kawai-publishing.jp/onsei/01/index.html

※ファイルはZIP形式で圧縮されていますので，解凍ソフトが別途必要です。

※ファイルの形式はMP 3 形式になります。再生するには，Windows Media Player やiTunesなどの再生ソフトが必要です。

音声データに関する注意

本書は問題英文の総語数が「**700～800語程度**」の英文をまとめた問題集です。同じシリーズとして①（400-500words）・②（500-600words）・③（600-700words）も用意していますが，英文の長さを除いて難度にそこまでの差はありません。どの問題集も最高の問題を用意していますので，読解力と語彙力の両方を確実に鍛えることができます。

皆さんの夢の実現に本書が少しでも役に立つことを切に願っています。

著者一同

もくじ

巻末語句リストのもくじ

本書の使い方

読解問題について

各問題ですべての設問を解き終えたら，まずは**【解答】**を見て答え合わせ・採点をしてください。記述問題については**【配点と採点基準】**を参照して，どの要素は含まれていて，どの要素が足りていないのか，と“自分の解答を客観視”してみてください。この客観視は入試本番で自身の解答を見返す際に必ず役立ちます。

【設問別解説】は冗長になりすぎないように，要点のみに絞っています。長く予備校講師として指導してきた経験に基づく解説なので，熟読しておくように。

また，“１文１文の意味を確認する”ことも重要です。本書の問題はすべて実際に出題された入試問題なので，皆さんが受験する入試本番と同等の英文です。このレベルの英文を正確に理解する経験を数多く積みましょう。英文の意味を理解できない箇所は，**【全訳】**や**【語句】**を参照してください。

《Vocabulary Building Exercise》について

左側の英文を見て答え合わせをした後は，まず【　】内の英語がどういう日本語訳になるのかを確認してください。【　】内は英英辞書をイメージした言い回しになっているので，皆さんが単語帳などで学んだ単語の“ニュアンスまで含み込んだ意味”を知ることができます。ニュアンスまで把握した後は，左側の英文を見て“正解の単語が実際にどういう文脈で使われるのか”を改めて確認してください。実際の英文を読む際には単語帳の訳語をあてはめるだけでなく，文脈に応じた理解が必要になります。たんに単語帳の訳を覚えるだけでなく，単語の実際の使われ方に慣れておくことが重要なのです。

各例文の日本語訳は付属の“赤シートで隠して和訳の練習”をすることができるようになっていますので，語彙力強化に役立ててください。

《Summary》について

答え合わせをした後は，要約文全体と【《Summary》の訳】を見て，“どう要約されているのか”を確認してみてください。要約文とは文章全体の内容を過不足なく簡潔にまとめ直したものです。自分の内容理解と比較することで，自分は正確に読解できていたか，内容的に過不足していなかったかなどを確かめることができます。

巻末の【語句一覧】について

本書掲載の問題英文に出てくる単語や語句は，この機会に確実に身につけておくべき重要なものばかりです。そのため，付属の“赤シートで意味を隠すことができる”ようにしました。一通り学習を終えた後には，“実戦的な単語帳”として本書を使うこともできます。

単語・語句は各回かつパラグラフ順に並べており，各問題英文の内容やテーマに即した訳をそのまま掲載しています。改めて見た時になぜそういう訳になるのかと疑問に思った場合には，該当回の解説を参照してください。

本書内の各種記号について

・(　) は省略可能な語句を，[　] はその前後で言い換えが可能であることを表す。
・S は主語，O は目的語，C は補語を指し，A や B は名詞を指します。
・*do* は動詞の原形，*to do* は不定詞，*doing* は動名詞あるいは現在分詞，*done* は過去分詞，*one's* は所有格，*A's* は主語と異なる所有格，*oneself* は所有代名詞，をそれぞれ表している。なお，実際には文脈に応じた単語が入る。

第１問　名古屋工業大学

得 点

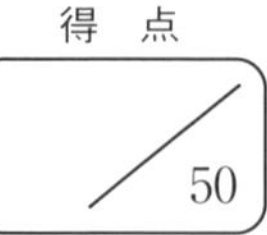

【解答】

問１．A ①　B ④　C ②　D ②

問２．(a) ④　(b) ①　(c) ②　(d) ③　(e) ④

問３．私たちの研究の原動力となった直感とは，誰かがあなたと異なる意見を持っていてあなたの目を長い間まっすぐに見た場合に，あなたは誰かがあなたを支配しようとしていると感じるということだった。

問４．人々が対面している時には，魅力があったりなかったりする聞き手に対して話す人が身を乗り出したりその他の反応を示したりするボディーランゲージなど，他にも多くのことが起こっている。

【配点と採点基準】（50点）

問１．20点（各５点×４）　解答通り

問２．10点（各２点×５）　解答通り

問３．10点

- The intuition that drove our research was that S V ... … 3点
- when someone disagrees with you … 1点
- and they look you in the eye in a prolonged, direct manner, … 3点
  - ＊等位接続詞 and による someone disagrees ... と they (= someone) look ... の並置関係をとらえていないものは２点減
  - ＊ look you in the eye の誤訳は２点減
  - ＊ in a prolonged, direct manner の誤訳は２点減
- it gives you the feeling of someone trying to dominate you … 3点
  - ＊ it gives you the feeling の誤訳は２点減
  - ＊ the feeling of someone trying to dominate you の誤訳は２点減

問４．10点

- When people are face-to-face, … 2点

・there are lots of other things going on, … 2 点
・like body language where S V ... … 2 点
・a speaker might lean in or respond in other ways to an attractive or unattractive recipient. … 4 点
＊ lean in の誤訳は 2 点減
＊ respond in other ways の誤訳は 2 点減
＊ to an attractive or unattractive recipient の誤訳は 2 点減

【設問別解説】

問 1 .

A 「ジュリア・ミンソンとフランシス・チェンの研究は，それ以前の研究とどのように異なっていたか」

① **「聞く人の観点に焦点を絞った」**→第 2 段落最終文と第 3 段落の内容に一致。

② 「聞く人の口に焦点を絞った」

③ 「『甘い状況』を調査した」

④ 「話す人の成功・失敗の感情に焦点を絞った」

B 「2 番目の調査によると，どちらの聞き手が話し手によって意見を変えられやすかったか」

① 「話す人の目をまっすぐじっと見ていた聞き手」

② 「話す人の目と口の間で視線を切り替えた聞き手」

③ 「話す人をまったく見ることのできなかった聞き手」

④ **「話す人の口だけをじっと見ていた聞き手」**→第 6 段落最終文の内容に一致。

C 「ミンソンによると，生のやりとりではなくビデオを使った 1 つの理由は何だったか」

① 「ビデオを使うことで，話す人と聞く人が異なる場所にいることが可能だった」

② **「ビデオを使うことによって，研究がアイコンタクトに集中することができた」**→第 8 段落の内容に一致。

③ 「ビデオを使うことによって，研究者がさまざまな形のボディーランゲージを含めることができた」

④ 「ビデオを使うことによって，聞く人が話す人に攻撃されるのを防いだ」

D 「本文によると，正しい文はどれか」

① 「説得力を持つためには，たえずアイコンタクトを保つことが重要だ」

② **「ほとんどの人の視線は，自然に場所から場所へと移動する」**→第７段落第２～３文に一致。

③「話す人は，アイコンタクトを行っている時には，自分の話の説得力が弱まっていると感じる」

④「感情的な状況にいる人たちは，アイコンタクトに対して同じように反応する」

問２.

(a) valid「正当な，有効な」(= correct「正しい」)

(b) potential「潜在的な，（…に）なる可能性がある」(= possible「可能な，見込まれる」)

(c) proposition「意見，命題」(= idea「考え」)

(d) instinctive「本能的な」(= natural「自然の，生まれながらの」

(e) at the outset「最初に」(= at the beginning「最初に」)

問３.

・intuition「直感」

・that drove our research は直前の the intuition を修飾する形容詞節。

・drive「…を推進する」，research「研究」

・disagree with A「A に賛成できない」

・look you in the eye「あなたの目を見る」

・in a prolonged, direct manner「長時間にわたる直接的なやり方で」

・the feeling of someone trying to dominate you「誰かがあなたを支配しようとしているという感覚」，someone は，動名詞句 trying to dominate you の意味上の主語。

問４.

・face-to-face「対面して，向き合って」

・there are lots of other things going on「他の多くのことが起こっている」(= lots of other things are going on there)

・like A「A のように」(= such as A)

・body language where S V ...「S が…するボディーランゲージ」(= body language in which S V ...)，where は関係副詞。

・lean in「身を乗り出す」

・respond in other ways「他のやり方で（身を乗り出す以外のやり方で）反応する」

・recipient「受ける側の人」，ここでは「聞き手の側の人」を意味している。

【全訳】

私たちの多くは，主張をしたい時には相手の目を見るべきだと思っている。配偶者，上司，車のセールスマン，政治家などはみな，相手が大勢であれ一人であれ，自分の立場が最も正当だということを相手に信じ込ませようとするときに，相手をまっすぐに見つめる。ところが今では，おそらくは違う方向に視線を向けるのがいいということがわかってきた。

集団の意思決定と交渉について研究している心理学者でありハーバード大学ケネディ政治大学院の准教授でもあるジュリア・ミンソンと，彼女の長年の共同研究者の心理学者でありブリティッシュ・コロンビア大学の准教授でもあるフランシス・チェンは，相手を見つめれば自分の主張がその人に伝わりやすいというこの一般通念のことを誰もまだ研究していないことに気づいた。今までは，学術研究の多くが，母親と赤ちゃんが互いに見つめあう（それによって，絆が強まる）ことや，結婚するかもしれない相手同士が互いに視線を交わす（これもまた，つながりを深める）という場合のような，「甘い状況」とミンソンが呼ぶ状況に焦点を当ててきた。だが，説得ということになると，研究者たちは実際は，アイコンタクトを行っていれば自分の言いたいことが伝わっているとほとんどいつも感じている話し手の観点からしか，やりとりを見てこなかったのだ。

雑誌『サイコロジカル・サイエンス』に発表されたばかりの新しい論文の中で，ミンソンとチェンは，話し手と意見の異なる人々をアイコンタクトが負かすことができるという命題の検証を行った。フライブルク大学でチェンによって行われた2つの異なる調査の中で，話し手が聞き手を斜めから見ていたり，相手の目ではなく口を見ていたりした時に，人々は反対意見により好意的に反応するということを研究データが示しているのだ。

ミンソンは，チェンも自分もその結果にはそんなに驚いていないと言う。動物の行動を研究する者たちは，犬などの多くの種が相手を睨みつけてから攻撃することによって相手を支配するということを証明してきた。「私たちの研究の原動力となった直感とは，誰かがあなたと異なる意見を持っていてあなたの目を長い間まっすぐに見た場合に，あなたは誰かがあなたを支配しようとしていると感じるということだった」とミンソンは言う。「私たちの反応は本能的なものかもしれない」と。

自らの理論を検証するために，ミンソンとチェンは2つの調査を行った。最初の調査で彼女たちは，女性の雇用率や，自殺幇助や，原子力発電の廃止などの意見の分かれる問題について人々が議論しているビデオを20人の学生が見る様子を観察した。彼女たちは，学生が話し手に賛成する傾向がある実例や反対する傾向がある実例を含めて，さまざまなシナリオを検証した。彼女たちは，視線の追跡によって，学生が話し手の目を見ているかどうかを計測した。いくつかのビデオでは，話し手はカメラを直視していた。別のいくつかのビデオでは，話し手が視線を45度逸らしていた。ミンソンとチェンが発見したことは，学生が最初から話し手の立場に反対している場合には，直接のアイコンタクトによって彼らが意見を変える可能性が低くなるということだった。「被験者がより多くのアイコンタクトを行った時には，彼らは説得されにくかった」とミンソンは言う。

2番目の調査では，さらに人数の多い42人の被験者グループに頼み，白い背景の中心に顔が来るようにしてカメラをまっすぐ見つめる4人の学生が登場する8本のビデオを見てもらった。今回も話し手は，女性の雇用の増大や農業のやり方など意見の分かれる話題について論じた。聞き手は全員，話し手の意見に反対だった。教授たちは聞き手に，話し手の目を直視するか口を見るかのいずれかにするように指示を与えた。この場合も，話し手の口を見ずに目を見ていた人は意見を変える可能性が低いということを，ミンソンとチェンは発見した。

このことは，私たちの中で主張を通したいと思う者にとって何を意味するのだろうか。ミンソンは，ほとんどの人はアイコンタクトを保ち続けるわけではないと言う。「視線は相手の目と口の間を自然に行ったり来たりする」と彼女は指摘する。「それにまた，視線がさまようだけの場合もある」と。不自然なほど相手の目を無理に見ようとするのはやめたほうがいい，と彼女は忠告する。

私は，この調査に関して1つの大きな疑問を持った。それは，ビデオの中のやりとりが実際に生の人間と行うコミュニケーションと同じなのかということだ。同じではない，とミンソンは言う。人々が対面している時には，魅力があったりなかったりする聞き手に対して話す人が身を乗り出したりその他の反応を示したりするボディーランゲージなど，他にも多くのことが起こっている。少なくともビデオの中のやりとりはアイコンタクトだけを切り離している。

次に私が主張を通したい時には，私は視線をさまよわせておこうと思う。

【語句】

第1パラグラフ

・make a point「主張する」

・look A in the eye「Aの目を見る」

・the other person「相手」
・spouse「配偶者」
・boss「上司」
・car salespeople「車のセールスマン」
・politician「政治家」
・gaze「凝視，注視」
・convince A that S V ...「A に…ということを確信させる」
・audience「聞き手，聴衆」
・position「立場，見解」
・valid「正当な，有効な」
・It turns out that S V ...「…ということがわかる」
・cast *one's* glance「視線を向ける」
＝ throw *one's* glance
・in a different direction「違う方向に」

第２パラグラフ

・psychologist「心理学者」
・assistant professor「准教授」
・government「政治，行政，政府」
・group decision making「集団の意思決定」
・negotiation「交渉」
・longtime「長年の，長期にわたる」
・collaborator「協同研究者，協力者」
・realize that S V ...「…だと（はっきりと）理解する」
・this piece of A「この１つのA」
※Aには不可算名詞が入る。
・conventional「月並みな，平凡な，従来型の」
・wisdom「（先人の）知恵，賢明な教え」
・stare at A「Aをじっと見る」
・(be) likely to *do*「…する可能性が高い」
・academic work「学術研究」
・focus on A「Aに集中する，Aに焦点を当てる」
・what S call C「SがCと呼ぶもの」
・lovey-dovey「ラブラブの，甘ったるい，ベタベタの」
・context「状況，文脈」
・gaze at A「Aをじっと見つめる」
＝ stare at A
・strengthen「…を強くする，…を強化する」
・bond「絆」
・potential「潜在的な，（…に）なる可能性のある」
・mate「配偶者，連れ合い」
・improve「…を向上させる」
・connection「つながり，関係（性）」
・when it comes to A「Aということになると」
・persuasion「説得」
・academic「学者，研究者」
・interaction「やりとり，相互作用」
・from the perspective of A「Aの視点［観点］から」
・get A across「Aを理解させる，Aをわからせる」

・make eye contact「アイコンタクトを行う」

第３パラグラフ

・paper「(学術) 論文, (研究) 論文」
・publish「…を発表する, …を公表する」
・proposition「意見, 命題」
・win over A「A を説き伏せる, A を味方に引き入れる」
・disagree with A「A に同意しない」
⇔ agree with A「A に同意する」
・conduct「(調査など) を行う」
・data「データ, 情報, 基礎資料」
※ datum の複数形。
・respond to A「A に反応する」
・favorably「好意的に, 好意を持って」
・opposing「反対の, 相反する」
・argument「主張, 論拠」
・at an angle「斜めに, 傾いて」
・recipient「受け取り手, 聞き手」
・focus A on B「A の焦点を B に合わせる, A を B に集中させる」
・counterpart「対応［相当］するもの, 対の片方」

第４パラグラフ

・totally「まったく, すっかり」
＝ entirely
・prove that S V ...「…ということを証明［立証］する」
・species「種」
※単複同形。
・control「…を支配する」
・stare A down「A をにらみつけて目をそらさせる」
・attack「攻撃する」
・intuition「直感」
・drive「…を推進する」
・research「研究, 調査」
・in a prolonged, direct manner「長時間にわたる直接的なやり方で」
※ prolonged は「長期の, 長引く」の意味を表す形容詞。
・dominate「…を支配する」
・reaction「反応, 反動」
・instinctive「本能的な, 直感的な」

第５パラグラフ

・run a study「調査［研究］を行う」
＝ conduct a study
・observe「…を観察する」
・controversial「賛否両論のある, 異論の多い」
・subject「話題, 問題, 主題」
・the percentage of women hired「女性の雇用率」
・assisted suicide「自殺幇助」
・nuclear power phase-out「原子力発電の段階的廃止」
・scenario「シナリオ, 筋書」
・including A「A を含めて」
・instance「実例, 例」
・a tendency to *do*「…する傾向」
・agree with A「A に同意する」

⇔ disagree with A「A に同意しない」
・through eye tracking「視線の追跡によって」
・measure whether S V ...「…かどうかを測定する」
・at the outset「最初は，最初に」
＝ at the beginning
・change *one's* mind「決心を変える，考えを変える」
・participant「被験者，参加者」
・persuade「…を説得する」

第6パラグラフ

・rely on A「A に頼る，A に依存する」
＝ depend on A
・with *one's* head centered「頭が中心の位置にあって」
※ with は「付帯状況」を表す。
・against a white background「白い背景を背にして」
・farming practice「農業のやり方，農業の実践」
・direct O to *do*「O に…するように指示する」
・those who S V ...「…する人々」
＝ the people who V ...
・B rather than A「A ではなく B」

第7パラグラフ

・consistent「一貫した，矛盾がない」
・go back and forth「行ったり来たりする」
・note「…と指摘する」
・wander around「(うろうろと) さまよう」
・force *oneself* to *do*「無理に…しようとする」
・look into A「A の中をのぞく」
・advise that S V ...「…ということを忠告する」

第8パラグラフ

・the same as A「A と同じもの［こと］」
・in-person「生の，ライブの」
・communication「コミュニケーション，意思疎通」
・face-to-face「対面して，向き合って」
・go on「起こる」＝ happen
・lean in「身を乗り出す」
・in other ways「別のやり方で」
・attractive「魅力的な」
⇔ unattractive「魅力的でない」
・at least「少なくとも」
・isolate「…を分離［隔離］する」

第9パラグラフ

・next time S V ...「今度…するときは」
・let O *do*「O を…するままにしておく」

《 Vocabulary Building Exercise 》

1. You, or your **spouse** , must be at least 60 to participate.

【a husband or wife】

2. Each party had its own quite **valid** reasons for its policies.

【based on what is logical or true】

3. Rents are agreed by **negotiation** .

【formal discussion between people who are trying to reach an agreement】

4. We are aware of the **potential** problems and have taken every precaution.

【that can develop into something or be developed in the future】

5. Trust that develops through social **interaction** between individuals can often be very important.

【the way that people communicate with each other】

1. 「参加するには，あなた，もしくはあなたの配偶者が60歳以上である必要があります」

【夫または妻】

2. 「各政党は，自らの政策について独自のまったく正当な理由を持っていた」

【論理的な，あるいは真実であることに基づいた】

3. 「賃貸料は交渉によって合意される」

【合意に達しようとしている人たちの間での正式な話し合い】

4. 「私たちは潜在的な問題に気づいていて，あらゆる予防措置を講じています」

【何かに発展する，あるいは将来発展する可能性がある】

5. 「個人間の社会的交流から生まれる信頼は，しばしば非常に重要なものになることがある」

【人がお互いに意思疎通を図る方法】

6. I'd like to put a business **proposition** to you.
【an idea or a plan of action that is suggested】

6. 「あなたにビジネスの提案をさせていただきたいと思います」
【提案されるアイデアや行動計画】

7. To make a decision quickly, people have to rely on their **intuition**.
【the ability to know something by using your feelings rather than considering the facts】

7. 「意思決定を迅速に行うには，自分の直感に頼る必要がある」
【事実関係を考慮せずに，自分の感覚を使って何かを知る能力】

8. Horses have a well-developed **instinct** for fear.
【a natural quality that makes people and animals tend to behave in a particular way using the abilities that they were born with】

8. 「ウマには，よく発達した警戒本能がある」
【ヒトや動物が生まれつき持つ能力を発揮して特定の行動をとるようにさせる先天的な性質】

9. From the **outset** he had put his trust in me, the son of his old friend.
【the beginning of something】

9. 「最初から，彼は旧友の息子である私に信頼を寄せていました」
【何かの始まり】

10. One weakness of the research was that interviewers were not **consistent** in the way they asked questions.
【always behaving in the same way, or having the same opinions or standards】

10. 「この調査の欠点の1つは，インタビュアーの質問の仕方が一貫していなかったことだった」
【常に同じように振る舞ったり，同じ意見や基準を持っていたりする】

《 Summary 》

It is commonly believed that we should look someone in the eye when we want to make a point. However, recent studies have shown that this is not actually effective. Instead, we should look in a different direction if we really want to convince someone that we are correct about something. Until now, researchers tended to focus on how direct gazes strengthened intimate bonds. Otherwise, they studied whether speakers felt like they were able to persuade others. But nobody had studied how the listeners felt. A new paper has tested the proposition that making direct eye contact is effective in changing the minds of people that disagree with you. The study used video interaction to avoid the influence of other factors like body language. It found that people respond more favorably if the speaker looks down at the mouth of his counterpart instead of looking directly into his eyes. (149 words)

【《Summary》の訳】

自分の主張を述べるときは相手の目を見るべきだと一般に考えられています。ところが，最近のいくつかの研究は，それが実際には効果的ではないことを示しています。そうする代わりに，何かについて自分が正しいことを相手に納得させたいならば，視線を別の方向に向けるべきなのです。これまで研究者たちは，相手を見つめることがいかにして親密な絆を強めることができるのかという点を重視する傾向がありました。さもなければ，話し手が相手を説得できたと感じたかどうかを調査していました。しかし，聞き手がどのように感じたのかを研究していた人は誰もいませんでした。ある新しい論文は，直接目を合わせることは，異なる意見を持つ人たちの考えを変えるのに効果的であるという説を検証しました。この研究では，ボディーランゲージなどの別の要素の影響を避けるためにビデオでのやり取りが用いられました。そこでわかったことは，話し手が相手の目を直視するのではなく，口元あたりに目を向けた方が好意的に反応してくれるということでした。

第２問　学習院大学

得　点
／50

【解答】

問１．第二次世界大戦の開戦直後に起こったロンドン市民によるペットの大量虐殺。（35字）

問２．英国政府もまた，より大きな大英帝国の利益のために自分たちのペットを殺すことなど国民に指示してはいなかった。むしろ，それは，戦争という新しい現実に恐怖を抱いた人たちによって起こった自発的と思われる集団行動だった。

問３．②

問４．③

問５．③

問６．④

問７．**that reveals a deep-rooted tendency**

問８．⑤・⑦（順不同）

【配点と採点基準】（50点）

問１．５点
・「第二次世界大戦の開戦直後」「第二次世界大戦の時」の内容 … 1 点
・「ロンドン市民によるペットの大量虐殺」の内容 … 4 点

問２．14点
・Nor did the British government issue instructions … 3 点
・telling its citizens to kill their pets … 2 点
・for the greater good of the Empire. … 2 点
・Rather, … 1 点
・it was a mass action that arose, … 2 点
・apparently voluntarily, … 2 点
・by a population terrified by the new reality of war. … 2 点

問３．４点　解答通り

問４．４点　解答通り

問５．３点　解答通り

問6．4点　解答通り
問7．4点　解答通り
問8．12点（各6点×2）解答通り

【設問別解説】

問1．

「このこと」とは，第1段落第1・2文の中の In early September 1939, the citizens of London set about killing their pets. During the first four days of World War Ⅱ, over 400,000 dogs and cats ... were put to death の内容を指す。

問2．

- Nor did the British government issue ... = The British government didn't issue ... either「英国政府もまた，…を発令しなかった」，否定の意味を含む副詞 nor が文頭に置かれたことによって，主節の S V が疑問文の語順［倒置形］となっている。
- issue instructions「指示を発令する」
- telling its citizens ... 以下は，直前の instructions を修飾する形容詞句。
- tell O to *do*「O に…するように告げる［命じる］」
- for the greater good of the Empire「もっと大きな大英帝国の利益のために」
- rather「むしろ」
- it は下線部(1)の this を受け，「ペットの大量虐殺」の内容を表す。
- mass action「集団行動，大衆行動」
- that arose ... 以下は，直前の名詞句 mass action を修飾する形容詞節で，that は主格の関係代名詞。
- apparently voluntarily「見たところ自発的らしい，自発的と思われる」
- terrified by the new reality of war「戦争という新しい現実におびえた」は直前の population を修飾する形容詞句。

問3．

- for no better reason than that S V ...「…という理由だけで」，inconvenient「不便な」
  「それら（＝ ペット）を生かしておくのが不便だからという理由だけで」

① 「英国政府が飼い主にペットを殺すように指示したからというだけの理由で」
② 「ペットを飼い続けることを，飼い主が面倒だと考えたからというだけの理由で」

③ 「ペットが凶暴で危険だと飼い主が考えたからというだけの理由で」
④ 「十分な食料と水がなかったからというだけの理由で」

問4.

「私たちは，ペットが私たちのために何ができるかではなく，私たちがペットのために何ができるかを問うようになった」

① 「ペットにできないことをペットがやってくれることを期待していたわけではなかったが，私たちはペットにあまりに多くのことをやるように強いた」
② 「私たちはペットが私たちのために何ができるかを考え始めたが，よい答えは見つからなかった」
③ 「私たちは以前は役立つからという理由で犬や猫を飼っていたが，犬や猫を伴侶として扱うようになった」
④ 「私たちは犬や猫に役立つことをするように望んだが，犬や猫は私たちが望むことができなかった」

問5.

be written out of history「歴史から削除される」

問6.

① 「RSPCA は正確な回答をした。そうすることが義務だったからだ」
② 「RSPCA は正確な回答をした。第二次世界大戦中にロンドン市民からの協力がもっと必要だったからだ」
③ 「RSPCA の回答は不正確だった。第二次世界大戦中にペットがどうなったかをロンドンにいるすべての人が知っているからだ」
④ 「RSPCA の回答は不正確だった。彼らは実際には，自らの雑誌の中で動物の殺処分について報じていたからだ」 →下線部を含む文の中の，A researcher ... was told that "there is no evidence in our surviving records of any 'massacre' of pets at the start of World War Ⅱ," despite the fact that the RSPCA's magazine *Animal World* had reported in October 1939 that "the work of destroying animals continued, day and night, during the first week of the war." の内容に一致する。

問7.

・reveal「…をさらけ出す，…を明らかにする」
・a deep-rooted tendency toward A「A への根深い傾向」
・コンマを挟んだ 2 つの名詞句 such an unhappy chapter in their history と one that reveals a deep-rooted tendency toward needless panic が同格関係にある。one = a chapter (in their history)。that は主格の関係代名詞。

問８.

① 「第二次世界大戦が始まった時に，ドイツが突然に英国を攻撃したために，ロンドン市民はペットを殺した」→第２段落第３文と矛盾。

② 「ロンドン市民は今でも，第二次世界大戦が始まった時にペットを殺すことによって自分たちはいいことをしたと考えている」→第３段落第１文と矛盾。

③ 「ロンドンで殺されたペットの数は，第二次世界大戦中に増加し続けた」→第３段落第４文と矛盾。

④ 「第二次世界大戦が始まった時のペットの殺処分に対して『タイムズ』紙は反対していたが，BBC のクリストファー・ストーンは殺処分は必要なことだと考えていた」→第３段落第３文と矛盾。

⑤ **「第二次世界大戦中に，一部の人間よりもいい待遇を受けているペットがいることを知って，かなり多くの英国人は複雑な気持ちになった」**→第５段落第１文の内容に一致。

⑥ 「第一次世界大戦中にはペットや動物は見捨てられたが，第二次世界大戦中には英国人にとってもっと重要な存在になった」→英文全体，特に第２段落と第５段落の内容と矛盾。

⑦ **「ロンドン市民たちは，第二次世界大戦が始まった時のペットの殺処分のことを思い出したがらない。それは彼らの誇り高いセルフイメージと合致しないからだ」**→最終段落の内容に一致。

【全訳】

1939年の９月初め，ロンドン市民は自分たちのペットを殺し始めた。第二次世界大戦の最初の４日間で，40万匹を超える犬と猫――ロンドンのペット全体の約26％――が殺されたが，その数は，この戦争の全期間中の爆撃による英国の民間人の死者数の６倍にのぼる。それは静かで秩序を保った大量虐殺だった。ある動物保護施設では，安楽死させるためにペットを引き渡す順番を待つ人たちで，１キロメートル近くにも及ぶ行列ができていた。動物福祉協会ではクロロホルムが足りなくなり，保護施設では埋葬地が足りなくなった。ある地方病院が用地を提供し，そこに50万匹のペットの遺体が埋められた。

こうしたことのいずれも，実際の必要に迫られて行われたものではなかった。食料供給はまだ不足してはいなかった。ドイツによる「電撃戦（空襲）」はまだ始まっておらず，それが本格的に始まったのは翌年の９月になってからのことだった。英国政府もまた，より大きな大英帝国の利益のために自分たちのペットを殺すことなど国民に指示してはいなかった。むしろ，それは，戦争という新しい現実に恐怖を抱いた人たちによって起こった自発的と思われる集団行動だった。

ほとんど瞬時に，人々は自分たちがいかに大きな間違いを犯したかに気づいた。11月までには，『タイムズ』紙は「単に生かしておくのが不便だからというだけの理由で，ペットとして飼われていた数多くの犬が今でも殺されている証拠が毎日のように見つかっている」と嘆いていた。同様にBBCのクリストファー・ストーンも，同じ月に彼の人気ラジオ番組でこの虐殺に抗議し，「忠実な友を必要もないのに殺してしまうのは，この戦争を自分の家の中に忍び込ませるもう1つのやり方だ」と言った。この頃までにはペットの大量殺処分は減っており，あの最初の4日間を生き抜いた犬の多くは戦争が終わるまで生き延びた。しかし，その犠牲はもう取り返しがつかなかった。

この殺害は，20世紀初めに起こった人間と犬や猫との関係の変化と大いに関係があった。ブタやニワトリ，ウシと同様に，人間は犬や猫が自分たちに役立つという理由から近くで飼うようになった。つまり，私たちは警護や狩猟のために犬を飼い，有害生物の駆除のために猫を飼うようになったのだった。コンパニオン（伴侶）動物としての犬や猫の地位は，最初は単なる副次的な恩恵だったが，都市化とともにそれは変わり始めた。都市の居住者は犬や猫に家の中で役立つ仕事をしてもらう必要がますます少なくなっていったのだが，それでも私たちは犬や猫をとにかく飼い続けた。従来の意味ではもはや役に立つものではなくなっていたが，犬と猫は単に家族の一員となり，私たちは，ペットが私たちのために何ができるかではなく，私たちがペットのために何ができるかを問うようになったのだ。

このような態度は平和な時代には問題がなかったが，第一次世界大戦中には，かなりの割合の英国人は，ペットが一部の人間よりもよい待遇を受けていると思うと落ち着かない気持ちになった。『タイムズ』紙は1916年にロンドンで開催された猫の品評会の画像を掲載したが，それはシルクのクッションの上にいるペットたちの姿で，「何匹かは太っていた」と指摘した。そのようなコメントが付けられた理由は，この時期に多くの人々が飢えかかっていて，ペットは人間と食べ物を奪い合うぜいたく品だというのが大方の意見だったからであるのは間違いない。

多くの点で，第二次世界大戦中に動物の運命を決めたのは第一次世界大戦の記憶だった。多くの人々が，飢えた猫や犬がロンドンの街をうろついている姿を覚えていた。しかしながら，当時は注目を集めたものの，それ以来ペットの虐殺は英国の歴史からほとんど削除されてしまっている。この殺害に関する情報を王立動物虐待防止協会（RSPCA）に求めたある研究者は，「当協会に残されている資料には，第二次世界大戦の開始時にペットが『虐殺』されたという証拠は一切ない」という回答を受け取った。そのRSPCAが発行する雑誌『アニマル・ワールド（Animal World）』が1939年10月に「戦争の最初の１週間に昼夜を問わず動物の殺処分の作業が続いた」と報じていたという事実があるにもかかわらずである。

もちろん，ロンドン市民が自らの歴史の中のそのような不幸な一章，つまり不必要なパニックを起こす根深い傾向をさらけ出す一章を思い出したくないのも無理はない。英国人は今日にいたるまで，戦争に直面しても失わない自制心を誇りにしていて，それは，「平静を保ち，（普段の生活を）続けよ」というフレーズの中に表現されている遺産である。奇妙だが重大なパニックが起きたこの時期のことは，このセルフイメージを壊してしまうものであり，「我慢強さ」の下に恐怖心と理性の欠如が潜んでいることを示唆してしまうのだ。

【語句】

第１パラグラフ

・citizen「市民」
・set about *doing*「…することにとりかかる」
・pet「ペット」
・put A to death「A を殺す」
・the number of civilian deaths「民間人の死者数」
・the UK「英国」＝ the United Kingdom
・bombing「爆撃」
・entire「全体の，全部の」
・calm「穏やかな」
・orderly「整然とした，秩序のある」
・shelter「避難所，収容所」
・line「列」
・stretch「広がる，伸びている」
・turn A over「A を引き渡す」
・animal welfare society「動物福祉協会」
・run out of A「A を切らす，A を使い果たす」
・burial ground「埋葬地」
・local hospital「地方病院」
・body「遺体，死体」
・bury「…を埋葬する，…を埋める」

第２パラグラフ

・out of necessity「必要に迫られて，必要から」
・food supply「食料供給」
・scarce「乏しい，少ない」
・following「次の，次に来る」
・Nor did S *do* ...「S はまた…しなかった」
　※接続詞 Nor が文頭に来ると疑問文の語順［倒置形］になる。
・government「政府」
・issue「…を発する，…を出す」
・instruction「指示，命令」
・tell O to *do*「O に…するように命じる」
・for the good of A「A の（利益の）

ために」
※ good は「利益」の意味を表す名詞。
・the Empire「大英帝国」
・rather「むしろ」
・mass action「集団行動，大衆行動」
・arise「起こる」＝ happen
※活用は【arise / arose / arisen / arising】
・apparently「見たところ（は）…らしい，どうやら…らしい」＝ seemingly
・voluntarily「自発的に，任意に」
・population「住人，人々」
・terrify「…をひどく怖がらせる，…をぞっとさせる」
・reality「現実」＝ actuality

第 3 パラグラフ

・immediately「すぐに，直ちに」＝ at once
・realize「…をはっきり理解する，…を悟る」
・complain that S V ...「…だと不満［不平］を言う」
・There is evidence that S V ...「…という証拠がある」
※ evidence は不可算名詞で that は同格を表す。
・daily「毎日の，日単位の」
・large numbers of A「非常に多くの A」
・be being destroyed「殺されている」
※ be being *done* は進行形の受動態の形。
・for no better reason than that S V ...「…という理由だけで」
・inconvenient「不便な」
⇔ convenient「便利な」
・keep O alive「O を生かしておく」
・likewise「同様に」⇔ similarly
・argue against A「A に反する結論を下す」
・faithful「忠実な，献身的な」
・There is no need to *do*「…する必要がない」
・let O *do*「O に…させる，O を…するままにしておく」
・creep into A「A の中に忍び込む」
・mass killing「大量殺処分」
・lessen「減る，少なくなる」＝ decrease
・survive「…を切り抜ける，生き残る」
・last「持ちこたえる，生き延びる」
・The damage is already done「その損害［犠牲］はもう取り返しがつかない」

第 4 パラグラフ

・have a great deal to do with A「A と大いに関係がある」
・the relationship of A to B「A と B の関係」
・human「人間，人類」
＝ human being

・like A「Aのように」
・cattle「ウシ」
※集合名詞で複数扱い。
・be useful to A「Aに役立つ」
・security「警備，防護，安全」
・hunting「狩猟」
・status「地位，身分」
・companion animal「伴侶動物，連れ合いとしての動物」＝ pet
・initially「最初に，初めに」
・side benefit「副次的な恩恵」
・with urbanization「都会化とともに」
・less and less「ますます（…）ない」
・no longer「もはや（…）ない」
・in the traditional sense「従来の意味で」

第5パラグラフ

・attitude「態度，姿勢」
・(all) well and good「よろしい，しかたない」
※やむを得ない同意・承諾を表す。
・peacetime「平時，平和時」
・significant「かなりの，相当数の，重大な」
・portion「部分，割り当て」
・treatment「待遇」
・run an image「画像を掲載する」
・silk pillow「シルクのクッション」
・note that S V ...「…だと指摘する」
・make a comment「コメントをする，批評する」
・no doubt「疑いなく，確かに」
・widespread「広範囲に及ぶ」
・luxury item「ぜいたく品」
・compete with A「Aと競争する，Aと張り合う」

第6パラグラフ

・memory「記憶」
・determine「…を決定する」
＝ decide
・fate「運命」
・wander「さまよう，歩き回る」
・despite A「Aにもかかわらず」
＝ in spite of A
・attention「注目，注意」
・all but「ほとんど」＝ almost
・write A out of history「歴史からAを削除する［消す］」
・researcher「研究者，調査員」
・ask A for B「AにBを（くれるよう）頼む」
・the Royal Society for the Prevention of Cruelty to Animals「王立動物虐待防止協会」
・despite the fact that S V...「…だけれども」
＝ in spite of the fact that S V ...
・report that S V ...「…だと報告する」
・continue「（間断なく）続く」
・day and night「昼も夜も，昼

夜の別なく」

第7パラグラフ

- It makes sense that S V ...「…は理屈に合う，…は理解できる」
  ※ It は形式主語。
- chapter「章」
- reveal「…をさらけ出す，…を明らかにする」
- a deep-rooted tendency toward A「A への根深い傾向」
- needless panic「不必要なパニック」
- pride *oneself* on A「A を誇る」
  = take pride in A, be proud of A
- self-control「自制，克己」
  = self-restraint
- in the face of A「A に直面して(の)」
- legacy「遺産」
- phrase「フレーズ，言い回し」
- carry on「(仕事などを) 続ける」
- odd「奇妙な，変わった」
- weaken「…を弱くする」
  ⇔ strengthen「…を強くする」
- suggest「…を示唆［提案］する」
- terror「恐怖」
- the lack of reason「理性の欠如」

《 Vocabulary Building Exercise 》

1. The share of **civilian** casualties in armed conflict has increased.
【connected with people who are not members of the armed forces or the police】

1.「武力紛争における民間人の犠牲者の割合が増えてきている」

【軍隊や警察に属さない人たちに関連する】

2. They are seeking an **orderly** and peaceful resolution to the crisis.
【arranged or organized in a neat, careful and logical way】

2.「彼らはその危機に対し，秩序ある平和的解決を模索している」

【きちんとし，注意深く，論理的な方法で配置されたり構成されたりしている】

3. The squirrels started to **bury** nuts and seeds in the ground.
【to place something in the ground, especially a dead body in a grave】

3.「そのリスたちは木の実や種を地中に埋め始めた」
【(特に死体を墓に埋葬するなど) 地中に何かを安置する】

4. Skilled workers were becoming increasingly **scarce**.
【there being not enough of something and it is only available in small quantities】

4.「熟練労働者がますます不足してきていた」
【何かが足りなくなり，わずかな数量しか手に入らない】

5. Refugees have not **voluntarily** chosen to leave their country of origin.
【willingly; without being forced】

5.「難民たちは，生まれた国を離れることを自発的に選んだわけではない」
【自ら進んで／強制されずに】

6. More people have been infected than was **initially** thought.
【at the beginning】

6.「当初考えられていたよりも多くの人たちが病気に感染した」
【最初に】

7. All animals **compete** with other members of their species.
【to try to be more successful than others】

7.「あらゆる動物は，自分たちと同じ生物種に属する仲間と競争する」
【ほかの者よりも成功しようと努める】

8. The new job doesn't pay as much, but we won't **starve**.
【to suffer or die because you do not have enough food to eat; to make somebody suffer or die in this way】

8.「その新しい仕事は前のものほど給料は高くないが，飢えることはないだろう」
【食べ物が十分にないために苦しんだり死んだりする／そのようにして誰かを苦しめたり死なせたりする】

9. The collapse of the USSR ended one **chapter** of human history.
【a period of time in history or a person's life; a separate section of a book, usually with a number or title】

9. 「ソビエト連邦の崩壊は，人類の歴史における１つの章を終わらせた」
【歴史や人生における１つの時代／書物の中の独立した部分で，たいてい番号やタイトルが付けられている】

10. These photos **capture** the spirit of those times.
【to succeed in accurately expressing a feeling, an atmosphere, etc. in a picture, piece of writing, film, etc.】

10. 「これらの写真は，当時の精神をとらえています」
【写真や文章，映画などで，ある感情や雰囲気などを正確に表現できている】

《 Summary 》

During the first few days of World War II, over 400,000 dogs and cats were put to death. This was done even though food supplies were not scarce yet. People may have done it because they were terrified by the beginning of a new war or they may have remembered seeing starving dogs and cats during World War I. Almost immediately, people regretted the mistake. Reporters argued that it was wrong to destroy faithful friends. In part, the reason it happened was that people's relationships with the animals around us changed due to urbanization. People living in cities did not need dogs and cats to be useful. They simply became part of the family. But some people became uneasy during the war because pets seemed like an unnecessary luxury. Despite reports of the massacre in magazines at the time, it has been written out of British history. This is probably because British people don't want to admit that they panicked at the beginning of the war. (166 words)

【《Summary》の訳】

第二次世界大戦が始まって最初の数日の間に，40万匹以上の犬と猫が殺処分されました。このようなことは，食料の供給がまだ不足していなかったにもかかわらず行われました。人々がそうしたのは，新たな戦争の開始に恐怖を覚えたためなのか，あるいは第一次世界大戦中に飢えた犬や猫を見かけたことを覚えていたせいなのかもしれません。ほとんどすぐに，人々は過ちを後悔しました。記者たちは，人間に忠実な友を殺すのは間違いだと主張しました。こうしたことが起こった理由の一つは，都市化によって人間と周りにいる動物との関係が変化したことです。都市に住む人々にとって，犬や猫が何かの役に立つ必要はありませんでした。犬や猫はただ家族の一員になったのです。ところが，ペットの動物は不必要な贅沢のように思えて，戦争中は落ち着かない人々もいました。当時の雑誌でそうした虐殺が報告されていたにもかかわらず，それは英国の歴史から抹消されました。これはおそらく，イギリス人が戦争が始まってパニックに陥ったことを認めたくないからです。

第3問　早稲田大学

得点
/50

【解答】

問1.「野球は90%が精神的なもので，残りの半分（50%）は身体的なものだ」という言葉があるが，90%と50%を足すと100%にならないということ。

問2. ③

問3. ①

問4. ③

問5. 私たちはスポーツにおける精神力をめぐる偏見の代替案を提示し，一見するときわめて常識的に思われるためにめったに調べられることのない多くの見過ごされている考え方に光を当てる必要がある。

問6. (a) ②　(b) ①　(c) ②　(d) ①　(e) ④

【配点と採点基準】（50点）

問1. 6点
- ・「50% と90% を足し合わせると140% になってしまう（100% にならない）」の内容 … 6点

問2. 3点　解答通り

問3. 3点　解答通り

問4. 3点　解答通り

問5. 10点
- ・We need to offer alternatives to the biases … 2点
- ・surrounding mentality in sports … 2点
- ・and shed light on many overlooked concepts … 2点
- ・that are rarely investigated … 2点
- ・because of how commonsense they seemingly are. … 2点

問6. 25点（各5点×5）解答通り

【設問別解説】

問1.

「この数学的に間違いのあるフレーズ」とは，第2段落で引用された“Baseball is 90% mental, and the other half is physical.”という，ヨギ・ベラの言葉を指す。90%と50%を合計すると140%となり，100%にならないので，「数学的に間違いがある」と筆者は言っている。

問2.

there is more to sports than ... は，「スポーツは，…だけがすべてではない」という意味を表す。「スポーツにおいては身体的な要素だけでなく精神的要素も重要だ」という第2・3段落の文脈から判断する。

①「健康上の利点」 ②「精神力」 **③「身体的な才能」** ④「圧倒的な勝利」

問3.

at face value「額面通りに」

①「疑うことなく見える通りに」

②「適切な忠告に基づいて」

③「深い意味に目を向けることによって」

④「他者との議論を通して」

問4.

make-or-break「成否を左右する」

①「混乱を招くような」 ②「無益な」 **③「極めて重要な」** ④「不必要な」

問5.

- alternatives to A「Aに代わる選択肢」
- bias「偏見」
- surrounding mentality「精神力を取り巻く」は直前の名詞biasesを修飾する形容詞句。
- offer alternatives ... in sports と shed light ... they seemingly are が等位接続詞によって併置されている。
- shed light on A「Aに光を投げかける，Aを解明する」
- overlooked concepts「見過ごされている考え方」
- that are ... they seemingly are は，直前の名詞句 many overlooked concepts を修飾する形容詞節。
- are rarely investigated「めったに調べられることがない」
- because of how commonsense they seemingly are「一見するときわめて常識的に思われるために」

問6.

(a)「ヨギ・ベラは，(　　)」

① 「奇抜な名言で子ども時代の筆者を魅了した」

② **「プロのスポーツ心理学者だった」**→第1段落第2文の内容と矛盾する。

③ 「考え方が十分に理解されていなかった」

④ 「人生とスポーツに対する考えについて記述した」

(b)「イソップの寓話は，(　　)」

① **「身体的トレーニングの重要性を支持する主張をした」**→第4段落の内容と矛盾する。

② 「賢明なのに当たり前のことと思われてしまうメッセージを含んでいる」

③ 「今日でもまだ適切な深いメッセージを持っていた」

④ 「最初のオリンピックが終わってまもなく書かれた」

(c)「スポーツの精神的な面は，(　　)」

① 「成功のために必要なものとして，長い間受け入れられてきた」

② **「データがなかったのに，広く研究されてきた」**→最終段落の内容と矛盾する。

③ 「現代のスポーツ界において，多くの決まり文句の一部となっている」

④ 「その重要性に関して実際には理解されていない」

(d)「筆者は，(　　)」

① **「ベラの異常な人生哲学ゆえにベラを批判している」**→第3段落の内容と矛盾する。

② 「イソップの寓話の大部分を覚えてはいない」

③ 「しばしば祖父母のバスルームで読み物をした」

④ 「子どもの頃に熱烈な野球ファンだった」

(e)「スポーツ心理学は，(　　)」

① 「スポーツの精神的な面の役割を調べる」

② 「精神の複雑さをまだ理解することができていない」

③ 「科学を利用して，精神的な側面と身体的な側面の関連を探求する」

④ **「精神と肉体を切り離す初めての試みだ」**→第3段落第7文の内容と矛盾する。

【全訳】

私の祖父母のバスルームは，他の多くのバスルームとは異なり，時間をつぶすためにパラパラめくるための雑誌が取り揃えてあったりはしなかった。額縁に入った，ちょっと変わったリンゴ売りの男のスケッチ画以外では，私の気を引くのに値しそうなものは1つしかなかった。それは，*The Yogi Book* というタイトルのペーパーバックだった。私は子どもの頃には熱狂的なヤンキースファンだったので，歴代最高のヤンキースの選手の一人であるヨギ・ベラの名言集のページをめくるのが大好きだった。私はその短い本を百回以上読んだに違いない。私が読んだ数多くのヨギ流の名言のうち，そのいくつかは今日まで私の頭から離れずにいる。「分かれ道に来たら，その道を行け」「もうここに来るものはいない。混雑し過ぎているからだ」そして，最も有名なものは「終わるまでは終わってはいない」などだ。だが，私にとって特に際立っていた名言がもう1つあった。

「野球は9割が精神で，残りの半分は体力だ」

数字を足しても計算が合わず，ベラの哲学を解き明かそうとする人はほとんどいないが，そこには彼の明確な主張が表れている。野球には精神力が重要だ。ベラは，精神力が肉体の役割よりもずっと重要だと示唆しているのだが，それはクレイジーな考えのように思われるかもしれない。この数学的には間違っているフレーズは，どのスポーツにおいても価値を保っている。今日，精神力がスポーツにおいて一定の役割を果たすという考えは常識になっていて，「試合に集中しろ！」とか「もっと貪欲になれ！」など，スポーツ界で最もよく使われる決まり文句の多くにも入り込んでいる。スポーツは純粋な身体的才能だけではないというのは，どこでも受け入れられている事実だ。スポーツ心理学とは，スポーツにおけるパフォーマンスと関わり方に精神がどのように影響するかを幅広く研究するもので，20世紀初めに注目を集め始めたのだが，それ以前には人々は精神と運動を行う肉体とを別のものと見なしていたと考えるとしたらそれは愚かなことだろう。単にこの2つの関連を科学的に検証する方法がなかっただけであって，それは私たちの現時点の革新的な技術を持ってしても，今でも研究者が苦労する障壁なのだ。

理論を検証する方法はなかったのだが，運動競技における精神と肉体の区別は古代ギリシャのオリンピック競技にまでさかのぼることができる。2500年近く前にギリシャで歴史上で最初のオリンピックが開催された直後に，イソップは有名ないくつかの寓話を書いた。1つだけ私が覚えているイソップの物語は『ウサギとカメ』だ。この物語の教訓は明白だ。遅くても着実な者が勝つということだ。私たちは，これを何千回となく聞いてきた。イソップが示した区別は単純であり，そのメッセージは今日でも妥当なものだ。一方の側がどんなに身体能力に優れていて技術が高くても，チームの精神的なアプローチによって勝つ可能性を高めることができるのだ。精神力は，身体的なスキルとは関係なく，競争の条件を平等にし，結果に影響を及ぼすことが可能なのだ。

ベラが正しいとすると，私たちがアスリートの精神についてほとんど理解していないというのは驚くべきことだ。スポーツの最高レベルで成功できる精神的な強さを持つということは何を意味するのだろうか。そして，統計，分析，データが爆発的に増えている今の時代にあって，競技の精神的な側面について私たちの理解がこんなに乏しい理由は何なのだろうか。

私たちは，自分たちが行うすべてのことにおいて精神力が極めて重要だということを知っている。精神がスポーツにおいては活用されないと言うのは馬鹿げたことなのだが，イソップの時代から，私たちはこの考え方を当然のことのようにしてきた。私たちは精神的な側面が重要であることは知っているのだがその理由は知らず，理由を知らないために精神を脇に置いてしまう。それの意味していることや複雑なところは忘れたまま，私たちはこの定説を額面通りに受けとる。スポーツ界は，そのファンを含め，精神力の重要性を十分に理解していない。それは運動選手にとって運命を左右する要因だとは見なされず，その一方で身体的な技能と運動能力が決定的な特徴となっている。運動選手が運動選手であるのは，常に3割前後の打率を残したり，ゴルフボールを200ヤード以上飛ばしたりできるからであって，プレッシャーのもとでどのようにして成果を出すかによってではないのだ。精神力は，常に身体的技能や身体的な外見によって過小に評価されるのだ。私たちはスポーツにおける精神力をめぐる偏見の代替案を提示し，一見するときわめて常識的に思われるためにめったに調べられることのない多くの見過ごされている考え方に光を当てる必要がある。

【語句】

第1パラグラフ

- grandparents「祖父母」
- unlike A「Aと違って」
- have a wide selection of A「Aを豊富に取りそろえている」
  ※ selection は「品ぞろえ」の意味。
- magazine「雑誌」
- flip through A「Aをすばやくめくる，Aをざっと読む」
- pass the time「時間をつぶす」
  = kill time
- other than A「A以外に」
- slightly odd「少し変わっている」
- framed sketch「額縁に入ったスケッチ画」
- object「物，物体」
- warrant「…を保証する」
- attention「注意，注目」
- paperback「ペーパーバック，紙表紙本」
  ⇔ hardback「堅い表紙の本，ハードカバー」
・entitle O C「OにCという題を付ける」
・crazed Yankee fan「熱狂的なヤンキースファン」
・as a kid「子どもの頃（の）」
・quote book「名言集，格言集」
・one hundred times over「100回以上」
・stick「（心に）とどまる，（心から）離れない」
※活用は【stick / stuck / stuck / sticking】
・crowed「混み合った」
・It ain't over「それは終わらない」
＝ It isn't over
※ ain't は is［am/are］not の短縮形。
・saying「格言，ことわざ，言い習わし」
・stand out「きわ出つ，傑出している」

第2パラグラフ
・mental「精神の」
⇔ physical「肉体の」
・the other half「残りの半分」

第3パラグラフ
・add up「計算が合う，（数字が）一致する」
・attempt to *do*「…しようと試みる」
＝ try to *do*
・unpack「…の意味を解明する」
・philosophy「哲学」
・make a point「主張する」
・mentality「精神力，精神構造」
・suggest that S V ...「…ということを示唆［暗示］する」
・concept「概念，考え」＝ idea
・mathematically「数学的に」
・erroneous「誤った，間違った」
＝ mistaken
・phrase「表現，言い回し，フレーズ」
・retain「…を保つ，…を保持する」
＝ keep
・the idea that S V ...「…だという考え」
・strength「強さ」
⇔ weakness「弱さ」
・have a role in A「Aにおいて役割を果たす」
・common knowledge「常識，共通の知識」
・find *one's* way into A「Aにたどりつく，Aに入り込む」
・cliché「（陳腐な）決まり文句」（フランス語由来）
・universally accepted truth「広く受け入れられている事実」
・there is more to A than B「AにはB以上のものがある，AはBだけがすべてではない」
・pure physical talent「純粋な身体的才能」
・psychology「心理学」
・broad study「幅広い研究」
・mind「精神」⇔ body「肉体」

- affect「…に影響する」
- performance「パフォーマンス，出来ばえ」
- participation「参加，加入」
- silly「愚かな」= foolish
- assume that S V ...「…だと思い込む，…だと決めてかかる」
- consider O separate「O を 別物だと考える」
- athletic body「運動を行う肉体」
- scientifically「科学的に」
- the link between the two「その 2 つの関連（性）」
- obstacle「障害（物）」
- researcher「研究者，調査員」
- current「今の，現在の」
- technological innovation「 技術革新」

第 4 パラグラフ

- despite A「A にもかかわらず」= in spite of A
- the absence of A「A がないこと」
- method「方法，手段」= way
- the distinction between A and B「A と B の区別」
- athletic competition「運動競技」
- trace A back to B「A を B までさかのぼらせる」
- ancient「古代の，太古の」
- soon after S V ...「…したあとすぐに」
- be held「開催される，行われる」= take place
- Aesop「イソップ」※古代ギリシアの寓話作家。
- fable「寓話，たとえ話」
- The Tortoise and the Hare「『ウサギとカメ』」
- moral「教訓」= lesson
- Slow and steady wins the race「遅くても着実な者が勝つ」
- message「伝えたいこと，メッセージ」
- hold true「有効である，当てはまる」
- physically equipped「身体能力が備わって」
- skilled「技術を身につけて」
- approach「取り組み（方），アプローチ」
- enhance「…を高める」
- chance「可能性」= possibility
- level「…を平等にする，…を平らにする」
- playing field「競技場，運動場」
- regardless of A「A とは関係なく」
- skill「技能，スキル」

第 5 パラグラフ

- remarkable「注目に値する，驚くべき」
- athlete「運動選手，アスリート」
- What does it mean to *do*?「…するということはどういう意味なのか」※ it は形式主語。

・thrive「栄える，繁栄する」
・era「時代，時期」
・exploding「爆発的に増加している」
・statistic「統計」
・analysis「分析」
・date「資料，データ」
※ datum の複数形。

第6パラグラフ

・vital「極めて重要な」
・utilize「…を利用する，…を役立たせる」
・ridiculous「馬鹿げた, おかしな」
・take A for granted「A を当然のことと思う」
・cast A aside「A を脇に置く，A を捨てる」
・implication「含意，意味すること」
・intricacy「複雑（さ），込み入っていること」
・dogma「定説，教義」
・at face value「額面通りに」
・including A「A を含めて」
・fan「熱烈な支持者，ファン」
・significance「重要性」
= importance
・see A as B「A を B だと見なす」
= regard A as B
・make-or-break「成否を左右する」
・whereas S V ...「(～)，だが一方で…」
・athleticism「運動能力」
・defining「決定的な，典型的な」
・feature「特徴」
= characteristic
・consistently「一貫して，常に」
・bat「…の打率を上げる」
・drive「（ボール）を強く打つ，飛ばす」
・over A「A 以上」
= more than A
・perform「やってのける，成果を出す」
・under pressure「プレッシャーのもとで」
・undermine「…を弱体化させる，…をひそかに傷つける」
・constantly「絶えず」= always
・appearance「外見」
・alternative to A「A に取って替わるもの，A に代わる選択肢」
・bias「偏見」= prejudice
・surround「…を取り巻く，…を囲む」
・shed light on A「A に光を投げかける，A を解明する」
・overlook「…を見過ごす，…を見落とす」
・investigate「…を調査する，…を調べる」
・commonsense「常識に富む，常識的な」
・seemingly「一見（…）のように思える，見かけは」
= apparently

《 Vocabulary Building Exercise 》

1. This **fable** is well known to children around the world.
【a story which teaches a moral lesson】

2. It was certain that the condition did not **warrant** antibiotic therapy.
【to make something necessary or appropriate in a particular situation; justify something】

3. A simple comparison between species can lead to **erroneous** conclusions.
【not correct; based on wrong information】

4. Until recently, this additive was widely used to **enhance** engine performance.
【to increase or further improve the good quality, value or status of somebody/something】

5. Today his company continues to **thrive**.
【to become, and continue to be, successful, strong or healthy】

1. 「この寓話は世界中の子どもたちによく知られている」
【道徳的な教訓を教えてくれる物語】

2. 「その状態は，抗生物質による治療法を必要としないことは明らかだった」
【特定の状況において何かを必要または適切なものにする／何かを正当化する】

3. 「生物種の間での単純な比較は，誤った結論をもたらす可能性がある」
【正しくない／間違った情報に基づいた】

4. 「最近まで，この添加剤はエンジンの性能を高めるために広く使われていた」
【誰か，あるいは何かの質，価値，地位などを高めたりさらに改善したりする】

5. 「今や，彼の会社は成功を重ねている」
【成功したり，強くなったり，あるいは健康になったりして，その状態を維持する】

6. The **statistics** show that the number of complaints has declined in recent years.
【a collection of information shown in numbers】

7. Sound engineers **utilize** a range of techniques to enhance the quality of the recordings.
【to use something, especially for a practical purpose】

8. It's **ridiculous** to suggest that she was involved in anything illegal.
【not at all sensible or reasonable】

9. We do not allow the teaching of religious **dogma** in our schools.
【a belief or set of beliefs held by a group or organization that others are expected to accept without argument】

10. Offering advice on each and every problem will **undermine** her feeling of being an adult.
【to make something gradually weaker or less effective】

6.「その統計によると，苦情の件数は近年になって減少している」
【数値で示される一連の情報】

7.「音響技師は録音の品質を高めるために，さまざまなテクニックを駆使する」
【特に実用的な目的のために何かを使う】

8.「彼女が何か違法なことに関わっていたのではないかと言うのはばかげている」
【まったく分別がなかったり不合理だったりする】

9.「私たちの学校では宗教的な教義を教えることを許可しません」
【ある集団や組織が持っている考えまたは一連の思想で，誰もが異議なく受け入れることを期待されているもの】

10.「あらゆる問題についてアドバイスを与えることは，彼女の大人である感覚を徐々に弱らせるでしょう」
【何かの力や効果を次第に弱める】

《 Summary 》

The baseball player Yogi Berra is known for saying strange things like, "Baseball is 90% mental, and the other half is physical." Obviously, this is mathematically [erroneous], but he makes an important point: Mental strength plays a vital role in sports. However, in spite of our current technological [innovation], it is still too difficult to scientifically test the link between mind and body in athletes. Even so, the importance of a strong mental approach to sports was understood by the ancient Greeks. The [moral] of Aesop's story "The Tortoise and the Hare" is that a good mental strategy can [enhance] an athlete's chance of winning. It is [ridiculous] to say that athletes don't use their minds, but we tend to ignore the [implications] and intricacies of the mental side of sports and believe that physical skill and athleticism are the most important factors. We need to re-examine this attitude. (149 words)

【《Summary》の訳】

野球選手のヨギ・ベラは，「野球は９割が精神，残りの半分は体力だ」というような奇妙な発言をすることで知られています。明らかに，これは数学的には間違っていますが，彼は重要なことを指摘しています。つまり，精神的な強さはスポーツでは非常に重要な役割を果たすのです。しかし，私たちの最新の技術革新をもってしても，スポーツ選手の心と体の関係を科学的に検証することはとても難しいままです。そうだとしても，スポーツにおいては強い精神力の重要さは，古代ギリシャ人によっても理解されていました。イソップ物語にある『ウサギとカメ』から得られる教訓は，優れた心構え次第でスポーツ選手が勝利する可能性を高めることができるということです。スポーツ選手が精神を使わないなどと言うのはばかげていますが，私たちはスポーツの精神面が持つ影響や複雑さを軽視しがちで，身体能力と運動能力が何よりも重要な要素だと信じています。私たちは，このような態度を再検討する必要があります。

第４問　同志社大学

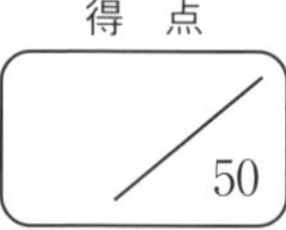

【解答】

問１．④
問２．③
問３．・複雑な作業を処理する能力が高い。
・注意力を維持することに優れている。
・（晩年になって）認知症の発症の時期が遅くなる。
問４．だが，それらの副次的な効果がなくても，バイリンガルの子どもが持つ親族や他の文化とのつながりは，それ自体がよいことだ。
問５．①
問６．(a)　③　　(b)　④　　(c)　③　　(d)　④　　(e)　②
問７．③・⑥（順不同）

【配点と採点基準】（50点）

問１．５点　解答通り
問２．５点　解答通り
問３．６点（各２点×３）
「複雑な作業の処理能力が高い」の内容…２点
「注意力（集中力）の維持能力が高い」の内容…２点
「認知症の発症の時期が遅くなる」の内容…２点
問４．７点
・Even without those side-effects, …２点
・though, …１点
・a bilingual child's connection to relatives and another culture …２点
・is a good thing in itself. …２点
問５　５点　解答通り
問６．10点（各２点×５）解答通り
問７．12点（各６点×２）解答通り

【設問別解説】

問１．

「子どもは言語を吸収するスポンジのようなものだ」という意味を表している。

① 「子どもは自分たちの言語を柔軟に作り出す」

② 「子どもは当然ながら言語を使うことに抵抗する」

③ 「子どもは言語を使わずに自由にコミュニケーションを行う」

④ 「子どもはとても簡単に言語を吸収する」

問２．

「制度的な圧力」とは，同段落の中で言及される「第一言語以外の言語の習得を妨げようとする学校からの圧力」を意味している。

① 「父母や祖父母を喜ばせようという子どもたちのニーズ」

② 「異なる語彙や文法のシステムを習得することの困難さ」

③ 「学校が一つの言語を優先させること」

④ 「バイリンガルになるように生徒を促そうとする教師たちの努力」

問３．

「バイリンガルの人の認知能力上の利点」については，直後の文の中で① be more skillful at complex tasks，②（be）better at maintaining attention，③（at the other end of life）suffer the onset of dementia later の３つの具体的項目が列挙されている。the onset of A は「A の発症」の意味。

問４．

・even without A「A がなかったとしても」，side-effect「副次的な効果，副作用」

・though「だが，しかしながら」，ここでの though は副詞（= however）。

・A's connection to B「A の B とのつながり」，relative「親族，身内」

・in itself「それ自体」

問５．

the one that needs support = the language that needs support「サポートを必要とする言語」つまり，「まだ習得できていない言語」のことを表している。

① 「出会う頻度が低い言語」

② 「その地域で以前には話されていた言語」

③ 「その子どもの学校で話されている言語」

④ 「公用語として話されている言語」

問６．

(a) accumulate「積もる，増える」（= increase「増える」）

(b) conspire「共謀する，（悪い方向に）重なる」（= work together「いっしょ

に作用する」)

(c) comply「(規則などに) 従う」(= obey「(…に) 従う」)

(d) imposed by ...「…によって課せられた」(= required by ...「…から要求された」)

(e) be restricted「制限される」(= be limited「…制限される」)

問7.

① 「移民である親たちの多くは，我が子が今暮らしている場所の公用語をうまく習得するための最善の方法を見つけさせせることに苦労している」

② 「外国語を推進しようとする政府の方針の結果として，4分の1ものアメリカ人が別の言語を話している」

③ **「アメリカで生まれた移民の子どもたちはしばしばバイリンガルであるが，孫たちの多くはモノリンガルであり継承言語を話すことができない」**→第4段落最終文の内容に一致する。

④ 「多言語使用の望ましさに関する見解が変わってきたのにつれて，移民の子どもたちの大半は今では継承言語を習得するようになっている」

⑤ 「二人の親が異なる言語を話す場合は，家で1つの言語を話し車の中ではもう1つの言語を話す方がいいが，子どもがひとり親家庭に暮らしている場合は，1つの言語を習得することに集中するのが最善だ」

⑥ **「サビーネ・リトルは，子どもたちが第二言語をリラックスした雰囲気の中で好きな活動を通して学習することを薦める。というのも，彼女は，言語との感情的なつながりの大切さを信じているからだ」**→第8段落の内容に一致する。

【全訳】

「ねえ，あなたはおばあちゃんが話す言葉がわかるんだよね」その女の子はうなずく。私たちがその子と，その子のデンマーク人の母親とイギリス人の父親に会ったのは，デンマークへ向かう途中の空港だった。その子の両親はロンドンで娘をバイリンガルに育てた経験についてしきりに議論したがった。それは容易なことではないのだ。夫のほうはデンマーク語を話さないから，その子は母親からしかデンマーク語を聞かない。母親は，娘が英語で応えることになることを受け入れるようになっている。

こういうことは苦痛になりかねない。自分にとっての第一言語を最愛の人たちと共有できないのは辛いことだ。それを自分の子どもに伝えられないというのは，特に辛いことにもなり得る。国外移住した移民の親たちの多くが，挫折感を味わう。彼らは，両手を固く握りしめながら，子育てフォーラムやソーシャルメディアで話を語り合うのだが，バイリンガルの子どもをうまく育てられる秘訣を見つけられることを願っているのだ。

子どもは言語を吸収するスポンジのようなものだが，だからと言って，いい加減に言語にさらしておけばそれで十分だというわけではない。ある言語を理解するためにはその言語をたっぷり聞かなければならないし，ある言語を楽に話せるようになるためにはその言語を頻繁に使わなければならない。そういうのは頭を使う作業だから，必要性であれ強い欲求であれ，何か言語を話す動機を持たない子どもは，多くの場合はそれを避けるだろう。子どもたちの脳はすでに十分に忙しいのだ。

だから，親が国外へ移住すると，言語は衰弱して死んでしまう。アメリカの場合を考えてみよう。海外で生まれた人の全人口に占める比率は現在13.7%で，これまでに1970年の4.7%を下回ったことは一度もない。ところが，外国語の話者の数は増えていないのだ。今日，別の言語を話すのは全人口の25%に過ぎない。その理由は，一般に，アメリカで生まれた第一世代はバイリンガルであっても，第二世代はモノリンガルであり英語だけを話すからだ。そのような子どもたちは移民の祖父母とスムーズに会話を行うのに苦労している場合が多いのだ。

過去には，移民の家族が自分たちの言語を使い続けないように政府が仕向けていた。テディ・ローズベルト（セオドア・ローズベルト）は，アメリカが「多国語の飛び交う下宿屋」になるのではないかと心配していた。最近では，役人たちも昔ほどは干渉しない傾向がある。移民の言語能力を貴重な資源と見る者さえいる。とは言え，多くの要因が重なって，今でも，子どもたちが親の言語を失ったり，一度も習得しなかったりすることを確実にしてしまうのだ。

１つの大きな要因が，制度的な圧力だ。子どもが第二言語を使って過ごす時間は，第一言語に費やされていない時間である。だから，しばしば教師は，親が自分の言語を子どもに向かって話さないように仕向ける。第二言語に威信がない場合は，特にそれが当てはまる。親は，自分の子どもの教育のことを心配して，しぶしぶ従う場合が多い。これは残念なことだ。実際には，子どもたちは２つの，あるいはもっと多くの言語でさえマスターできるのだ。確かに，それぞれの言語において子どもたちの語彙が一定期間は多少少なくなることを調査は示している。だが，別の研究の中には，バイリンガルの人の認知能力に関する利点を示唆しているものもあるのだ。バイリンガルの人のほうが，複雑な課題を処理する能力が高く，注意力を維持することに優れ，（晩年になって）認知症の発症の時期が遅くなるかもしれないのだ。

だが，それらの副次的な効果がなくても，バイリンガルの子どもが持つ親族や他の文化とのつながりは，それ自体がよいことだ。それをどうやって生み出せばよいのだろうか。継承言語を両親が共有する場合は，家庭ではその言語を話し家庭の外ではその国の言語を話すことが戦略だ。だが，両親が異なる言語を話す場合には，最も一般的なアプローチは「一人の親が1つの言語を話す」ということかもしれない。スイスのヌーシャテル大学の言語学者フランソワ・グロジャンは，必要性を強調する。彼は，使われるかもしれない言語がサポートの必要な言語しかないような機会を用意しておくことを勧める。

シェフィールド大学のドイツ人言語学者であるサビーネ・リトルは，別の点を強調する。彼女は，継承言語を，親から課せられたまた一つの課題にしてしまうことは，拒絶という結果に終わる可能性があると言うのだ。彼女は，子どもなりの言語との感情的なつながりを子ども自身に築かせることを勧める。彼女の息子は，ドイツ語を数年間やめていた後に，ドイツ語に戻ってきたのだった。彼女は息子に，どんな時に二人でいっしょにドイツ語を話すかを決めさせた。彼は，母親の車に乗って放課後の活動に向かう時がいいと決めた。その時であればドイツ語を話さない父親が除け者にならないからだった。彼らは英語とドイツ語のごちゃ混ぜをジョークにしながら，それを彼らの語彙に組み入れる。多くの若者がそうであるように，彼がYouTubeを見る時間は制限されている。だが，ドイツ語で見る場合には，もっと長い時間見てもいいことになっている。リトルは，ネイティブ・スピーカーのために作られたアプリや娯楽を通して学習することを提案する。彼女は，教育目的のタイプのものは宿題に似ていると考えている。

言語は，アイデンティティの私的な一部だ。言語を子どもに伝えようとして挫折するのは痛ましいことだ。成功するかどうかは，言語が，子どもの頭の中に詰め込むべき単なるもう1つのことではなく，心の問題なのだということを覚えておくかどうかの問題なのかもしれない。

【語句】

第1パラグラフ

- grandmother「祖母，おばあちゃん」
- darling「あなた，お前」
  ※呼びかけの表現。
- nod「うなづく」
- Danish「デンマーク人の，デンマーク語（の）」
- be eager to *do*「しきりに…したがる，…することを切望する」
  ＝ be anxious to *do*
- bring up A「Aを育てる」

= raise A
- bilingually「二カ国語を話せるように」
- come to *do*「…するようになる」
- accept that S V ...「…であることを認める」
- reply「返事をする，答える」

第2パラグラフ
- painful「苦痛を与える，痛ましい」
- share「…を共有する，…を分かち合う」
- loved ones「最愛の［身内の］人たち」
- pass A on to B「AをBに伝える」
- tough「骨の折れる，難しい」
- immigrant「移民（の）」
- feel a sense of failure「挫折感を味わう」
- wring *one's* hands「両手を固く握りしめる」
- parenting「子育て，育児」
- forum「公開討論（の場），フォーラム」
- social media「ソーシャルメディア」
- nurture「…を育てる」
  = bring up, raise
- successfully「首尾よく，うまく」

第3パラグラフ
- linguistic「言語の，言葉の」
- sponge「吸収する人［物］，スポンジ」
- mean that S V ...「…ということを意味する」
- exposure「（身を）さらすこと，さらされること」
- quite a bit「かなり」
- comfortably「気楽に，心地よく」
- mental work「頭を使う作業」
- have a motive to *do*「…する動機を持つ」
- either A or B「AであれBであれ」
- avoid「…を避ける」

第4パラグラフ
- wither「衰える，しぼむ」
- move abroad「国外に移動［移住］する」
- foreign-born「海外で生まれた」
- share「割り当て，割合」
- accumulate「積もる，増える」
  = increase
- That is because S V ...「それは…だからだ」
- typically「一般的に，主として」
- the first generation「第一世代」
- monolingual「単一言語の，一言語使用の」
- struggle to *do*「…するのに苦労する」
- grandparent「祖父母」

第5パラグラフ
- in the past「過去には」
- government「政府」

・discourage A from *doing*「A に…するのを思いとどまらせる」
　= dissuade A from *doing*
・official「役人，官僚」
・valuable resource「貴重な資源」
・factor「要因，要素」
・conspire「共謀する，（悪い方向に）重なる」
・ensure that S V ...「確実に…するようにする」
　= make sure that S V ...

第6パラグラフ

・institutional pressure「制度的な圧力」
・lack prestige「威信を欠く」
・reluctantly「しぶしぶ」
・comply「（規則などに）従う」
・offspring「子，子孫」
・shame「残念なこと，遺憾なこと」
　※ a shameの形で使うのが原則。
・research「研究，調査」
・suggest that S V ...「…ということを示唆［暗示］する」
・vocabulary「語彙」
・somewhat「いくぶん，多少」
・for a while「しばらくの間」
・hint at A「A をほのめかす，A をそれとなく言う」
・cognitive advantage「認知能力に関する利点」
・bilingual「二カ国語を自在に使える人，バイリンガル」
・be skillful at A「A がうまい，A が上手だ」
・complex task「複雑な仕事［課題］」
・be good at A「A が得意だ」
・maintain attention「注意力を維持する」
・at the other end of life「晩年になって」
・suffer「…を受ける，…をこうむる」
・onset「（通例よくないことの）開始，（病気の）発症」

第7パラグラフ

・even without A「A がなかったとしても」
・side-effect「副次的な効果，副作用」
・though「しかしながら」
　= however
　※副詞の though は文中・文末で用いる。
・*A's* connection to B「A と B とのつながり」
・in itself「それ自体」
・bring A about「A を生み出す，A をもたらす」
・heritage language「継承言語」
・strategy「戦略，方針」
・national language「（その）国の言語」
・the most common approach「最も一般的な取り組み［アプローチ］」
・linguist「言語学者」
・emphasize「…を強調する」

・necessity「必要性」
・recommend *doing*「…することを勧める」
・reserve「…を取っておく」
・occasion on which S V ...「…する機会」

第8パラグラフ

・emphasis「重点，強調」
・impose「…を課す」
・lead to A「Aにつなげる，Aを引き起こす」= cause A
・rejection「拒絶，却下」
・argue that S V ...「…だと主張する」
・let O *do*「（望み通り）Oに…させる」
・emotional「感情的な」
・give up on A「Aに見切りをつける」
・return to A「Aに戻る」
・determine when S V ...「いつ…かを決める」
・decide on A「Aに決定する」
・trip to A「Aへの移動」
・after-school activity「放課後の活動」
・exclude「…を除外する，…を排除する」
・joke about A「Aについて冗談を言う」
・incorporate A into B「AをBに組み入れる」
・youngster「若者，子ども」
・restrict「…を制限する」
= limit
・allow O_1 O_2「O_1にO_2を許す」
・app「アプリ，アプリケーション」
・entertainment「娯楽」

第9パラグラフ

・intimate「個人的な，私的な」
= personal
・identity「アイデンティティ，自分であること」
・fail to *do*「（意志に反して）…しない［できない］」
・drill A into B「AをBに徹底的に教え込む」
・young mind「子どもの頭脳［知力］」
・a matter of A「Aの問題」

《 Vocabulary Building Exercise 》

1. Parents want to know the best way to **nurture** their child to adulthood.
【to care for and protect somebody/something while they are growing and developing】

1. 「親というものは，自分の子どもを大人になるまで育てる最善の方法を知りたがる」
【誰か，あるいは何かが成長し発達している間，その世話をしたり守ったりする】

2. The report recommends that people avoid prolonged **exposure** to sunlight.
【the state of being in a place or situation where there is no protection from something】

2. 「その報告書は，人が日光に長時間さらされることを避けるよう勧めている」
【何かから保護されていない場所または状況に置かれている状態】

3. Dust and dirt soon **accumulate** if a house is not cleaned regularly.
【to gradually increase in number or quantity over a period of time】

3. 「家屋は定期的に掃除をしないと，ほこりや汚れがすぐに溜まってしまう」
【一定の期間にわたって徐々に数や量が増える】

4. High interest rates will **discourage** investment.
【to make somebody feel less confident or enthusiastic about doing something】

4. 「高い金利は投資を思いとどまらせるだろう」
【誰かが何かをすることに自信や意欲をなくさせる】

5. They will never **conspire** to overthrow the government.
【to secretly plan with other people to do something illegal or harmful】

5. 「彼らは決して政府を転覆させようと陰謀をたくらむことはしないだろう」
【違法であったり害があったりすることを他人と密かに計画する】

6. Some companies failed to **comply** with environmental regulations.
【to obey a rule, an order, etc.】

6. 「一部の企業は，環境規制を順守しなかった」
【規則や命令などに従う】

7. Among those surviving **offspring**, 15 were females.
【the young of an animal or plant; someone's child/children】

7. 「生き残っていた子孫のうち，15人が女性だった」
【動物や植物の子／誰かの子ども(たち)】

8. Even minor head injuries can cause **cognitive** impairments.
【connected with the mental processes of understanding】

8. 「頭部への軽度な外傷であっても，認知機能障害を引き起こす可能性がある」
【理解するという精神機能に関する】

9. These laws **impose** additional financial burdens on many people.
【to force somebody/something to deal with something that is difficult or unpleasant】

9. 「これらの法律は，多くの人々にさらなる経済的負担を課すものである」
【誰か，あるいは何かに対して困難であったり不快であったりすることに対処するよう強制する】

10. We **restrict** the number of students per class to ten.
【to limit or control the size, amount or range of something】

10. 「私たちは，1クラスあたりの生徒数を10名に限定しています」
【何かのサイズや量，範囲などを制限したり抑制したりする】

《 Summary 》

In families where the parents speak different languages, it can be difficult to raise a bilingual child. Even when parents make every effort to [nurture] children who speak two languages, their children will avoid learning a second language unless they have a strong [motive] to speak it. That is why foreign-language speakers haven't accumulated in America, even though over 10% of the population was born in a different country. One factor that may [conspire] to ensure that children in the U.S. only learn English is that teachers often discourage parents from speaking their native languages to their children. Parents often [comply], even though mastering two languages can give bilinguals [cognitive] advantages. But when parents do try to pass on their language, their children may reject it if it is [imposed] on them like homework. It may be best to allow children to find their own ways to make an emotional connection with a second language. (155 words)

【《Summary》の訳】

両親が異なる言語を話す家庭では，バイリンガルの子どもを育てることが難しい場合があります。親が2か国語を話す子どもを育てるためにあらゆる努力を払ったとしても，子どもに第二言語を話す強い動機がなければ，それを学ぼうとはしないでしょう。人口の10%以上が外国生まれであるにも関わらず，外国語を話す人間がアメリカで増えていかないのはそのためです。アメリカの子どもたちが英語だけを学ぶことを裏で助長している要因の1つは，親が子どもに彼らの母国語を話させることを思いとどまらせようとする教師が多いことです。2か国語を習得した人間が認知能力の点で優位に立つことができるにもかかわらず，親はしばしば従います。しかし，親が実際に自分の話す言語を教えようとしても，それを宿題のように押しつけられるならば，子どもたちはそれを拒絶するかもしれません。最善の方法は，子どもたち自身に第二言語との感情的なつながりを築く方法を発見させることなのかもしれません。

第5問　お茶の水女子大学

得点
/50

【解答】

問1．人間の耐久力の限界を試し，人類が地球の支配者だと宣言し，この類のことではどの国家が一番すぐれているのかをはっきりさせること以外には，極地へ行く理由などなかった。

問2．**was made all the more unbearable**

問3．スコットは不安になる必要などなかった。というのも，彼は敗北と死によって，おそらくは成功していた場合よりも確実に，英雄になったからだ。いや，むしろ彼の物語によって，人々は成功と失敗が何を意味するのかを見直さざるを得なくなったのだ。

問4．(a) ④　(b) ①　(c) ①　(d) ④　(e) ②
(f) ①　(g) ②

問5．④

【配点と採点基準】（50点）

問1．11点

・There was no reason to go there, … 2点
＊ there が the Poles「極地」「北極と南極」のことだと理解していないものは2点減

・except to *do* … 2点
＊ 3つの to 不定詞の並置関係をとらえていないものは2点減

・to test the limits of human endurance, … 2点

・to declare that mankind was master of the planet, … 2点

・and to establish which nation was really the best at this kind of thing. … 3点

問2．4点　解答通り

問3．13点

・Scott need not have feared, … 2点

・for … 1点

・failure and death made him a hero … 2点

・perhaps even more securely … 1点
・than success could have, … 2点
・or rather … 1点
・his story forced people to *do* … 2点
・re-examine what success and failure mean … 2点

問4．14点（各2点×7）解答通り

問5．8点　解答通り

【設問別解説】

問1．

・There was no reason to go there「極地（北極や南極）へ行く理由はなかった」
there = to the Poles
・except to *do*「…するためという理由以外には，…すること以外には」ここでは，to test ..., to declare ..., to establish ... の3つのto不定詞が等位接続詞andによって併置されている。
・endurance「忍耐力」
・declare that S V ...「…だと宣言する」, mankind「人類」, master of A「Aの支配者」
・establish「…をはっきりさせる，…を立証する」
・was the best at Aはbe good at A「Aに優れている」の最上級表現。

問2．

・all the +比較級「（ある理由によって）それだけ…」，本文の場合はby his sense of failure「自らの敗北感によって」が理由を表す語句となっている。
・His fate was made all the more unbearable to him by his sense of failureは，His sense of failure（S）/ made（V）/ his fate（O）/ all the more unbearable to him. を受動態を用いて表したもの。

問3．

・need not have *done*「（実際に行ったことに対して）…する必要はなかった」
・forは「理由」を表す接続詞。for S V ...「というのも…だからだ」
・failure and death made him a hero「失敗と死が彼を英雄にした」「失敗と死によって彼は英雄になった」
・even more securely「いっそう確実に，よりしっかりと」
・than success could have = than success could have made him a hero「（仮に彼が成功していたと仮定して）成功が彼を英雄にしたであろうと思わ

れる以上に」

・or rather「いやむしろ，というより」

・S force O to *do*「S は O に…することを強いる，S によって O は…せざるを得なくなる」

・re-examine「…を再検証する，…を見直す」

・what success and failure mean「成功と失敗が何を意味するのか，成功と失敗が意味するもの」

問 4．

(a) defy「…に従わない，…を寄せ付けない」(= resist「…に抵抗する」)

(b) disturbing「心を掻き乱すような」(= distressing「悩ませるような，痛ましい」)

(c) perish「死滅する」(= die「死ぬ」)

(d) appropriate「…を占有する，…を私物化する」(= take over「…を奪取する」)

(e) drift「漂流する，漂う」(= float「浮かぶ，浮遊する」)

(f) narrative of A「A の物語，A についての叙述」(= account of A「A についての説明，記述」)

(g) vanity「虚栄心」(= conceit「うぬぼれ」)

問 5．

① 「自身の異常な北極冒険についてのノルウェー人フリチョフ・ナンセンの記述は，健全さと良質のユーモアを特徴としている」→第 2 段落最終文の内容に一致。

② 「スコットは死後になって，高貴な理想のために自己を犠牲にするというイギリス人の理想を具現化するものとなった」→最終段落の最後から 2 つ目の文の内容に一致。

③ 「ヨーロッパ人を北西航路の探検へと駆り立てたのは，商業的・軍事的な重要性よりも国家のプライドだった」→第 1 段落最終文の内容に一致。

④ **「スコットの日記の記載は全部がとても短く事実に即していて，失敗に終わった自身の探検に関する疑念や不安については一度も言及していない」**→第 3 段落最終文，第 4 段落第 1 ～ 2 文の内容と矛盾。

【全訳】

20世紀は19世紀に完成しなかった 1 つの事業とともに幕が開いた。それは，極地探検だった。北極および南極大陸は，ヨーロッパの探検家や科学者や冒険家を寄せ付けない地球上の最後の地域であり，1850年代になってもまだ，古くからの北西航路の夢は商業上の，そして帝国の野望を抱かせる魅力を失っていなかった。1846年にカナダ領の北極圏でジョン・フランクリン卿の率いる探検隊が消息を絶ったことはイギリスでは有名な事件となり，十数年にわたって十数回の救援隊が送り込まれた後に，ようやく真実が明らかになった。その真相は心を掻き乱すようなものだった。イギリス人全員が死亡していて，中には氷に閉ざされた船中で死んだ者もいたが，大部分は助けを求めて氷上をさまよい歩き，イヌイットの人々がはるか昔から暮らし繁栄することのできた環境に無力に屈したのだった。未亡人となったフランクリン夫人は，遠征隊の130人の男たちは，戦いで死を遂げたのと同じくらいに忠実に，国への奉仕のために命を捧げたのだという声明を発表した。だが，北西航路を必要とする根拠となっていた商業的および海軍的重要性は神話であって，本当の動機は国家のプライドであり，政治的にではないにせよ心理的に，そのような遠い地域でさえも奪取しようというヨーロッパ人の衝動にあったのだ。

同じことは，独特ではあるが何の地形的特徴もない地球上の２つの地理的地点である両極地そのものにも当てはまっていて，その近づくことができないところが何世代にもわたる探検家たちを引きつけていた。人間の耐久力の限界を試し，人類が地球の支配者だと宣言し，この類のことではどの国家が一番すぐれているのかをはっきりさせること以外には，そこへ行く理由などなかった。北極点へは1909年にアメリカ海軍士官のロバート・ピアリーが最初に到達したのだが，それよりも10年前にノルウェーのフリチョフ・ナンセンはおそらく最も異常な極地の旅を生き抜いていた。彼は，約2,000マイルにわたって漂流を続けながら，氷で閉ざされた船の中に３年間のあいだ閉じこめられていた。そのようにして彼は，北極圏が陸地ではなく動く氷冠であることを証明していた。*Farthest North*（『極北』）に書かれているこの無人の地での体験を語ったナンセンの話は，クマの肉とセイウチの脂身を食べて生きる不潔な野蛮人に変わり果てる自らの姿を見ながらも，きわめて正気で，感情を乱さず，ユーモラスだ。

南極は一般に，それよりも陰鬱ながらも気高い類の文献を生んだ。その中では，旅をする者は探検者は激しい肉体的苦痛と，「なぜ私はここにいるのか」という哲学的な疑問に直面することになる。ロバート・スコットが死に至ることになった1912年の最後の探検の日記は，彼の死体とともに発見されたが，逃れられないと彼が悟った運命を合理化しようとして，その記載はたいてい短く事実に基づいている。「イギリス人は（このような状況になっても）まだ大胆な精神を持って死ぬことができるということを，我々は示そうとしている」と。しかし，士官として訓練を受けた仮面が外れ，単に自分自身の選択によって，おそらく自分自身の虚栄心によってこの地に来てしまったという事実と向き合うときに，日記の記載にはもっと強い痛恨の思いが表れている。「空想はすべて消え去らなければならない … 神よ，ここは恐ろしいところだ」

南極点へ先に到達するレースで自分がロアルド・アムンゼンに敗れたことがわかり，自らの敗北感によって，彼の運命はいっそう耐え難いものになった。それに加えて，自分の家族も含めて一般の人々が同情してくれて，何が自分たちを駆り立てたのかを理解してくれるのかどうかという疑問によって，さらに苦しめられたにちがいない。「間違いなく，我が国のようなきわめて豊かな国は，私たちを頼っている者たちが養われるよう取り計らってくれるだろう」そして，最後に記された項目は，家族に対する自責の念に苦しんでいるように思われる。「お願いだから，私たちの家族の面倒を見ていただきたい」スコットは不安になる必要などなかったのだ。というのも，彼は敗北と死によって，おそらくは成功していた場合よりも確実に，英雄になったのだ。いや，むしろ彼の物語によって，人々は成功と失敗が何を意味するのかを見直さざるを得なくなったのだ。というのも，彼は究極の目標への理想像を追及し，ある理念に自分の生涯を捧げていたからだった。この種の理想主義は，国家を作る過程や，それ以上に帝国を作る過程には不可欠であるとみなされていた。崇高な大義における個人の自己犠牲，それこそがスコットが象徴するようになったものであり，間違いなくそれ以上に崇高な運命などありえないだろう。スコットは英国人気質の神話の一部となり，この犠牲の理想は第一次世界大戦中に何百万もの人々が考えることを，受け入れるか拒絶するかを，求められる理想となった。

【語句】

第１パラグラフ

- polar exploration「極地探検」
- Arctic「北極の」
- Antarctic「南極の」
- continent「大陸」
- region「地域，地方」
- defy「…に従わない，…を寄せ付けない」
- explorer「探検家」
- adventurer「冒険家」
- as late as the 1850s「1850年代になっても」
- lure「魅力」= temptation
- commercial「商業（上）の」
- imperial「帝国の」
- ambition「野望，野心」
- disappearance「消滅，消えること」
- expedition「探検，遠征隊」
- famous case「有名な事件」
- initiate「…を開始する，…を始める」

- a dozen A「十数（回）の A」
- rescue「救助（の）」
- as many (as) A「同数の A」
  ※ A は複数名詞。in as many years は「数十年において」の意味。
- disturbing「心を掻き乱すような」
- ice-bound「氷に閉ざされた」
- while *doing*「…しながら」
- trek「(徒歩で) 骨の折れる旅をする」
- overland「陸上［陸路］で」
- seek aid「助けを求める」
- succumb to A「A に屈する」
  = yield to A
- helplessly「無力に」
- environment「環境」
- dwell「住む，居住する」= live
- permanently「永久に，恒久的に」
- flourish「栄える，繁栄する」
- widow「未亡人」
- proclaim that S V ...「…だと宣言［公言］する」
- lay down *one's* life「命を捧げる」
  ※活用は【lay / laid / laid / laying】
- in the service of A「A の役に立つために，A に奉仕するために」
- as truly as if S V ...「…かのように忠実に」
- perish「死滅する」= die (out)
- naval「海軍の」
- claim A for B「B に対して A があると主張する」
- myth「神話」
- motive「動機」= incentive
- drive to *do*「…したいという衝動」
- appropriate「…を占有する，…を自分のものにする」
- psychologically「心理的に」
- B if not A「A でなくとも B」
- politically「政治的に」
- remote「遠い，遠方の」

第 2 パラグラフ

- be true of A「A に当てはまる」
  = apply to A
- unique「独特な，唯一の」
- featureless「特徴［特色］のない」
- geographical「地理的な，地理学上の」
- the planet「地球」
  = the earth
- inaccessibility「近づきにくいこと」
- generations of A「数世代の A」
- limit「限界，限度」
- endurance「忍耐力」
- declare that S V ...「…だと宣言する」
  = proclaim that S V ...
- mankind「人類」
  = humankind
- master of A「A の支配者」
- establish「…を立証する，…をはっきりさせる」

・officer「士官，武官」
・the Norwegian「ノルウェー人」
・survive「…を（切り抜けて）生き残る」
・extraordinary「異常な，普通でない」
⇔ ordinary「普通の」
・lock「…を閉じ込める」
・drift「漂流する，漂う」
・demonstrate that S V ...「…ということを証明する」
＝ prove that S V ...
・not A but B「A ではなく B」
・land-mass「大陸，広大な土地」
・ice cap「氷冠」
・narrative「物語，記述」
・wilderness「荒野，未開［無人］の地」
・remarkably「著しく，際立って」
・sane「正気な」
⇔ insane「正気でない，狂気の」
・good-tempered「温厚な，気立ての良い」
・humorous「ユーモアのある」
・transform A into B「A を B に変形させる，A を B に変質させる」
・filthy「汚れた，不潔な」
・savage「野蛮人」
・fat「脂肪，脂身」

第3パラグラフ

・produce「…を生み出す」
・literature「文献，文学（作品）」
・bleak「暗い，わびしい」
・face to face with A「A に直面して」
・intense physical suffering「激しい肉体的苦痛」
・philosophical question「哲学的疑問」
・fatal「致命的な，命取りになる」
・body「死体」
・entry「記載，記入」
・factual「事実に基づく」
・rationalise「…を合理的に説明する」＝ rationalize
・fate「運命」＝ destiny
・bold spirit「大胆な精神」
・officer-trained mask「士官として訓練を受けた仮面」
・slip away「消える，なくなる」
・confront「…に直面する」
・solely「単に」＝ only
・vanity「虚栄心」
・day-dream「空想，白昼夢」
・awful「恐ろしい，すさまじい」

第4パラグラフ

・all the ＋比較級「（ある理由によって）それだけ…」
・unbearable「耐えられない」
・*one's* sense of failure「自らの敗北感，自分が失敗したことに気づくこと」
・beat「…を打ち負かす」
＝ defeat
・additionally「その上，さらに」
＝ in addition
・torment「…をひどく苦しめる」

・including A「A を含めて」
・sympathise「同情する」
　= sympathize
・drive A on「A を駆り立てる」
・see (to it) that S V ...「…するように取り計らう［気をつける］」
・be dependent on[upon] A「A に頼っている」
　⇔ be independent of A「A に頼らない」
・provide for A「A を養う」
・ache「心を痛める，悲しむ」
・a sense of personal guilt「自責の念」
・for God's sake「お願いだから」
・look after A「A の世話をする」
　= care for A, take care of A
・need not have *done*「…する必要はなかった」
・fear「心配する，恐れる」
・securely「確実に，安心して」
・force O to *do*「O に…することを強いる」= compel O to *do*
・re-examine「…を再検証する，…を見直す」
・pursue「…を追求する」
・vision「理想像」
・the ultimate end「究極の目標」
・idealism「理想主義」
・see A as B「A を B だと見なす」
　= regard A as B
・essential「不可欠の，絶対必要な」
　= indispensable
・process「過程，プロセス」
・sacrifice「犠牲」
・individual「個人の」
・self「自己，自分自身」
・noble cause「崇高な大義」
・come to *do*「…するようになる」
・symbolise「…を象徴する」
　= symbolize
・destiny「運命」= fate
・mythology「神話」
・Britishness「英国人気質」
・call on[upon] O to *do*「O に…するように求める」
・embrace「…を受け入れる」
　= accept
・reject「…を拒絶する」

《 Vocabulary Building Exercise 》

1. This was the first time that I dared to **defy** my father.
【to refuse to obey somebody/something】

1.「私が父にあえて逆らったのはこの時が初めてでした」
【誰か，あるいは何かに従うことを拒否する】

2. Few can resist the **lure** of adventure.
【something that you find attractive】

2.「冒険が持つ魅力に逆らえる人はほとんどいない」
【魅力的だと感じるもの】

3. He said his country would never **succumb** to pressure.
【to be unable to fight an attack, a temptation, etc.】

3.「彼は，自分の国が圧力に屈することは決してないと言った」
【攻撃や誘惑などに逆らうことができない】

4. Most of the butterflies **perish** in the first frosts of autumn.
【to die, especially in a sudden violent way; to be lost or destroyed】

4.「ほとんどのチョウは，秋の初霜の頃に命が尽きる」
【特に突然，無惨な形で死ぬ／失われたり破壊されたりする】

5. This book offers no coherent **narrative** of the American Civil War.
【a story or an account of a series of events】

5.「この本は，アメリカ南北戦争について首尾一貫した説明を提供していない」
【一連の出来事についての物語や説明】

6. Why are the streets so **filthy** in this part of the city?
【very dirty; very unpleasant and disgusting】

6.「市内のこの地域の街路はなぜそんなに不潔なのですか」
【とても汚れている／とても不快で気分が悪くなる】

7. He fails to distinguish **factual** information from opinion.
【based on or containing facts】

7.「彼は事実に基づく情報と意見を区別できない」
【事実に基づいていたり事実を含んでいたりする】

8. No doubt the idea appealed to his **vanity**.
【the fact of being too proud of your own appearance, abilities or achievements】

9. At times the memories returned to **torment** her.
【to cause somebody extreme mental suffering】

10. He dedicated his life to fighting for the **cause** of animal rights.
【an organization or idea that people support or fight for】

8. 「その考えが彼の虚栄心を刺激したことは間違いない」
【自分の外見や能力，功績を過度に誇りに思うという事実】

9. 「ときどき，その記憶がよみがえって彼女を悩ませた」
【人に非常に大きな精神的苦痛を与える】

10. 「彼は，動物の権利という大義のために闘うことに一生を捧げた」
【人が支援したりそのために闘ったりする組織や考え】

《 Summary 》

At the beginning of the 20th century, the Arctic and Antarctic continents were the last places remaining for Europeans to explore. A British expedition to the Canadian Arctic in 1846 became famous when it was learned that every Englishman had succumbed to the harsh environment. In the end, it turned out that the commercial and naval importance of the Northwest Passage which the group had been searching for was a myth. However, explorers were still attracted to the remotest regions of the planet, like the North and South Pole, for psychological reasons. They wanted to prove which nation was best at exploration. Fridtjof Nansen wrote about his experience of being trapped on a ship surrounded by polar ice for three years in a surprisingly sane and humorous way. Narratives about the South Pole are often bleak, but philosophical. In Robert Scott's diary of his fatal expedition, he confronts the fact that his own choices led him to the fate he cannot escape. In the end, Scott became a hero who symbolised the ideal of self-sacrifice for a noble cause. (179 words)

【《Summary》の訳】

20世紀の初頭，北極と南極大陸は，ヨーロッパ人が探検するのに残された最後の場所でした。1846年に行われたイギリスによるカナダ北極圏への探検旅行は，すべてのイギリス人乗組員が過酷な環境で命を落としたことがわかって有名になりました。結局，この探検隊が探し求めていた北西航路の商業上，そして軍事上の重要性は根拠がなかったことが判明しました。しかしながら，探検家たちは，それでも心理的な理由から，北極や南極などの地球の最も遠い地域に引きつけられていました。彼らは，どの国が探検で最も優位に立っているのか証明したかったのです。フリチョフ・ナンセンは，極地の流氷に囲まれた船に3年間も閉じ込められた経験について，驚くほど冷静でユーモラスな語り口で書き残しています。南極に関する話は暗いものが多いものの，哲学的でもあります。ロバート・スコットが命を落とした遠征時の日記の中で，彼は自分自身の選択のせいで避けることのできない運命に陥ったという事実を直視しています。結果的に，スコットは高貴な大義のための自己犠牲という理想を象徴する英雄となりました。

第６問　北海道大学

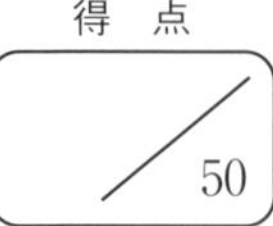

【解答】

問１．１万２千年前に起こった定住型農業の発達が都市化のきっかけとなったが，現生人類が現れたのはそれよりもはるか以前の約20万年前だから。（65字）

問２．私たちの感情や本能は，より定住性の高い農工業型のライフスタイルよりも，狩猟採集民のライフスタイルに適している。

問３．①

問４．③

問５．②

問６．②・④・⑦（順不同）

【配点と採点基準】（50点）

問１．12点
- 「約20万年前に現生人類が現れた」… 4 点
- 「約１万２千年前に定住型農業（農業革命）が始まった」… 4 点
- 「定住型農業の発達（農業革命）の後に都市化が起こった」… 4 点

問２．８点
- Our feelings and instincts are suited to a hunter-gatherer lifestyle, … 4 点
  - ＊ be suited to A の誤訳は 2 点減
  - ＊ hunter-gatherer lifestyle の誤訳は 2 点減
- rather than a more settled agricultural-industrial one. … 4 点
  - ＊ rather than の誤訳は 2 点減
  - ＊ more settled の誤訳は 2 点減
  - ＊ agricultural-industrial one の誤訳は 2 点減

問３．３点　解答通り

問４．３点　解答通り

問５．６点　解答通り

問６．18点（各６点×３）解答通り

【設問別解説】

問１.

「都市の成長は人類の歴史においては比較的最近に起こった進展だ」と言える根拠を説明するためには，①第１段落第３文 Modern humans ... have been around for about 200,000 years の内容，②第２段落第１文の前半の The development of cities only began following the agricultural revolution の内容，③第２段落第１文の後半の which（= the agricultural revolution）took place in different parts of the world from about 12,000 years ago の内容の３項目を記述する必要がある。

問２.

・instinct「本能」
・be suited to A「A に適している」
・hunter-gatherer lifestyle「狩猟採集民のライフスタイル［生活／生活様式］」
・rather than ...「…よりも，…ではなくて」
・more settled「より定住性の高い」
・agricultural-industrial one（= agricultural-industrial lifestyle）「農工業型のライフスタイル［生活／生活様式］」

問３.

「今日私たちが緊急事態と見なすかもしれない状況は，狩猟採集民であった私たちの祖先（　　　）」

① **「(狩猟採集民であった私たちの祖先）にとっては日常的な現実だった」**
② 「(狩猟採集民であった私たちの祖先）にとっても無理な負担だった」
③ 「(狩猟採集民であった私たちの祖先）の一つの利点だった」
④ 「(狩猟採集民であった私たちの祖先）の想像を超えるものだった」

問４.

筆者は，直前の第４～５段落で「狩猟採集民たちが現代人よりも環境に適応した生活を行っていた」という意見を述べている。空所を含む第６段落第１文で狩猟採集民の生活の短所に触れた後で，次の第２文（But ... ）以下では再び狩猟採集民の生活の利点が話題になっている。空所には「譲歩」の目印となる Of course を補うのが最適である。

問５.

「しかし，別の点では彼ら（狩猟採集民）が私たち（現代人）よりも豊かだったのかもしれない」と筆者が語る理由は，第３～６段落の内容（本文全体の主旨）そのものである。

① 「大都市では，狩猟採集民が高給の仕事を見つけることは困難ではなかった」

② **「狩猟採集民だった私たちの祖先は，生活の中のストレスがほとんどなかった」**

③「狩猟採集民のライフスタイルは，食料を集める最も効率的なやり方だった」

④「部族のメンバーは互いをよく知っていたので，狩猟採集民のライフスタイルはとても生産性が高かった」

問６.

①「狩猟採集民の生活様式は都市の発展に起因していた」→第２段落第１文の内容と矛盾する。

② **「誰もが同じレベルの富を所有していたので，狩猟採集民は互いをそれほど妬むことがなかった」**→第６段落第２文の内容に一致する。

③「歴史の大部分を通して，人類は遊牧生活よりも定住生活を好んだ」→第１段落最終文の内容と矛盾する。

④ **「ハラーリは，１日のスケジュールを厳しく制限されている工場労働者の姿を鮮明に描いている」**→第５段落第２文以下の内容に一致する。

⑤「狩猟採集民だった私たちの祖先は，今日の私たちよりも物質的に豊かな暮らしをしていた」→第６段落最終文の内容と矛盾する。

⑥「筆者は，田園地帯の農業中心のライフスタイルと都市部の工業中心のライフスタイルを対比している」→本文に言及なし。

⑦ **ハラーリの著書からの引用例は，狩猟採集民のライフスタイルの好ましい面を強調する傾向がある」**→第４～５段落の内容に一致する。

【全訳】

国連は，2050年までに人類の66％が都市部に住むようになると概算している。これほどの高い比率は，人間にとってそのような暮らし方が普通であることを示唆しているのかもしれない。しかしながら，都市の成長は人類の歴史においては比較的最近に起こった進展なのだ。現生人類（つまり，解剖学的に私たちに似ていると私たちが認識する人間）が登場してから約20万年になる。この期間の大半にわたって，人類は狩猟採集民として存在してきた。

都市の発達が始まったのは，世界のさまざまな場所で約12,000年前から始まった農業革命の後のことに過ぎない。これに伴う根本的な変化は，（動物の移動や植物の豊作パターンを追いかけながら）食べ物を求めてあちこち動き回るのではなく，人間が特定の場所で作物を育て動物を飼い始めたことだった。徐々に人間は，大きな部族集団の中で一緒に暮らすのではなく，個々の家族で暮らすようになった。

12,000年というのは，人間が新しいライフスタイルに適応するのには長い時間ではない。私たちの感情や本能は，より定住性の高い農工業型のライフスタイルよりも，狩猟採集民のライフスタイルに適している。都市に住むことには，食べ物や水の迅速な供給，野生動物からの安全，広範囲の医療サービスの利便性，そして便利な輸送システムなど，多くの物質的な利点がある。しかし，都市環境は，狩猟採集民だった私たちの祖先が経験する可能性が高くなかった感情面の問題，つまり，憂うつや孤独感や，過密環境での生活から生じるストレスなどの問題を生み出す。人間は社会的動物であるため，例えば長時間労働のせいで親しい友人や家族と接する時間を定期的に持てないと，私たちは気持ちが沈んでしまう。私たちの大部分が都市に住んでいるかもしれないが，私たちはそこで本当に幸せなのだろうか。

それを判断するため，イスラエル人の著者ユバル・ノア・ハラーリは，2014年の著書『サピエンス』の中で，昔の狩猟採集民の生活と現代の都市居住者の生活とを比較している。ハラーリは，狩猟採集民たちが自由に活動していた様子を記述している。彼らはいつ働くか（食べ物を探すか），また誰と働くか（家族や友人）を決めていた。彼らには皿洗いやアイロンがけなどの行うべき家事がなかったし，請求書の支払いをすることも，銀行に行くことも，自分を叱る上司の声を聞くことも必要なかった。汚染や交通事故や路上強盗など，心配すべき問題もなかった。狩猟採集民はさまざまな食物を食べていたし，また人々が密集した状態で暮らしていなかったために感染病も一般的ではなかった。狩猟採集民は必要なすべてのものを買うのではなく作らなければならなかったので，多くの面で高い技術を持っていたし，また自分の足以外に移動手段がなかったことを考えると，肉体的にも非常に健康だった。彼らはまた，自分たちの環境について精通していた。今日，あなたが自宅から100キロメートルのところで立ち往生して，電話も，お金も，交通手段も，食べ物も水もない状況になった場合を想像してみてほしい。あなたはパニックに陥るだろうか。あなたは生き残れるだろうか。今日私たちが緊急事態と見なすかもしれない状況は，狩猟採集民であった私たちの祖先にとっては日常的な現実だったのだ。

現代人のほとんどは，自分で食べ物を見つけたり作ったりするのではなく，食べ物と交換できるお金を稼ぐために働く。『サピエンス』の中で，ハラーリは，今日の都市の労働者が，朝早く自宅を出て，毎日同じ道を歩いて行って誰も話をしていない地下鉄に乗り，工場では機械の前の一か所に座って何時間も同じ作業を行うかもしれない有様を記述している。その労働者は，飲食できる時間や仕事が終わる時間を告げられる。夜になって，おそらくはその日の朝に家を出た12時間後に家に着くと，その労働者は，料理をして（その日3度目の同じ種類の食べ物を食べるのかもしれない），それから掃除をして，洗濯をして，騒々しく明るいアパートで安らかに眠ろうと努めなければならない。

もちろん，狩猟採集民のライフスタイルには短所があった。食べ物が足りなくなった時期もあっただろう。乳幼児の死亡率も高かったし，医療は高度に発達しているわけではなかった。しかし，狩猟採集民の精神的健康は良好で，「仕事」に対する満足感は高く，嫉妬心はほとんどなかった。それは，他の者より多くを持つ者が誰もいなかったからだ。狩猟採集部族のメンバーは，自分の生死が集団の他のメンバーたちに依存していたから，互いのことをとても親密に知っていた。これは，見知らぬ人とオフィスで働く現代人には到達するのが困難な感覚だ。狩猟採集民だった私たちの祖先は，物質的には私たちより貧しかったかもしれないが，別の点では彼らは私たちがなり得ないほど豊かだったのかもしれない。

【語句】

第1パラグラフ

・the United Nations「国際連合（国連）」
・estimate that S V ...「…だと概算する」
・human beings「人類，人間」= humans
・high percentage「高い比率」
・comparatively「比較的」
・development「進展，発展」
・modern humans「現生人類」
・that is「つまり，すなわち」= that is to say
・recognize A as B「AをBだと認める［認識する］」
・anatomically「解剖学的に」
・(be) similar to A「Aと似て（いる）」
・be around「（人が）生きている，存在している，活動している」
・the vast majority of A「Aの大部分，Aの大半」
・hunter-gatherer「狩猟採集民」
・existence「生活」= life

第2パラグラフ

・follow「…の後に来る，…に続く」
・agricultural revolution「農業革命」
・take place「起こる，生ずる」
・fundamental「基本的な，根本的な」
・involved in A「Aに伴う，Aに関係している」
・rather than *doing*「…するのではなく」
・wander「歩き回る，さまよう」
・from place to place「あちこちに［を］」
・in search of A「Aを捜して」

・animal migration「動物の移動」
・fertility pattern「豊作[繁殖]のパターン」
・plant「植物」
・crop「作物」
・breed「…を飼育する」
・particular location「特定の場所」
・separate family「別個の家族，独立した家族」
・B rather than A「AではなくB」＝ not A but B
・tribal「種族の，部族の」

第3パラグラフ

・adapt to A「Aに順応する」
・instinct「本能」
・be suited to A「Aに適している」
・settled「安定した，落ち着いた，定着した」
・agricultural-industrial「農工業の」
・material advantage「物質的な利点」
・ready「素早い，迅速な」
・supply「供給」
⇔ demand「需要」
・access to A「Aの利用［入手］の権利，Aへのアクセス」
・a large range of A「広範囲に及ぶ［さまざまな］A」
・medical service「医療（サービス）」
・convenient「便利な」
⇔ inconvenient「不便な」
・transport system「輸送システム」
・urban condition「都市環境」
・produce「…を生み出す，…を生じさせる」
・emotional「感情的な」
⇔ rational「理性的な」
・ancestor「祖先，先祖」
・be less likely to *do*「…する可能性がそれほど高くない」
・depression「憂うつ，意気消沈」
・loneliness「孤独」
・overcrowded environment「過密環境」
・have regular contact with A「Aと定期的に接触する」

第4パラグラフ

・judge「…を判断する」
・compare A with B「AとBを比較する」
・city-dweller「都市居住者」
・describe「…を記述する，…を描写する」
・be free to *do*「自由に…する（ことができる）」
・household chore「家事」
・bill「勘定，請求書」
・boss「上司」
・scold「…をしかる」
・pollution「汚染，公害」
・varied「さまざまな，変化に富んだ」
・diet「食事」
・infectious disease「感染病」

・common「普通の，よく起こる」
・skilled「熟練した，技術を身につけた」
・physically「肉体的に」
⇔ mentally「精神的に」
・fit「体調がよい」= healthy
・given that S V ...「…ということを考慮すると」
・extremely「とても，きわめて」
・imagine if S V ...「もし…だったらと想像する」
・strand「(人を) 立ち往生させる」
※通例受け身で使用される。
・panic「うろたえる，パニックになる」
・survive「生き残る」
・situation「状況，事態」
・consider O C「O を C だと考える［見なす］」
・emergency「緊急事態」
・daily reality「日常的な現実」

第 5 パラグラフ
・exchange A for B「A を B と交換する」
・relate「…を述べる，…を物語る」
・walk the same route「同じ道を歩いて行く」
・subway train「地下鉄の列車」
・perform the same process「同じ作業を行う」
・peacefully「安らかに，穏やかに」

第 6 パラグラフ
・disadvantage「不利」
⇔ advantage「有利」
・period「期間，時期」
・infant mortality「乳幼児の死亡率」
・medical care「医療」
= medical service, medical treatment
・develop「…を発展［発達］させる」
・mental health「精神的健康」
・satisfaction「満足（感）」
・jealousy「嫉妬（心）」
・tribe「種族，部族」
・depend on A「A に依存する，A に頼る」= rely on A
・achieve「…を獲得する，…を勝ち取る」
・stranger「見知らぬ人」

《 Vocabulary Building Exercise 》

1. Often it is not possible to **estimate** the probability of a catastrophe.
【to approximately calculate or judge the value, number, quantity or extent of something】

1. 「大災害が起こる確率を見積もることは，多くの場合不可能だ」
【何かの価値や数量，程度などを大まかに計算したり判断したりする】

2. The company is a **comparative** newcomer to the software market.
【measured or judged by how similar or different something is to something else】

2. 「その会社は，ソフトウェア市場への比較的最近の参入者である」
【何かと別の何かとがどのくらい似ているかあるいは違うかで測定されたり判断されたりするような】

3. There are some minute **anatomical** differences between these insects.
【relating to the structure of the bodies of people and animals】

3. 「これらの昆虫の間には，いくつか身体構造上のごく小さな違いがある」
【人や動物の体の構造に関する】

4. Those policies resulted in massive internal rural-to-urban **migration**.
【the movement of large numbers of people or animals from one place to another】

4. 「これらの政策の結果，国内の農村部から都市部への大規模な人口移動が発生した」
【多くの人々や動物の，ある場所から別の場所への移動】

5. This curriculum is especially **suited** to middle-grade students.
【right or appropriate for a particular purpose or a particular job】

5. 「このカリキュラムは特に中学生に適している」
【特定の目的や特定の作業に合っている，あるいは適切な】

6. The extra money should be spent on improving public **transport**.
【a system for taking people or goods from one place to another】

6. 「余分な資金は，公共交通機関を改善することに費やすべきだ」
【人々や物資をある場所から別の場所に運ぶための仕組み】

7. Shopping is a real **chore** for me.
【a task that you do regularly; an unpleasant or boring task】

7. 「買い物は私にとってまったくの雑用です」
【人が定期的に行う作業／楽しくない，あるいは退屈な作業】

8. **Infectious** diseases are a major global threat.
【that can be passed easily from one person or animal to another】

8. 「伝染性の疾病は，世界にとって重要な脅威の１つだ」
【人から人，あるいは動物から動物へと簡単に受け渡される】

9. She tries to keep **fit** by jogging every day.
【in good physical or mental condition】

9. 「彼女は，毎日ジョギングすることで健康を保とうとしている」
【体や心の状態が良好な】

10. Reduced **mortality** among newborns led to an increase in life expectancy.
【the number of deaths in a particular situation or period of time】

10. 「新生児の死亡率の減少は，平均余命の延長をもたらした」
【特定の状況，あるいは期間における死亡者の数】

《 Summary 》

By 2050, 66% of human beings will live in cities. Given the fact that modern humans have existed for about 200,000 years, living in cities is a very recent change for us. For most of human history, we have been hunter-gatherers. Although we have not changed [anatomically], we have completely changed our way of life. Most of us no longer live in [tribal] groups, wandering from place to place to find food. Now we have convenient [transport] systems and ready access to medical services, along with basic necessities like food and water. However, our feelings and [instincts] are still suited to a hunter-gatherer lifestyle, not an [urban] one. We have lost a lot of our freedom and our close ties to others. In many ways, our hunter-gatherer [ancestors] might have been richer than we are. (135 words)

【《Summary》の訳】

2050年までに，人類の66%が都市に住むようになるでしょう。現生人類がおよそ20万年前から存在してきたという事実を考慮すると，都市部に住むことは私たちにとってごく最近になって起きた変化です。人類の歴史のほとんどの期間，私たちは狩猟採集民でした。私たちは身体の構造では変わっていませんが，私たちの暮らし方はすっかり変わりました。私たちの大半は，もはや部族集団として暮らしておらず，食べ物を探すためにあちこちを歩き回ることもありません。今では，私たちは便利な移動手段を有しており，食料や水などの基本的な生活必需品に加え，医療サービスも迅速に利用できます。しかしながら，私たちの感覚や本能は，今なお都会のライフスタイルではなく，狩猟採集のライフスタイルに適しています。私たちは多くの自由や他者との密接な結びつきを失ってしまいました。いろいろな点で，私たちの狩猟採集民の祖先は，今の私たちよりも豊かだったのかもしれません。

第7問　一橋大学

得点

／50

【解答】

問1．②

問2．私たちの表情は，心の中で起こっていることを映す鏡というよりは，次に起こってほしいと私たちが望んでいることに関して送っている合図だ。

問3．感情は根源的で本能的なものであり私たちの顔に表われるものだという考え方。

問4．私たちが顔を,隠された感情を映し出しているものというよりも,積極的に私たちに話しかけようとしているものと見なすとしたら，私たちはもっとうまくコミュニケーションが行えるかもしれないということになる。

問5．彼は私たちを操り人形使いに例え，私たちの表情は「相手を操るためにあなたが使おうとしている見えないワイヤーやロープのようなものだ」と言う。

問6．a ④　b ①　c ⑤　d ⑥

【配点と採点基準】（50点）

問1．6点　解答通り

問2．8点

・our expressions are less a mirror of what's going on inside than ... …4点

＊ expressionsの誤訳は2点減

＊ less A than Bの誤訳は2点減

＊ a mirror of Aの意味を理解していないものは2点減

＊ what's going on insideの意味を理解していないものは2点減

・a signal we're sending about what we want to happen next …4点

＊ we're sending ... 以下が形容詞節であることを理解していないものは2点減

＊ what we want to happen next の意味を理解していないものは2点減

問3． 6点

・「感情は根源的で本能的なものだ」の内容 … 2点

・「感情は顔に表われる」の内容 … 4点

問4． 10点

・It turns out that S V ... … 2点

・we might communicate better … 2点

・if we saw faces not as mirroring hidden emotions … 4点

＊仮定法過去で書かれていることを理解していないものは2点減

＊ see A as B の誤訳は2点減

＊ mirroring hidden emotions の誤訳は2点減

・but rather as actively trying to speak to us. … 2点

＊ not A but rather B の誤訳は2点減

＊ actively の誤訳は2点減

＊ trying to speak to us の誤訳は2点減

問5． 8点

・He compares us to puppeteers, … 2点

・with our expressions like "invisible wires or ropes … 3点

＊ with O C の形を理解していないものは2点減

＊ invisible wires or ropes の誤訳は2点減

・that you are trying to use to manipulate the other." … 3点

＊この部分が直前の invisible wires or ropes を修飾する形容詞節であることを理解していないものは2点減

＊ manipulate the other の誤訳は2点減

問6． 12点（各3点×4）解答通り

【設問別解説】

問1．

「顔の表情は，単に感情が表に出てきたものではなく，相手とのやり取りの方向性に影響を及ぼそうという動機を含んでいる」という本文全体の趣旨に合致するものを選ぶ。

「それらの顔の表情は私たちの（　　）を表す」

① 「信念や道徳的な価値観」

② **「意図や対人的な目的」**

③「好き嫌い」

④「意見や知能レベル」

問２.

・less A than B「A というよりも B」(= not so much A as B)

・a mirror of A「A を映し出すもの［鏡］」

・what's going on inside「内面で起こっていること，心の中の状態」

・a signal we're sending about ...「…について私たちが送っている信号［シグナル］」, we're sending ... 以下は a signal を修飾する形容詞節，a signal と we're ... の間に目的格の関係代名詞が省略されている。

・what we want to happen next「次に何が起こることを私たちが望んでいるか，私たちが次にどうなってほしいと望んでいるか」, S want O to *do* の表現が用いられていて，what は want の目的語が前に出たもの。

問３.

this viewpoint「この見解」とは，直前の文の中の The idea that emotions are fundamental, instinctive, and expressed in our faces を指している。

問４.

・It turns out that S V ...「…ということがわかる，(結果的に) …ということになる」

・we might communicate better if we saw ... は，仮定法過去を用いている。現状では実現されていないというニュアンスを伝えている。

・see A as B「A を B だと見なす［考える］」

・mirroring hidden emotions「隠された感情を映し出している」，他動詞 mirror「…を映し出す」の現在分詞を用いた形容詞句。

・not A but rather B「A ではなく，(むしろ) B」

・actively「能動的に，積極的に」，顔の表情は感情が表に出てきたというような受動的なものではないことを表している。

問５.

・compare A to B「A を B に例える」

・with our expressions like "invisible wires or ropes「私たちの表情は目に見えないワイヤーやロープのようなものだ」は with O C「O が C である」の表現を用いている。

・that you are trying ... 以下は，名詞句 invisible wires or ropes を修飾する形容詞節。that は目的格の関係代名詞で，形容詞節の中の他動詞 use の目的語になっている。

・to manipulate the other「相手を操るために」

問6.

a　identify「…を特定する，…を認定する」

b　attribute A to B「A（性質など）がBにあると考える」

c　respond to A「Aに反応する」

d　reveal「(隠されていること）を明らかにする」

【全訳】

2015年，パプアニューギニアで感情と顔の表情に関する研究を行っている時に，心理学者カルロス・クリヴェッリは驚くべきことを発見した。彼はトロブリアンド諸島の住民に西洋では標準的な恐怖の顔 —— 目を見開き，口を大きく開けた顔 —— の写真を見せて，彼らに何を見たかを特定するように求めた。トロブリアンドの住民が見たのは，恐怖におびえた顔ではなかった。そうでなく，彼らが見たのは威嚇と攻撃性を示すものだった。言い換えれば，私たちが普遍的な恐怖の表情と考えるものは，まったく普遍的なものではないのだ。だが，トロブリアンドの住民が表情について異なる解釈をするのであれば，そのことは何を意味するのだろうか。新しく登場し，そして支持を広げつつある1つの理論は，顔の表情は私たちの感情を反映するものではないというものだ。表情は，私たちの感情の状態を示すものとして信頼できるものではなく，それらは私たちの意図や対人的な目的を示すものなのである。

顔は「通過していく交通に影響を与える道路標識のように」作用すると，最近，クリヴェッリとの共同研究を執筆した心理学教授のアラン・フリドルンドは言う。「私たちの顔は，対人的なやり取りを方向づける手段だ」と。だからと言って，私たちが自分の顔の表情を使って積極的に他人を操作しようとしているということではない。私たちのほほ笑みとしかめっ面はたぶん無意識なものだろう。しかし，私たちの表情は，心の中で起こっていることを映す鏡というよりは，次に起こってほしいと私たちが望んでいることに関して送っている合図なのだ。例えば，あなたの最高に「うんざりしている」顔は，あなたが会話の進み方に満足していないこと，そして，会話の方向が変わることをあなたが望んでいるということを示しているのかもしれない。

この理論は賢明な理論だと思えるかもしれないが，長い期間を経てやっと生まれたものだ。感情は根源的で本能的なものであり私たちの顔に表われるものだという考え方は，西洋文化に深く定着している。だが，この見方は常に批判されてきた。新しい研究は，基本的な感情理論の2つの主要な論点に異議を唱えている。1つ目は，いくつかの感情は普遍的に共有され認識されるという考えだ。2つ目は，表情はそれらの感情を反映するものとして信頼できるという考えだ。

その新しい研究には，クリヴェッリによる最近の研究が含まれている。彼はパプアニューギニアのトロブリアンド諸島の住民とも，モザンビークのムワニ族たちとも，数か月を共に過ごした。彼はいずれの原住民の集団に関しても，被験者たちが西洋人のように顔が感情を持つと考えているわけではないということを発見した。それは単に恐怖の顔だけでもなかった。微笑んでいる顔を見せられてその顔は幸せだと明言したトロブリアンド諸島の住民はわずかしかいなかった。自分の言葉で何の顔かを言い表すように求められた住民の約半数は，「笑っている」と言い表した。それは，感情ではなく行為を表す言葉だ。言い換えれば，クリヴェッリは，顔の表情の背後にあるものが普遍的に理解されるという証拠を何も見つけられなかったのだ。

さらに問題を複雑にするのだが，私たちの顔の表情がある特定の感情を示していると他人が解釈した場合でも，その人は私たちが実際には感じていない感情を特定するかもしれないのだ。約50件の研究についての2017年の分析の中で，顔が実際の感情を反映する人がとても少ないことを研究者たちは発見した。

顔の表情が気持ちを実際には反映しないとすると，その影響はとても大きい。1つは人工知能（AI）の分野，特にロボット工学においてだ。「非常に多くの人々が，心理学の教科書に載っている顔の実例を使って人工知能や対人ロボットを訓練している」とフリドルンドは言う。だが，ロボットに向かってしかめっ面をする人が単なる不機嫌以外のことを伝えようとしているような場合に，AIはそれらに対し間違った反応をするかもしれない。

しかしながら，私たちのほとんどにとって新しい研究は，私たちが社会的相互作用をどのように解釈するかということに関して大きな影響を与えるのかもしれない。私たちが顔を，隠された感情を映し出しているものというよりも，積極的に私たちに話しかけようとしているものと見なすとしたら，私たちはもっとうまくコミュニケーションが行えるかもしれないということになる。人々は「道路標識のようなもの」として顔を読み取るべきだとフリドルンドは言う。「それは鉄道線路の上の切替器のようなものだ。会話の中で，こっちに行くのか，あっちに行くのか」と。あなたの友人の顔に浮かぶしかめっ面は実際の怒りではないかもしれない。もしかすると，彼女はあなたに，彼女の見解に同意することを望んでいるだけなのかもしれない。

笑いを例にとってみようと，ブリジット・ウォラーは言う。「社会的相互作用の中では，いつ笑うかということと，どのように笑うかということが絶対的に重要だ」と。タイミングの悪い笑いは今起こっていることに対するあなたの心の中の喜びを表さずに，むしろ，あなたがその会話に細心の注意を払っていないか，または敵意を伝えることにさえなるかもしれない。

クリヴェッリにとって，私たちの顔はそれ以上に計算高いものなのかもしれない。彼は私たちを操り人形使いに例え，私たちの表情は「相手を操るためにあなたが使おうとしている見えないワイヤーやロープのようなものだ」と言う。そしてもちろん，そのまま逆に，その相手は私たちを操作しているのだ。結局のところ，私たちは社会的な生き物なのだ。

【語句】

第１パラグラフ

・conduct research on A「A を研究する」
・emotion「感情，情緒」
・facial expression「(顔の) 表情」
・psychologist「心理学者」
・startling「びっくりさせる，仰天させる」
・photograph「写真」＝ photo
・fear「恐怖感，おびえ」
・wide-eyed「目を大きく開いた」
・identify「…を特定する，…を見分ける」
・frightened face「おびえた顔」
・indication「表示，徴候」
・threat「おどし，威嚇」
・in other words「言い換えれば」
・think of A as B「A を B だと考える［見なす］」
＝ regard A as B
・universal「普遍的な，一般的な」
・interpretation「解釈」
・emerging「新生の，新興の」
・increasingly「ますます，だんだん」
・support「…を支持する」
・reflect「…を反映する」
・instead of A「A ではなくて」
・reliable「信頼できる」
・display「表示，示すもの」
・state「状態，様子」
・intention「意図，意志」

第２パラグラフ

・act like A「A のように行動する」
・road sign「道路標識」
・affect「…に影響する」
・traffic「交通」
・psychology professor「心理学教授」
・direct the course of A「A を方向づける」
・social interaction「対人的なやりとり，社会的相互作用」
・That is not to say that S V ...「そうだからといって…ということではない」
・actively「積極的に，活発に」
・manipulate「…を操作する，…をたくみに扱う」
・frown「しかめっ面，渋い顔」
・may well be C「たぶん C だろう」

・unconscious「無意識の，意図していない」
・less A than B「A というよりむしろ B」
= B more than A, not so much A as B
・a mirror of A「A を映し出すもの［鏡］」
・go on「起こる」= happen
・signal「合図」
・disgusted face「うんざりした顔」
※ disgust は「…に嫌気を起こさせる」の意味。
・conversation「会話」

第 3 パラグラフ

・sensible「賢明な，分別のある」
= wise
・fundamental「根源的な，基本となる」
・instinctive「本能的な」
・fix「…を定着［固定］させる」
・viewpoint「見地，見方」
・criticize「…を批判する」
・challenge「…に異議を唱える」
・share「…を分かち合う，…を共有する」
・recognize「…を認識する」
・reflection「反映，反映するもの」

第 4 パラグラフ

・include「(全体の一部として)…を含む」
・recent work「最近の研究」
・B as well as A「A と同様 B も」
= not only A but (also) B
・native「原住民の」
・study participant「被験者，研究の参加者」
・attribute A to B「A（性質など）が B にあると考える」
・in the same way S V ...「…するのと同じように」
・declare that S V ...「…だと明言［断言］する」
・describe「…を説明［表現］する」
・deal with A「A を扱う，A に関係がある」
・B, not A「A ではなく B」
= not A but B
・evidence that S V ...「…という証拠」

第 5 パラグラフ

・make matters more complicated「問題をさらに複雑にする」
・exhibit「…を表す，…を見せる」
・analysis「分析」
・researcher「研究者，調査員」
・a minority of A「A の少数（の者）」

第 6 パラグラフ

・enormous「非常に大きい，莫大な」
・consequence「影響，帰結」
= effect
・field「分野」
・artificial intelligence「人工知能」
・specifically「特に，とりわけ」

・robotics「ロボット工学」
・a good number of A「かなりの数のA，非常にたくさんのA」
・social robot「対人ロボット」
・example face「顔の実例」
・frown「しかめっ面をする，まゆをひそめる」
・signal「…に合図を送る，…に信号を送る」
・B other than A「A以外のB」
・unhappiness「不機嫌，不幸，不運」
・respond to A「Aに反応する，Aに応答する」
・incorrectly「不正確に，不適切に」

第7パラグラフ
・though「しかしながら」
＝ however
※副詞のthoughは文中，文末で用いる。
・have most of an effect on A「Aに大いなる影響を与える」
・interpret「…を解釈する」
・It turns out that S V ...「…ということがわかる，（結果的に）…ということになる」
・communicate「コミュニケーションを行う」
・see A as B「AをBだと見なす」
＝ regard A as B
・mirror「…を映し出す」
・not A but rather B「Aではなく（むしろ）B」
・hidden「隠れた，隠された」
・kind of like A「Aのようなもの」
・railroad track「鉄道線路」
・agree with A「Aに同意する」
⇔ disagree with A「Aに同意しない」
・*one's* point of view「自分の見方」

第8パラグラフ
・take laughter「笑いを例にとる」
・absolutely「絶対的に，完全に」
・crucial「決定的な，きわめて重大な」
・poorly-timed「タイミングの悪い」
・reveal「（隠されていること）を明らかにする」
・inner joy「心の中の喜び」
・pay close attention to A「Aに細心の注意を払う」
・hostility「敵意」

第9パラグラフ
・calculating「打算的な，抜け目のない」
・compare A to B「AをBに例える」
・invisible「目に見えない」
・wire「ワイヤー，金属線」
・the other「相手」
＝ the other person
・right back「まったく逆に」
・social creature「社会的な生き物」
・after all「結局」

《 Vocabulary Building Exercise 》

1. Did you **identify** all those species correctly?
【to recognize somebody/something and be able to say who or what they are】

2. While apes sometimes **interpret** staring as friendly, as humans do, most monkeys find staring threatening.
【to decide that something has a particular meaning and to understand it in this way】

3. You should **direct** your attention to the next task.
【to aim something at a particular goal or person, or in a particular direction】

4. I'm **disgusted** with the way that he was treated.
【feeling a strong sense of dislike and disapproval at something】

5. Given the difficult situation, their approach seems **sensible** and appropriate.
【done or chosen with good judgment based on reason and experience rather than emotion】

1. 「あなたは，それらすべての生物種を正確に見分けられましたか」
【誰か，あるいは何かを認識し，その正体を明らかにすることができる】

2. 「霊長類は人間と同様，相手を見つめることを親愛の情の表われだと解釈することがあるが，たいていのサルは見つめることを威嚇だと感じる」
【何かに特定の意味があると判断し，そのようなものとして理解する】

3. 「あなたは次の任務に注意を向けるべきです」
【何かを特定の目標や人物，あるいは特定の方向に向ける】

4. 「私は，彼の扱われ方に対して，とても腹が立っている」
【何かに対して強い嫌悪や不満を感じている】

5. 「困難な状況を考えると，彼らのやり方は賢明で適切なように思える」
【感情ではなく，理性や経験に基づいて適切な判断で行われたり選択されたりする】

6. They **challenge** the belief that obesity represents wealth.
【to question whether something is right, legal or true; to refuse to accept or believe something】

6.「彼らは，肥満が富の象徴だとする考え方に異議を唱えている」
【何かが正しいか，合法か，真実かどうか疑う／何かを受け入れたり信じたりすることを拒否する】

7. They **attribute** magical properties to the stones.
【to regard a quality or feature as belonging to somebody/something】

7.「彼らは，その石に不思議な特性があると考えている」
【ある性質や特徴が誰か，あるいは何かに備わっていると見なす】

8. The **interaction** between performers and their audience is very interesting.
【the way that people communicate with each other】

8.「演奏者と聴衆とのやり取りはとてもおもしろい」
【人がお互いに意思疎通を図る様子】

9. A thorough search failed to **reveal** the murder weapon.
【to show something that previously could not be seen】

9.「徹底的な捜索をしても，凶器を明らかにすることはできなかった」
【今まで見えなかったものを示す】

10. As a politician, he knows how to **manipulate** public opinion.
【to control or influence somebody/something, often in a dishonest way so that they do not realize it】

10.「政治家として，彼は世論を操作する方法を知っている」
【人に気付かれないように，しばしば不正な方法で誰か，あるいは何かをコントロールしたり影響を与えたりする】

《 Summary 》

Recent research supports the emerging theory that facial expressions don't reflect our feelings. Instead, they show what our intentions or social goals are. The idea that we express our emotions instinctively on our faces and that these emotions are universally shared and recognized is fixed in Western culture. But new research is challenging these points. In places like Papua New Guinea and Mozambique, the native people did not recognize emotions on faces in the same way that Westerners do. This proved that facial expressions are not universally understood. This may have enormous consequences in fields like the AI used in social robots. It may also help people to interpret social interactions. If we think of expressions as social signals instead of instinctive reflections of our real emotions, we may be able to communicate better with others. (136 words)

【《Summary》の訳】

最近の研究は，顔の表情は私たちの感情を反映してはいないとする新たな学説を支持しています。むしろ，表情は私たちの意図や対人的な目標が何であるかを示しているというのです。私たちは自分の感情を本能的に顔に表し，そうした感情は広く共有され，理解されるという考えは，西洋文化に深く根づいています。しかし，新たな研究はそのような主張に疑問を投げかけています。パプアニューギニアやモザンビークのような場所では，先住民たちは顔に表れる感情を西洋人と同じ方法で認識していませんでした。これは，顔の表情がどこでも同じように解釈されるわけではないことを証明するものでした。このことは，ソーシャル・ロボットに使われる人工知能などの分野に大きな影響を与える可能性があります。それはまた，人が対人的な交流を解釈するのに役立つかもしれません。顔の表情は私たちの真の感情を本能的に反映したものではなく，社会的な合図であると考えると，私たちは他人とのコミュニケーションをより円滑にすることができるかもしれません。

第8問　大阪大学

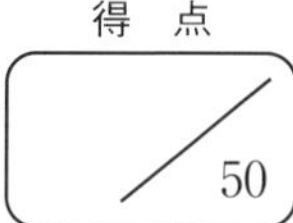

【解答】

問1．我慢しきれずに目の前の菓子を食べたということ。
　（別解）目の前の菓子を食べたいという誘惑に負けたということ。

問2．この子どもたちは，おいしいマシュマロから目を逸らして，ご馳走のことを考えずにいられる方法を見つけた。

問3．④

問4．結局のところ，私たちは情報化の時代に生きていて，そのために重要な情報に焦点を絞る能力は信じられないほど重要になるのだ。

問5．A　①　　B　④　　C　①　　D　③

問6．(a)　②　　(b)　①　　(c)　①　　(d)　④

問7．②

【配点と採点基準】（50点）

問1．6点
- 「我慢しきれずに菓子を食べた」「菓子を食べたいという誘惑に負けた」などの内容…6点
  - ＊「菓子」の代わりに「マシュマロ」「おやつ」「ご馳走」などと記述したものも可。

問2．7点
- These kids found a way to *do* … 2点
- keep themselves from thinking about the treat, … 3点
  - ＊ keep O from *doing* の誤訳は2点減
  - ＊ treat の誤訳は2点減。ただし訳語は「ご馳走」「菓子」「おやつ」など可。
- directing their gaze away from the delicious marshmallow. … 2点
  - ＊ direct *one's* gaze away from ... の誤訳は2点減

問3．6点　解答通り

問4．　9点

・We live, ... , in the age of information, … 2点

・after all … 1点

・which makes the ability to focus on the important information incredibly important. … 6点

＊関係代名詞 which がコンマの前の内容を指すことを理解していないものは2点減

＊ S make O C の文構造を理解していないものは2点減

＊ the ability to *do* の誤訳は2点減

＊ focus on A の誤訳は2点減

問5．　8点（各2点×4）解答通り

問6．　8点（各2点×4）解答通り

問7．　6点　解答通り

【設問別解説】

問1．

lost the battle「戦いに負けた」の主語になっている children who tried to postpone the treat「おやつを先延ばしにしようと頑張った子どもたち」とは，第1段落最終文から「実験者が戻ってくるまで我慢して待つことによって，さらにお菓子をもらうことに挑んだ子どもたち」であることを理解することがポイント。

問2．

・find a way to *do*「…する方法を見つける」

・keep *oneself* from *doing*「…しないようにしておく」

・treat「ご馳走，（子どもが与えてもらう）おやつ」

・direct *one's* gaze away from A「A から目を背ける，A から視線を逸らす」

問3．

These correlations「これらの相関関係」とは，直前の第5段落に引用された追跡調査の結果を指している。

① 「生徒たちが常に目標に集中しようと頑張れば頑張るほど，学校生活で学業に成功する可能性が高くなる」

② 「大学進学適性試験で高得点を達成した生徒たちは，以前に15分以内にマシュマロを食べてしまった生徒たちだった」

③ 「子どもたちは，可能な限りたくさんのマシュマロを食べることを許された場合には，他の子どもたちと友情を維持することが困難になる可能性が高く

なる」

④ **「自分の欲しいもの以外のものに注意を逸らすことのできた子どもたちは，後に学業面でより良い成績を達成した」**→第５段落最終文の内容に一致する。

問４.

・We live in the age of information「私たちは情報（化）の時代に生きている」

・after all「結局のところ，そもそも」

・which makes O C「そのことがＯをＣにする，そのためにＯがＣになる」which はコンマの前の内容を先行詞とする関係代名詞。

・the ability to *do*「…する能力」

・focus on A「Ａに集中する」，incredibly「信じられないほど」

問５.

A　participate in A「Ａに参加する」

B　follow up (with A)「（Ａについて）追跡調査をする」

C　improve odds「可能性[確率]を高める」，odds against A「Ａに勝つ可能性，Ａにならない可能性」

D　still「それでもやはり」

問６.

(a)　inherently「本質的に，もともと」（= innately「本質的に，生まれつき」）

(b)　allocation「配分，割り当て」（= assignment「割り当て」）

(c)　parse「…を分析する」（= analyze「…を分析する」），文脈から判断する。

(d)　erode「…を侵食する」（= wear away「…を磨耗させる」）

問７.

① 「ウォルター・ミシェルによる一連の心理学の実験は，人間の意志力が日常生活のさまざまな誘惑に抵抗できるぐらい十分本質的に強いということを発見した」→第２段落最終文と矛盾する。

② **「科学者たちは以前は，未来の利益のためにその場の欲求を犠牲にする際に強い決意が重要な役割を演じると信じていた」**→第２段落第１文の内容に一致する。

③ 「スポットライトが当たるところに身を置きたいという欲求は，キャリアの中で成功するために重要だ」→本文に言及なし。

④ 「ウォルター・ミシェルが発見したことは，セルフ・コントロールは注意力を適切に扱う能力とはほとんど関係がないということだった」→本文全体の趣旨と矛盾する。

【全訳】

1960年代後半に，心理学者ウォルター・ミシェルは，4歳児に簡単な実験を始めた。彼は机と椅子がある小さな部屋に子どもたちを招き入れ，マシュマロとクッキーとプレッツエル・スティックが載ったお皿からおやつを1つ取るように求めた。それから，ミシェルは4歳児たちにある提案をした。すぐに1つのおやつを食べてもよいし，彼が数分間部屋を出ている間もしも待つ気があるなら彼が戻ってきた時に2つのおやつをもらうこともできるというものだった。当然のことながら，ほとんどすべての子どもが待つことを選んだ。

当時，心理学者たちは，その2つめのマシュマロやクッキーをもらうために満足を先延ばしにする能力は，意志の力によるものだと想定していた。単純に他の人々よりも多くの意志力を持つ人々がいて，そのために，彼らは魅惑的なお菓子に抵抗できたり，退職後に備えて貯金することができたりするというわけである。しかしながら，数百人の子どもたちがマシュマロ実験に参加するのを観察した後に，ミシェルはこの標準モデルが間違っていると結論づけた。意志の力はもともと弱いものであって，誘惑をものともせずに歯を食いしばりながらおやつを先延ばしにしようとした子どもたちは，すぐに，多くの場合は30秒以内にその戦いに負けてしまうことがわかってきたのだった。

その代わりにミシェルは，2つめのおやつをちゃんと待つことができたごく一部の子どもたちを調べた時に，ある興味深いことを発見した。こうした「先延ばし上手」たちはみんな例外なく，同じ精神的戦略に頼っていたのだった。この子どもたちは，おいしいマシュマロから目を逸らして，ご馳走のことを考えずにいられる方法を見つけたのだ。目を覆い隠したり，かくれんぼをして机の下にもぐる子どももいた。『セサミ・ストリート』の歌を歌ったり，何度も靴ひもを結び直したり，昼寝のふりをしたりする子どももいた。彼らの欲求は打ち負かされたのではなく，ただ忘れられただけだったのだ。

ミシェルはこの能力を「戦略的注意配分」と呼び，それはセルフ・コントロールの根底にある能力なのだと主張する。私たちは，意志力とは強い道徳心を持つことに関係していると思い込んでいる場合があまりに多い。だが，それは間違いだ。実際には，意志力とは，注意力のスポットライトを適切な方向に向けて，作業メモリの中にリストアップされている少数の思考をどのようにしてコントロールするかを習得することに関係している。私たちがマシュマロのことを考えるとマシュマロを食べたくなる，だから目を逸らす必要がある，ということに気づくことに関係しているのだ。

興味深いのは，この認知能力がダイエットをしている人だけに役立つものではないということだ。それは，実社会において，成功の核心部分であるように思われる。たとえば，ミシェルが最初の被験者たちを13年後，彼らがもう高校の最上級生になっていた時に追跡調査した時に，あのマシュマロ・テストの成績が，非常に広範囲にわたる基準に関してきわめて予言的なものだったということがわかった。4歳の時に待つのに苦労した子どもたちのほうが，学校と家庭の双方において行動上の問題を抱えている可能性も高かった。彼らはストレスの多い状況で苦労し，しばしば集中することに苦労し，友情を維持することが困難だった。おそらく最も印象的なのは，学業成績の数字だった。マシュマロをもらうために15分待つことができた子どもたちは，30秒しか待てなかった子どもたちと比較して，大学進学適性試験の点数が平均で210点高かったのだ。

こうした相関関係は，注意を戦略的に配分できるようになることの重要性を実証している。私たちが（注意の）スポットライトを適切にコントロールする時には，否定的な考えや危険な誘惑に抵抗することができる。争いを避けて，中毒に陥らない可能性を高めることができる。私たちの決定は，頭の中を跳び回るさまざまな事実や感情によって動かされるものであり，注意の配分をすることによって，私たちは自分が考える対象にしたいと望む思考を意識的に選択しながら，この偶然性の強い過程に方向を与えることができるのだ。

さらに言えば，この精神的能力はいっそう価値を増しているのだ。結局のところ，私たちは情報化の時代に生きていて，そのために重要な情報に焦点を絞る能力は信じられないほど重要になるのだ。（ハーバート・サイモンは，「情報の豊かさは注意力の貧しさを生み出す」と，このことを見事に言い表している）脳は限界のある機械であり，世界はデータや気を散らすものに満ちたまぎらわしい場所だ。知性とは，そうしたデータがほんの少しでももっと論理的に理解できるものになるように，データを分析する能力のことだ。意志力と同じように，この能力には戦略的な注意力の配分が必要になるのだ。

最後に1つ。この数十年に，心理学と神経科学が自由意志に関する伝統的な概念を著しく侵食してきた。無意識の精神が精神の大部分だということになるのだ。だが，それでも私たちは自分が成功する助けとなるような考えに焦点を絞ることによって，注意力のスポットライトをコントロールすることはできるのだ。結局は，このことが私たちにコントロールできる唯一のことなのかもしれない。私たちは，マシュマロに目を向ける必要はないのだ。

【語句】

第 1 パラグラフ

・psychologist「心理学者」
・experiment「実験」
・invite A into B「A を B に招き入れる」
・tiny「小さな」
・contain「(中味の全体として)…を含む」
・treat「おやつ，ご馳走」
・tray「お皿，お盆」
・marshmallow「マシュマロ」
・pretzel stick「プレッツェル・スティック」
・offer「提案，申し出」
・right away「すぐに，ただちに」
・be willing to *do*「…するのをいとわない，進んで…する」
・step out「外出する，席をはずす」
・not surprisingly「驚くことではないが，当然のことながら」

第 2 パラグラフ

・assume that S V ...「…だと思い込む」
・delay「…を遅らせる」
・gratification「満足」
　= satisfaction
・depend on A「A によって決まる，A にかかっている」
・willpower「意志力」
・allow O to *do*「O が…するのを可能にする」= enable O to *do*
・resist「…に抵抗する」
・tempting「魅力的な，誘惑する」
　= attractive
・save money「貯金する」
・retirement「退職，隠居」
・participate in A「A に参加する」
　= take part in A
・conclude that S V ...「…だと結論づける」
・standard model「標準モデル」
・come to realize that S V ...「…ということがわかるようになる」
・inherently「本質的に，もともと」
・postpone「…を先延ばしにする」
・grit *one's* teeth「歯をくいしばる」
・in the face of A「A にもかかわらず」
・temptation「誘惑」= lure

第 3 パラグラフ

・without exception「例外なく」
・high delayer「先延ばしが上手な人」
・rely on A「A に頼る」
　= depend on A
・mental strategy「精神的戦略」
・find a way to *do*「…する方法を見つける」
・keep *oneself* from *doing*「…しないようにしておく」
・direct *one's* gaze away from A「A から目を背ける，A から視線を逸らす」
・delicious「(とても) おいしい」
・cover *one's* eyes「目を覆い隠す」

・hide-and-seek「かくれんぼ」
・tie *one's* shoelaces「靴ひもを結ぶ」
・pretend to *do*「…するフリをする」
・take a nap「昼寝をする」
・defeat「…を打ち負かす」

第4パラグラフ

・refer to A as B「AをBと呼ぶ」
・strategic「戦略的な，戦略上の」
・allocation「配分」
・attention「注意（力）」
・argue that S V ...「…だと主張する」
・underline「…の根底にある，…の基礎となる」
・self-control「自制，克己」
＝ self-restraint
・be about *doing*「…するということだ，…することに関係している」
・properly「適切に」
・direct「…を方向づける，…を向ける」
・spotlight「スポットライト，注目」
・look away「目を逸らす」

第5パラグラフ

・cognitive skill「認知能力」
・dieter「ダイエットをする人」
・core part「核心部分」
・follow up (with A)「(Aについて) 追跡調査をする」
・initial「最初の」
・subject「被験者」
・high school senior「高校の最上級生」
・performance「成績，(テストなどの) 出来ばえ」
・task「(課された) 作業［仕事］，課題」
・predictive「予言的な」
・a vast range of A「非常に広範囲にわたるA」
・struggle to *do*「…しようともがく，…するのに悪戦苦闘する」
・be likely to *do*「…する可能性が高い」
・behavioral problem「行動上の問題」
・stressful situation「ストレスの多い状況」
・have trouble *doing*「…するのに苦労する」
＝ have difficulty (in) *doing*
・pay attention「注意を払う」
・maintain「…を維持する」
・impressive「印象的な」
・academic number「学業成績の数字」
・score「得点，点数」
・on average「平均して」

第6パラグラフ

・correlation「相関関係」
・demonstrate「…を実証する，…を示す」
・strategically「戦略的に」

・allocate「…を配分する」
・resist「…に抵抗する」
・negative「否定的な」
⇔ positive「肯定的な」
・improve odds against A「A に勝つ可能性を高める」
・addiction「中毒」
・drive「…を駆りたてる，…の原動力となる」
・bounce「弾む，活発に動く」
・process「過程」
・consciously「意識的に」
・select「…を選ぶ」

第7パラグラフ

・furthermore「さらに,その上に」
＝ moreover, besides
・mental skill「精神的能力」
・valuable「貴重な，価値のある」
⇔ valueless「価値のない」
・the age of information「情報(化)の時代」
・focus on A「A に集中する，A に焦点を当てる」
・incredibly「信じられないほど」
・a wealth of A「豊富な A」
・create「…を生む，…を引き起こす」
・poverty「貧困，貧しさ」
・bounded「限界のある」
・confusing「困惑させる，混乱させる」
・be full of A「A でいっぱいである」
＝ be filled with A
・data「データ」
※ datum の複数形。ただし単数扱いが標準。
・distraction「気を散らすもの」
・intelligence「知性」
・parse「…を分析する」
＝ analyze
・make sense「道理にかなう，意味をなす」

第8パラグラフ

・in recent decades「この数十年に」
・psychology「心理学」
・neuroscience「神経科学」
・severely「著しく，激しく」
・erode「…を侵食する」
・classical notion「伝統的な概念」
・free will「自由意志」
・unconscious mind「無意識の精神」
・It turns out that S V ...「(結果として)…ということになる」
・help O (to) *do*「O が…するのに役立つ」
・in the end「結局は，つまるところ」

《 Vocabulary Building Exercise 》

1. It is a misconception to **assume** that the two continents are similar.
【to think or accept that something is true without having proof of it】

1. 「その２つの大陸が似ていると見なすのは間違った考え方だ」
【証拠がないにもかかわらず，何かを真実であると考えたり受け入れたりする】

2. A feed will usually provide instant **gratification** to a crying baby.
【the state of feeling pleasure when something goes well for you or when your desires are satisfied】

2. 「授乳はたいてい，泣いている赤ん坊に瞬時に満足感を与えるだろう」
【何かがうまくいったときや欲望が満たされたときに喜びを感じている状態】

3. He believed there was no **inherent** contradiction between religion and science.
【that is a permanent, basic or typical feature of somebody/something】

3. 「彼は，宗教と科学の間には固有の矛盾は存在しないと信じていた」
【誰か，あるいは何かに関して永続的，基本的，あるいは典型的な特徴となっている】

4. I couldn't resist the **temptation** to open the door.
【the desire to do or have something that you know is bad or wrong】

4. 「私はそのドアを開けたいという誘惑に逆らえなかった」
【悪いとか間違っているとわかっていることをしたい，あるいは手に入れたいという欲求】

5. We should **allocate** more money for famine relief.
【to give something officially to somebody/something for a particular purpose】

5. 「私たちはもっと飢饉救済のために資金を割り当てるべきです」
【特定の目的のために，誰か，あるいは何かに正式に何かを与える】

6. The housing market continues to **struggle**.
【to try very hard to do something when it is difficult or when there are a lot of problems】

6.「住宅市場は引き続き悪戦苦闘している」
【困難な状況にあるときや問題がたくさんあるときに，何かを一生懸命にしようとする】

7. There is a direct **correlation** between exposure to sun and skin cancer.
【a connection between two things in which one thing changes as the other does】

7.「日光にさらされることと皮膚ガンの間には，直接的な相関関係がある」
【一方が変化すれば他方も変化するという，2者間の関係】

8. He is now fighting his **addiction** to alcohol.
【the condition of being unable to stop using or doing something as a habit, especially something harmful】

8.「彼は今，アルコール依存症と闘っている」
【特に有害な何かを使ったりしたりすることが習慣となってやめられない状態】

9. Television is a **distraction** when we are reading.
【a thing that takes your attention away from what you are doing or thinking about】

9.「私たちが読書をするとき，テレビは気を散らすものとなる」
【人が今していることや考えていることから注意をそらすもの】

10. Repeated failures began to **erode** her confidence in herself.
【to gradually destroy the surface of something through the action of wind, rain, etc; to gradually destroy something or make it weaker over a period of time】

10.「繰り返された失敗が，彼女の自信を損ない始めた」
【風や雨などの作用によって，何かの表面を徐々に破壊する／一定の期間にわたって何かを徐々に破壊したり，弱くしたりする】

《 Summary 》

Psychologists used to believe that the ability to delay gratification depended on each individual's willpower. However, an experiment in which children were told they could get another marshmallow or cookie if they could wait for a few minutes made it clear that this standard model was wrong. After watching hundreds of kids participate in the experiment, a researcher realized that all children have weak willpower, but those who successfully resisted temptation used the same mental strategy: They didn't look at the marshmallow. They realized that if they were thinking about the marshmallow, they would eat it, so they thought about something else. This experiment turned out to be highly predictive. The children who waited the longest got much higher scores on tests thirteen years later. This demonstrates the importance of allocating our attention, which is a very valuable skill now that we live in an age of information. With so much information around us, we need to be able to focus on things that are important and not become distracted by everything else. (173 words)

【《Summary》の訳】

かつて心理学者は，欲望を抑えることのできる能力は，それぞれの個人の意志の力に左右されると考えていました。しかし，子どもたちにあと数分待てばマシュマロやクッキーをもう１つ手に入れられると告げた実験によって，この定説が間違っていることが明らかになりました。この実験に参加する数百人の子どもたちを観察した研究者は，どの子どもも自制心が弱いことに気づきましたが，誘惑にうまく抵抗できた子どもたちは同じような思考戦略を用いていました。すなわち，そうした子どもたちはマシュマロを見ていませんでした。その子らはマシュマロのことを考えていたら，それを食べたくなることに気づいたので，別のことを考えたのです。この実験は将来をかなりの確率で予測するものであることが判明しました。最も長く待つことのできた子どもたちは，13年後に行ったテストではるかに高い得点を取ったのです。これは注意力を配分することの重要性を示すものですが，情報化の時代に生きている今では，非常に重要な能力です。私たちの周りは非常に多くの情報であふれているので，大切なことにだけ集中し，それ以外のすべてことに惑わされないようにする必要があるからです。

第９問　慶應義塾大学

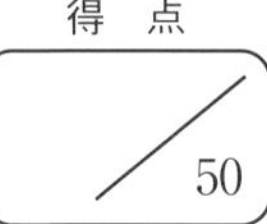

【解答】

問１．③

問２．それだけにとどまらず，人間関係や自分の感情に注意を向けると気が散って神の意志を生産的に実行することに集中できなくなるという理由で，仕事中に人付き合いをすることは避けるべきだ主張する者さえいた。

問３．自分の仕事を主に余暇を楽しむための手段だと考えているのであれば，仕事の外で友人関係を築く時間を確保するために効率性と生産性が最も重要だと思い込むのは簡単なことだ。

問４．a　①　　b　②　　c　④　　d　④

問５．①

問６．①

【配点と採点基準】（50点）

問１．６点　解答通り

問２．10点
- Some went even further, arguing that S V... … 2 点
- people should avoid socializing while working, … 2 点
- as S V ... … 1 点
- attention to relationships and emotions … 2 点
- would distract them productively doing God's will. … 3 点

問３．10点
- When we see our jobs primarily as a means to leisure, … 2 点
- it is easy to *do* … 2 点
- convince ourselves that S V ... … 2 点
- efficiency and productivity are most important … 1 点
- so that we have time for friendships outside work. … 3 点

問４．12点（各３点×４）解答通り

問５．６点　解答通り

問６．６点　解答通り

【設問別解説】

問１.

下線部は「彼ら（＝同僚）は一度限りの友人になる」という意味を表す。コロン（:）の前の「私たちは同僚を，飛行機や長距離列車で隣に乗り合わせて言葉を交わす見知らぬ人のように扱う」という内容から判断する。

① 「私たちは，自分の生活の一部しか彼らと共有しない」
② 「私たちは，ある特定の目的のために彼らと会話する」
③ 「私たちは，トラブルを避けるために彼らを無視する」
④ 「私たちは，友情が深まるのを良しとしない」

問２.

・go even further「さらにその先まで行く」「それだけにとどまらない」，コンマの後の arguing ... 以下は，分詞構文を用いて，その人たちが具体的に何をしたのかを説明している。Some went even further, arguing ... = Some went as far as to argue ...「…だと主張しさえする者もいた」
・avoid socializing「人付き合いをすることを避ける」
・while working「仕事をしながら」「仕事中に」
・as S V ...「…だからという理由で」「…なので」
・attention to relationships and emotions「人間関係や感情に注意を向けること」
・distract O *doing*「…することから O の注意を逸らす」「O の気を散らして…できなくする」(= distract O from *doing*)
・productively do God's will「生産的に神の意志を実践する」

問３.

・see A as B「A を B だと見なす[考える]」
・primarily「主に，第一に」
・a means to leisure「余暇活動のための手段」
・it is easy to *do*「…するのは簡単だ」「すぐに…してしまう」「…するのは無理もない」
・convince *oneself* that S V ...「…だと思い込む，…だと自分に言い聞かせる」
・so that S V ...「S が…するために」(「目的」を表す表現)
・outside work「仕事の外に[の]」「仕事以外で（の）」

問４.

a　get down to A「A に本気で取りかかる」
b　in touch with A「A（人）と連絡を取り合って」
c　outweigh「…よりも重要だ，…を上回る」
d　be taken for granted「当たり前のことと思われている」

問５.

① **「会社の同僚とさまざまな活動に参加することは，より良い職場の人間関係を育む可能性がある」**→最終段落の内容に一致する。

② 「職場で友人関係を作るアメリカ人労働者が少なくなっているのは残念なことだが，それは仕方のないことだ」

③ 「若い労働者たちは，年上の世代の労働者たち以上に友人を作る努力をする傾向がある」

④ 「若い労働者たちは，年上の世代の労働者たちに対してもっと敬意に満ちた態度を取るべきだ」

問６.

① **「職場の友人：アメリカ人の態度が変化した経緯と原因」**→本文全体の内容に一致する。

② 「職場での付き合いに対する肯定的な見解：宗教的な起源」

③ 「雇用政策が若い労働者に影響を及ぼした経緯」

④ 「アメリカの企業が職場の社会的相互作用をやめさせるべき理由」

【全訳】

数十年前のアメリカでは，仕事が友情の主な源だった。私たちは家族を会社主催のピクニックに連れて行き，同僚を自宅での夕食に招待した。今では，職場は以前に増してビジネスを行う場所となっている。私たちは，友人関係を築くためではなく，効率的に仕事をするためにオフィスに行く。生産性の高い会話はたっぷりするが，それに比べて有意義な人間関係は少ない。

1985年には，アメリカ人の約半数が職場に親しい友人がいると言っていた。しかし，2004年までには，それが当てはまるのはわずか30パーセントになった。卒業を控えたアメリカの高校生を対象にしたいくつかの全国調査では，友人を作ることのできる仕事を見つけることが非常に大切だと答えた割合は，1976年の54パーセントから2006年の41パーセントにまで減少した。友人と一緒に会社を始めることはあるかもしれないが，同僚とは友人にならないのだ。アメリカ人は職場の外で友情を築くことにますます重点を移しているのかもしれないが，それは世界中で標準となっているわけではない。たとえば，最近では，アメリカ人は最も親しい同僚のうち32％しか自宅に招待していないと答えたが，ポーランドの人たちは66％，インドの人たちは71％と答えている。

なぜ今のアメリカ人は，そんなにも仕事に本腰を入れようと意を決しているのだろうか。

経済学的な説明としては，長期雇用や終身雇用の大部分が消滅したことが挙げられる。アメリカ人は，1つの会社でキャリアを過ごすのではなく，数年ごとに別の会社に移るつもりでいる。1つの場所にずっととどまるつもりがないので，友情を築くことに時間や努力を費やそうとはしない。私たちは同僚を自分の人生における一時的な存在と見なし，礼儀正しく挨拶を交わすが適当な距離を保つ。本物の友情は職場以外のところにとっておくのだ。しばしば，私たちは同僚を，飛行機や長距離電車でたまたま隣に座って世間話を交わす見知らぬ人と同じように扱う。彼らは「一度限りの友人」になるのだ。

一部の評論家は，フレックスタイム制や在宅勤務の増加がその原因だとしている。リモートで働く人が増えると，友人関係を育てるのに不可欠な対面での出会いの機会が減る。しかし，最近の調査によると，少なくとも週に2.5日間オフィスに出勤している限りは，「在宅勤務が職場の人間関係の質に全般的な悪影響を及ぼすことはなかった」。それでも，テクノロジーは人間関係に影響を及ぼしている。私たちがソーシャルメディアで昔からの友人といつでも連絡を取り合っている —そして，いつでも訪ねることができる— のであれば，なぜわざわざ新しい友人を作ろうとするだろうか。私たちは24時間インターネットにつながっているために，どんどん酷くなる時間不足に直面しており，そうなると，仕事を片付けてしまわなければならないというプレッシャーのほうが，人付き合いをしたいという欲求を上回る。つまり，私たちは24時間制のスケジュールの奴隷になっているのだ。

社会学者のマックス・ウェーバーは，プロテスタントによる宗教改革がアメリカ人の仕事に独特の影響を及ぼしたと主張した。この改革の指導者たちは，どのような仕事であっても勤勉さは神から求められている義務だと信じていた。それだけにとどまらず，人間関係や自分の感情に注意を向けると気が散って神の意志を生産的に実行することに集中できなくなるという理由で，仕事中に人付き合いをすることは避けるべきだと主張する者さえいた。やがて，このような考え方がプロテスタントに影響を与え，彼らは職場を人間関係よりも生産性の方が重要な場所と見なすようになった。特にプロテスタントの男性は，仕事とは人付き合いが混ざってはならない真剣な活動だと教え込まれた。20世紀の後半になるまで，アメリカ人の職場は主にプロテスタントの男性によって仕切られていた。しかし近年では，アメリカのプロテスタントは著しく減少していて，1950年代のおよそ70パーセントから2014年の37パーセントにまで下がった。プロテスタントのCEOの数もまた減っている。今では職場での人種や性別の多様性が以前よりも一般的となり，当然のことと受け取られてさえいる。ビジネス文化が変わったのだ。では，なぜプロテスタント的な職業倫理が根強く残っているのだろうか。

性別や人種，宗教とは関係なく，世代交代によって，職場とは主にビジネスを行う場所だという考えが強まっている。余暇活動に置かれる価値は着実に増大している。最近の調査では，ミレニアル世代の31％が，２週間以上の休暇を取ることをとても重視すると言った。自分の仕事を主に余暇を楽しむための手段だと考えているのであれば，仕事の外で友人関係を築く時間を確保するために効率性と生産性が最も重要だと思い込むのは簡単なことだ。

しかし，私たちは，職場での友人関係が私たちの幸福感，そして私たちの能率性に及ぼす影響を過小評価しているのかもしれない。仕事が友情を育む機会を提供してくれる時には，仕事はより多くの満足感を与えてくれるものとなる。友人同士で仕事をすると，信頼感が強くなり，互いの成功に対する献身の度合いも強くなる。Google や Facebook などの企業は現在，従業員が一緒にゲームや運動，食事を楽しめる機会や施設を提供している —— 調査でも，一緒に遊んだり食事をしたりすることは職場の協力関係を促進する優れた方法だということが示されているのだ。

【語句】

第１パラグラフ

- decades ago「数十年前」
- major source「主要な源」
- invite A to B「A を B に招く」
- colleague「同僚」
- efficient「効率的な，能率的な」
- form a friendship「友人関係を築く」
- productive「生産的な，利益をもたらす」
- meaningful relationship「有意義な人間関係」

第２パラグラフ

- national survey「全国調査」
- graduating「卒業を控えている」
- proportion「比率，割合」
- drop from A to B「A から B に下がる」
- start a company「会社を起こす，起業する」
- co-worker「同僚」＝ colleague
- increasingly「ますます，だんだん」
- focus A on B「A を B に集中させる」
- outside of work「職場の外で」
- norm「標準，基準」＝ standard
- report *doing*「…したことを報告する」
- whereas S V ...「(〜)，だが一方…」＝ while S V ...

第３パラグラフ

- be determined to *do*「…することを決心している」
- get down to A「A に本気で取り

かかる」

第４パラグラフ

・economic explanation「経済的要因」
・long-term employment「長期雇用」
・lifetime employment「終身雇用」
・disappear「消える」
・instead of *doing*「…するのではなく」
・career「経歴，キャリア」
・expect to *do*「…するつもりである，…すると思っている」
・move on「（よい仕事に）移る」
・every few years「数年ごとに」
・forever「永久に」
・view A as B「AをBだと見なす」
　＝ regard A as B
・temporary「一時的な」
・presence「存在」
・greet「…にあいさつをする」
・keep A at arm's-length distance「Aと適当な距離を保つ」
　※ arm's-length は「親密でない」の意味。
・reserve「…を取っておく」
・treat「…を扱う」
・the way S V ...「…するように」
　＝ as S V ...
・stranger「見知らぬ人」
・sit next to A「Aの隣に座る」
・have a conversation with A「Aと会話する」
・on a long-distance train「長距離列車で」
・single-serving「一回限りの」

第５パラグラフ

・observer「評論家」
・blame「…のせいにする，…の責任にする」
・flexible working hours「フレックスタイム制」
・working from home「在宅勤務」
・remotely「離れて，遠くで」
・face-to-face「向かい合って（の）」
・encounter「出会い，遭遇」
・be critical to A「Aにとって極めて重要である」
・as long as S V ...「…する限り」
・per week「一週間につき」
・have an effect on A「Aに影響を及ぼす」
・negative「否定的な」
　⇔ positive「肯定的な」
・quality「質，性質」
・workplace「職場，仕事場」
・affect「…に影響する」
・be constantly in touch with A「Aと絶えず連絡を取り合う」
・on social media「ソーシャルメディアで」
・bother *doing*「わざわざ…する」
　＝ bother to *do*
・connect A to B「AをBにつなぐ，AをBに接続する」
・round the clock「24時間ぶっ通

しで」
- face「…に直面する」
- shortage「不足」
- the pressure to *do*「…せよという圧力［重圧］」
- get work done「仕事を終えてしまう」
- outweigh「…よりも重要だ，…を上回る」
- the desire to socialize「人付き合いをしたいという欲求」
- slave「奴隷」

第６パラグラフ
- sociologist「社会学者」
- argue that S V ...「…だと主張する」
- peculiar「独特の，特有の」
- demand「…を要求する」
- go even further「さらにその先まで行く，それだけにとどまらない」
- avoid *doing*「…することを避ける」
- attention to A「A に注意を向けること」
- emotion「感情」
- distract O *doing*「…することから O の注意を逸らす，O の気を紛らわせて…できなくする」
  = distract O from *doing*
- do God's will「神の意志を実践する」
- over time「やがて，時と共に」
- influence「…に影響を及ぼす」
- come to *do*「…するようになる」
- productivity「生産性」
- in particular「とりわけ，特に」
- mix A with B「A を B と混ぜる［混合する］」
- design「…を考案する」
- noticeably「著しく，目立って」
- fall from A to B「A から B に下がる」
  = drop from A to B
- the number of A「A の数」
- racial and gender diversity「人種や性別の多様性」
- common「ふつうの，ありふれた」
- take A for granted「A を当然だと見なす」
- work ethic「職業倫理」
- persist「根強く持続する」

第７パラグラフ
- regardless of A「A とは関係なく」
  = irrespective of A
- race「人種」
- religion「宗教」
- generational shift「世代交代」
- reinforce「…をより強力にする，…を強化する」
- the idea that S V ...「…という考え」
- place a value on A「A に価値を置く」
  = value A
- leisure time「余暇，自由時間」
  = free time

・steadily「着実に」
・more than A「A 以上」
⇔ less than A「A 未満，A 足らず」
・see A as B「A を B だと見なす」
= view A as B
・primarily「主に，第 1 に」
・means to A「A の手段」
※単複同形
・convince *oneself* that S V ...「…だと思い込む，…だと自分に言い聞かせる」
・efficiency「効率性」

第 8 パラグラフ
・underestimate「…を過小評価する」
⇔ overestimate「…を過大評価する」
・the impact of A on B「A が B に及ぼす影響」
= the effect of A on B
・effectiveness「能率性」
・satisfying「満足のいく，納得のいく」
・provide「…を提供する」
・opportunity to *do*「…する機会」
= chance to *do*
・trusting「信じやすい，信頼する」
・be committed to A「A に専心する，A に献身する」
・facilities「施設，設備」
※複数形が原則。
・employee「従業員」
⇔ employer「雇用者」
・share「…を分かち合う，…を共有する」
・research「研究，調査」
・suggest that S V ...「…ということを示唆［暗示］する」
・promote「…を促進する」
・cooperation「協力（すること）」

《 Vocabulary Building Exercise 》

1．Over the past decades, it has become the accepted **norm** for women to be in employment.
【a situation or a pattern of behaviour that is usual or typical】

1．「過去数十年間で，女性が仕事に就くことは広く受け入れられている規範となった」
【通常の，または典型的な状況や行動パターン】

2. The opposition to her plan made her more **determined** than ever.
【having made a definite decision to do something and not letting anyone prevent you】

2.「彼女の計画に対する反対勢力のせいで，彼女はそれまで以上に決心を固くした」
【何かを実行しようと固く決心し，誰にも妨害させようとしない】

3. I didn't **bother** trying to explain my feelings.
【to spend time and/or energy doing something】

3.「私は，自分の気持ちをわざわざ説明しようとはしなかった」
【何かをすることに時間やエネルギーを費やす】

4. The costs of such decisions are likely to far **outweigh** their benefits.
【to be greater or more important than something】

4.「そのような決断のコストは，その利点をはるかに上回る可能性が高い」
【何かよりも大規模に，あるいは重要になる】

5. The problem is by no means **peculiar** to America.
【belonging or relating to one particular place, situation, person, etc., and not to others】

5.「その問題は決してアメリカに特有なものではない」
【ほかではなくある特定の場所，状況，人などに属する，あるいは関連する】

6. If symptoms **persist**, surgery may be required.
【to continue to exist】

6.「症状が持続する場合は，手術が必要となるかもしれません」
【存在し続ける】

7. They fear that those reforms would only **reinforce** the power of the larger countries.
【to make a feeling, idea, habit or tendency stronger】

7.「彼らは，それらの改革が大国の力を強めるだけになるだろうと恐れている」
【感情や考え，習慣，傾向などを強める】

8. Don't **underestimate** what she is capable of.
【to think or guess that the amount, cost, size or importance of something is smaller or less than it really is】

8.「彼女ができることを過小評価しないでください」
【何かの量や費用，大きさ，重要性などを実際よりも小さいとか少ないと考えたり推定したりする】

9. He said the government remained **committed** to peace.
【willing to work hard and give your time and energy to something】

9.「彼は，政府は平和に熱心に取り組み続けていると述べた」

【一生懸命に働き，何かに自分の時間とエネルギーを費やすことをいとわない】

10. My time spent in the library was very **productive**.
【doing or achieving a lot】

10.「私が図書館で過ごした時間は，とても生産的なものでした」
【多くのことをする，あるいは達成している】

《 Summary 》

The workplace is no longer a major source of friendships. Decades ago, about half of Americans said they had a close friend at work, but by 2004 only 30% did. While in other countries, the majority of people said they invited work colleagues to their homes, only 32% of Americans did. This may be partly due to the fact that lifetime and long-term employment are disappearing, and so people view their co-workers as a temporary presence in their lives. Or it may because the rise of flexible working hours and working from home means that co-workers rarely see each other face-to-face. Additionally, social media platforms make it easier to keep in touch with old friends, so we don't need to make new ones. The sociologist Max Weber argued that the Protestant work ethic has made especially Protestant men avoid socializing at work, but in spite of the racial and gender diversity in the workplace today, the younger generation still does not place importance on forming friendships at work. Instead, they see work simply as a means to leisure and put emphasis on efficiency and productivity. (185 words)

【《Summary》の訳】

職場はもはや交友関係を築く主要な場所ではありません。数十年前にはアメリカ人の約半数が職場に親しい友人がいると答えていましたが，2004年までには，そう答えた人はわずか30%しかいませんでした。ほかの多くの国々では，大多数の人々が職場の同僚を自宅に招くことがあると答えましたが，アメリカ人の32%しかそうしていませんでした。これは，終身雇用や長期雇用がなくなりつつあるため，人々が同僚を自分の人生における一時的な存在と見なしていることも原因の一端なのかもしれません。あるいは，フレックス制や在宅勤務の普及によって，同僚たちが直接顔を合わせることがめったにないからなのかもしれません。それに加えて，ソーシャルメディア環境を利用すると，昔からの友人と簡単に連絡を取り合うことができるので，新たに友人を作る必要がなくなります。社会学者のマックス・ウェーバーは，プロテスタントの職業倫理のために，特にプロテスタントの男性は職場での交友を避けるようになったと主張しましたが，今日の職場での人種や性別の多様性にもかかわらず，若い世代は依然として職場で交友関係を結ぶことを重要視していません。その代わりに，彼らは仕事をただ余暇のための手段でしかないと考え，効率と生産性を重視しています。

第 10 問　早稲田大学

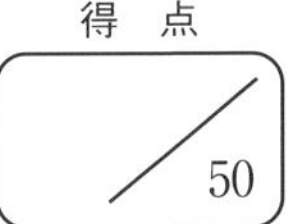

【解答】

問 1．米国における多様性の全体的な規模は国勢調査を行うたびに拡大し続けているのだが，2000年の国勢調査では，多くのアメリカ人が認識していたよりもはるかに大きな規模で人種や民族性による隔離が根強く存在することが明らかになった。

問 2．その一方で，アメリカ人は今でも機会の平等という理想を固く信じ続けていて，平等な成功のチャンスをすべての人に与えるための方法を追求し続けている。

問 3．a ⑤　b ⑥　c ④　d ②　e ①

【配点と採点基準】（50点）

問 1．12点

・Though the amount of diversity in the United States continues to grow … 2 点

・with each census, … 1 点

・the 2000 census revealed that S V... … 2 点

・segregation according to race and ethnicity has persisted … 3 点

＊ segregation according to race and ethnicity の誤訳は 2 点減

＊ has persisted の誤訳は 2 点減

・to a much larger degree … 2 点

・than many Americans had realized. … 2 点

問 2．8 点

・On the other hand, … 1 点

・Americans continue to believe strongly in … 2 点

・the ideal of equality of opportunity … 2 点

・and to search for ways to give everyone an equal chance at success. … 3 点

＊等位接続詞 and による並置関係を理解していないものは 2 点減

＊ search for A の誤訳は２点減
＊ ways to *do* の誤訳は２点減
＊ give O_1 O_2を理解していないものは２点減
問３．30点（各６点×５）解答通り

【設問別解説】

問１．

・the amount of diversity「多様性の総量，多様性の全体的な規模」
・continue to *do*「…し続ける」
・with each census「国勢調査のたびに」
・reveal that S V ...「…ということを明らかにする」
・segregation according to race and ethnicity「人種や民族性による隔離」
・persist「根強く存在［存続］する，固執する」
・to a much larger degree than ...「…よりもはるかに大きな規模で」
・than many Americans had realized「多くのアメリカ人が認識していたよりも」

問２．

・on the other hand「その一方で，他方で」
・believe in A「Aを（正しいと）信じる」
・the ideal of A「Aの理想，Aという理想[理念]」
・equality of opportunity「機会の平等」
・等位接続詞 and は，to believe strongly in the ideal of equality of opportunity と to search for ways to give everyone an equal chance at success の２つの to 不定詞をつないでいる。
・search for A「Aを探し求める」
・ways to give everyone an equal chance at success「すべての人に平等な成功のチャンスを与える方法」

問３．

a　第２段落では，アメリカでは民族による隔離が根強く存在していることを説明している。⑤で，一部民族の多様性が実現されている地区が存在することを認めた後で，直後の文では，それが例外的なものだと述べている。⑤の Of course, ... と，直後の文の However, ... にも注目。「譲歩」の後に「主張」に移る典型的なパターンを用いている。

b　第３段落では，アメリカ人の大多数が白人と有色人種が隔離された地区で暮らしていることを説明している。（ b ）では同じ流れの中で，その肌の色による壁が都市部から都市周辺部へ広がっている事実に言及する。さらに直後の文では，そのような地区では有色人種が同じ人種で集まって白人から離れて暮らす傾向を指摘している。⑥の中の In fact「いや実際は，それどころか」，the same color barrier「それと同じ肌の色の壁」，直後の文の中の in those areas「それらの地域では」などの語句も手がかりとなる。

c　第4段落では，民族・人種の隔離には肯定的な側面もあることを認めようとしている。直前の文で同じ人種・民族の人間が集まって暮らすのは悪いことなのだろうかと問うた後で，さらに④では個人には好きなところで生きる自由が認められるのではないかと疑問を投げかけている。

d　第5段落では再び，民族・人種の隔離の否定的な側面を説明する。（ d ）で否定的な側面というのは民族・人種間の格差 “gulf” の問題だということを示した後で，その後に政治参加，所得，教育，治安などの面の格差の現状を具体的に述べている。

e　直前の immigrants from the Middle East tend to have a higher socioeconomic level than the average white American を受けて，（ e ）に So do Asians, ... を補う。この表現は，肯定文＋ so ＋助動詞［be 動詞 / 完了形の have］＋ S「S もまたそうである」の形。So do Asians = Asians tend to have a higher socioeconomic level than the average white American too

【全訳】

公民権運動は，アフリカ系アメリカ人だけでなく，米国内のすべての少数民族 —— アメリカ先住民，ヒスパニック，アジア系 —— に恩恵をもたらした。雇用や住居に関する人種差別は法律で禁止された。公民権法はまた女性の権利を進展させ，その法律はすべてのアメリカ人にとっての機会の平等という理想をより強固にすることになった。

しかしながら，あるパラドックスが存在する。米国における多様性の全体的な規模は国勢調査を行うたびに拡大し続けているのだが，2000年の国勢調査では，多くのアメリカ人が認識していたよりもはるかに大きな規模で人種や民族性による隔離が根強く存在することが明らかになった。一方では，アメリカのほとんどの若者は，異なる人種の人や異なる民族的背景を持つ人と友人であったり，あるいは結婚したりすることさえ問題はないと言っている。世論調査によると，アメリカ人の大多数は隔離を悪いことだと考えている。他方，さまざまな人種や民族が今でも隔離されたコミュニティで暮らす傾向がある。これは都市部に見られる傾向だが，少数民族の集団が都市周辺部へ移住していく中でもそうした傾向は続いている。もちろん，民族的な多様性が存在する地区が実際に存在し，多くのアメリカ人が確かにそこに住むことを自ら選択している。しかしながら，そうした地区は，普通のことというよりもむしろ例外だ。

社会学の教授ジョン・ローガンはこの現象を研究してきたが，2000年の国勢調査で米国がこれまでと同じくらいに隔離が行われている国家であることがわかったと報告している。ローガンの発見によると，「アメリカ人の大多数は，白人と黒人，ラテン系アメリカ人，アジア系の人々を分離し続けている地区に住んでいる。それどころか，数十年にわたって都市コミュニティを支配してきたのと同じ肌の色の壁が，今は急激に拡大しつつある都市周辺部へと広がっている。そうした地域では，有色人種は白人から離れた地区や住宅団地に集まる傾向がある」とのことである。さらには，ローガンはこの傾向が未来へ続いていくと見ている。

人々の集団が自分と同じ人種や同じ民族的背景を持つ人たちのいるコミュニティに住むことを選ぶのは悪いことなのだろうか。個人は，どこであろうと，誰であろうと好きな人の近くに住む自由を持つべきではないのだろうか。民族によるコミュニティには，母国語の新聞やその民族料理のレストランや食料品店があって，新たな移民に貴重な支援を提供してくれることが多い。アメリカのほとんどの白人，特にその都市やその近郊に住む人たちは国際色豊かな食べ物を楽しんでいて，世界各地の文化的なお祭りイベントに参加する人も多い。そうした人たちは，この多様性を自分たちの生活を豊かにしてくれるものと考えている。

しかし，この状況には1つのマイナス面がある。悪いニュースは，異なる人種や民族の集団の間に依然として格差が存在するということだ。アフリカ系アメリカ人は人口の約12%を占めているが，連邦議会には今でも議員がきわめて少なく，同じことはヒスパニックにも当てはまる。フルタイムで働く黒人やヒスパニック系の既婚男性の収入の中央値は，今もなお白人の既婚男性のそれよりもかなり低い。隔離や差別は法律に違反するのだが，居住のパターンが，特に多くの都市部では，大きく隔離の進んだ地区の学校を生み出している。白人は黒人やヒスパニックよりも都市周辺部に住む傾向が強く，そこでは地区の学校は通常は他の場所よりも良い状況にあり，より良い教育を提供している。都心部に住む多くの黒人やその他の少数民族は，貧困，失業，暴力，絶望の循環から抜け出せないでいる。黒人は暴力犯罪の被害者となる頻度が最も多く，5人に1人もの若い男性が犯罪歴を持っているかもしれない。白人の子どもよりも黒人やヒスパニックの子どもの方が，貧困の中で暮らし，一人親世帯であることが多い。

その一方で，アメリカ人は今でも機会の平等という理想を固く信じ続けていて，平等な成功のチャンスをすべての人に与えるための方法を追求し続けている。アメリカンドリームは今でも移民を魅了し，あらゆる人種や民族的背景を持つ人たちを触発し続けている。現実に，一部の移民集団が他の移民集団よりも多くの成功を収めている。当然予想されることだが，歴史の示すところでは，経済的資産，高い学歴，必要な仕事のスキルを持ってやって来る移民は，最善の結果を出せる可能性が高い。例えば，中東からの移民は，平均的なアメリカの白人よりも社会経済的レベルが高い傾向がある。集団として見れば，アジア人も同様だ。しかしながら，経済的資産や強力な学歴を持たずにやって来る者たちは，それほどの成功は収めない。同じ国からやって来た移民でも，米国では異なる経験をするかもしれない。例えば，1970年代の半ばにやって来たベトナム人は教育を受けたエリート層で，その後でやって来たベトナム人の農民や漁師よりも成功した。1960年代の初めにやって来たキューバ人は，後からやって来た多くの貧しいキューバ人よりも多くの財産と教育を持った。ここでもまた，教育を受けたエリート層は，貧しい家庭の出身者よりも大きな成功を収めているのだ。

【語句】

第１パラグラフ

・the civil rights movement「公民権運動」
・benefit「…に利益を与える」
・not only A but (also) B「A だけではなく B も」
　= B as well as A
・minority「少数派，少数民族」
・Hispanic「ヒスパニック，ラテンアメリカ系の人」
・racial discrimination「人種差別」
・employment「雇用」
・housing「住宅（供給）」
・forbid「…を禁ずる」
　= prohibit
　※活用は【forbid / forbade / forbidden / forbidding】
・advance「…を前進させる，…を進める」
・reinforce「…を強化する，…をより強力にする」
・the ideal of equality of opportunity「機会の平等という理想」

第２パラグラフ

・paradox「パラドックス，逆説」
・the amount of diversity「多様性の総量，多様性の全体的な規模」
・continue to *do*「…し続ける」
・with each census「国勢調査のたびに」
・reveal that S V ...「…ということを明らかにする」
= show that S V ...
・segregation「隔離，分離」
= separation, isolation
・according to A「A に応じて，A によれば」
・race「人種」
・ethnicity「民族性，民族的背景」
・persist「根強く存在［存続］する，固執する」
・realize「…を（はっきり）理解する」
・on the one hand「一方で」
・be friends with A「A と友人である」
・marry「…と結婚する」
= get married to A
・ethnic background「民族的背景」
・poll「世論調査」
・the (vast) majority of A「大多数の A，A の大多数」
・on the other hand「他方で」
・segregate「…を隔離する，…を分離する」
= separate, isolate
・community「地域社会，コミュニティ」
・trend「傾向」= tendency
・move into A「A（の中）に移動する」
・suburb「郊外，都市の周辺部」
・ethnically「民族的に（見て）」
・diverse「異なった，多様な」
= various
・neighborhood「地区，区域」
= district
・do exist「実際に存在する」
※ do は exist を強調する助動詞。
・a number of A「たくさんの A」
・exception「例外」
・B rather than A「A というよりはむしろ B」
= not so much A as B
・the rule「普通のこと，常態」

第3パラグラフ

・sociology「社会学」
・phenomenon「現象」
・report that S V ...「…だと報告する」
・separate A from B「A を B から分離する」
・Latino「米国在住のラテンアメリカ人」
・descent「血統，家系」
・in fact「いや実際は，それどころか」
・color barrier「肌の色による壁」
・dominate「…を支配する，…を牛耳る」
・urban「都市の」
⇔ rural「田舎の」
・decade「10年間」
・spread to A「A まで広がる」

- fast-growing「成長の早い，急成長している」
- people of color「有色人種」
- housing development「(低所得者向けの) 住宅 (団) 地」
- B apart from A「Aから離れたB」
- continue into future「未来へ続く」

第4パラグラフ

- choose to *do*「…する方を選ぶ」
- individual「個人」
- have the freedom to *do*「…する自由を持つ」
- provide「…を提供する」
- valuable support「貴重な支援」
- immigrant「移民」
- grocery store「食料品店」
- particularly「とりわけ，特に」
- those in and near A「AとA近くに住む人々」
  = the people in and near A
- participate in A「Aに参加する」
  = take part in A
- cultural festival「文化的なお祭りイベント」
- see A as B「AをBだと見なす」
  = regard A as B
- enrich「…を豊かにする」

第5パラグラフ

- negative side「マイナス面」
- this picture「この状況」
  = this situation
- gulf「大きな隔たり，格差」
  = gap
- represent「…に相当する」
- grossly「大いに，極めて，著しく」
- under-represented「十分に代表されていない」
- Congress「(米国の) 連邦議会」
- be true of A「Aに当てはまる」
  = apply to A
- medium「中間の，中位の」
- income「収入」
- married「既婚の」
- work full-time「フルタイムで働く」
  ⇔ work part-time「パートタイムで働く」
- significantly「著しく，かなり」
- be against the law「法律に違反している」
- residential pattern「居住のパターン」
- create「…を生み出す」
- be likely to *do*「…する可能性が高い」
- condition「状況，状態」
- education「教育」
- trap A in B「AをBに閉じ込める」
- cycle「循環」
- poverty「貧困」
- unemployment「失業」
  ⇔ employment「雇用」
- violence「暴力」
- despair「絶望」
- frequent「頻繁な，常習的な」

・victim「犠牲者」
・violent crime「暴力犯罪」
・as many as A「A も」
※ A が「数」的に多いことを表す。
・male「男性」⇔ female「女性」
・criminal record「犯罪歴」

第6パラグラフ

・believe in A「A を（正しいと）信じる」
・search for A「A を探し求める」
= look for A
・chance「機会」= opportunity
・attract「…を引きつける，…を魅了する」
・inspire「…を鼓舞する，…を激励する」
・in reality「現実には」
・as one would expect「予想されるように，予想されることだが」
・financial resources「経済的資産」
・educational background「学歴」
・skill「技能」
・the Middle East「中東」
・socioeconomic level「社会経済的レベル」
・so do Asians「アジア人もそうだ」
※ so ＋助動詞［be 動詞］＋ S で，前述部分や相手の発言などを受けて，「S もまたそうだ」の意味を表す。
・experience「経験」
・the Vietnamese「ベトナムの人々」
= Vietnamese people
・the educated elite「教育を受けたエリート層」
・farmer「農民」
・fisherman「漁師」
・Cuban「キューバ人」
・wealth「富，財産」

《 Vocabulary Building Exercise 》

1. He was **trapped** in an unhappy marriage.
【being kept in a bad situation that you want to get out of but cannot】

1.「彼は不幸な結婚生活から抜け出せないでいた」
【抜け出したいのに抜け出せないという，悪い状況に置かれている】

2. There is a seeming **paradox** that people often feel advertising is untruthful, yet find it a useful source of information.
【a thing, situation or person that has two opposite features and therefore seems strange】

2. 「広告は真実を伝えていないと感じていながら，それを有益な情報源だと考えている人が多いという，一見すると矛盾に思える状況がある」
【2つの相反する特徴を持つために奇妙だと思える物や状況，または人物】

3. The 2000 **census** data show a ratio of 118 males to 100 females.
【the process of officially counting something, especially a country's population, and recording various facts】

3. 「2000年度の国勢調査データは，100人の女性に対して118人の男性が存在するという比率を示している」
【(特に国の人口など) 何かを公式に数えたり，さまざまな事実を記録したりする過程】

4. In retailing, a few large organizations tend to **dominate** the market.
【to control or have a lot of influence over something/somebody】

4. 「小売業界では，少数の大型店が市場を支配する傾向がある」
【何か，あるいは誰かを支配したり，それに大きな影響を及ぼしたりする】

5. Most European languages have a common **descent**.
【a person's family background】

5. 「ヨーロッパのたいていの言語には，共通の系統がある」
【人の家柄】

6. For many Americans today, weekend work has become the **rule** rather than the exception.
【the normal state of things; what is true in most cases】

6. 「今の多くのアメリカ人にとって，週末に働くことは例外ではなく普通のことになっている」
【通常の状態／ほとんどの場合に当てはまること】

7. He was a **victim** of racial prejudice.
【a person who has been attacked, injured or killed as the result of a crime, disease, accident, unpleasant circumstance, etc.】

7.「彼は人種的偏見の犠牲者だった」
【犯罪や疾病，事故，望ましくない状況などで，攻撃を受けたり，負傷したり，死亡したりする人】

8. At that time, the sea level was **significantly** higher than it is today.
【in a way that is large or important enough to be noticed】

8.「その当時，海面は現在よりもかなり高かった」
【はっきりと目立つくらい大きな，あるいは重要な形で】

9. They intend to bring a swift end to racial **segregation**.
【the act or policy of separating people from different groups, for example people of different races, religions or sexes, and treating them in a different way】

9.「彼らは人種隔離（政策）を速やかに終わらせるつもりだ」
【(たとえば人種や宗教，性別などが異なる人々など）異なる集団に属する人々を分離し，異なる扱いをする行為または政策】

10. We encourage students to **participate** fully in the running of the college.
【to take part in or become involved in an activity】

10.「私たちは，学生が大学の運営に全面的に参加することを奨励しています」
【ある活動に参加したり関わったりする】

《 Summary 》

While it is true that the civil rights movement benefited minorities and also women, there is a [paradox]. Even though most young Americans say they have no problem being friends with or marrying someone of a different race or ethnic background, Americans still tend to live in [segregated] communities. There are benefits to living in a community with members of your own race or ethnic background, such as the support new [immigrants] receive and international food and festivals that enrich all Americans' lives. But there is also a negative side. Married black and Hispanic men's [median] incomes are still significantly lower than those of married white men. Blacks are the most frequent victims of violent crime, and black and Hispanic children are more likely to live in [poverty] than white children. Americans believe in the ideal of equal opoortunity, but in reality, people from a higher [socioeconomic] level who have a better educational background are more likely to achieve success in America. (162 words)

【《Summary》の訳】

公民権運動がマイノリティや女性にも恩恵をもたらしたことは事実ですが，そこには矛盾があります。たいていのアメリカ人の若者は，人種や民族的背景が異なる相手と友人になったり，結婚したりすることに何ら問題はないと言っていますが，アメリカ人は依然として分離されたコミュニティで暮らす傾向があります。自分と同じ人種や民族的背景を持つ人たちのコミュニティで暮らすことには，新たな移民が支援を受けられたり，すべてのアメリカ人の生活を豊かにしてくれる国際色豊かな料理やお祭りがあったりするなどの利点があります。ただし，そこには負の側面もあります。黒人やヒスパニック系の既婚男性の収入の中央値は，今でもなお既婚の白人男性のものよりもかなり低いままです。黒人は暴力犯罪の犠牲者となることが最も多く，黒人やヒスパニック系の子どもは白人の子どもよりも貧困生活を送る可能性が高いのです。アメリカ人は機会均等という理想を信じていますが，現実では，アメリカではより高い学歴を持つ社会経済的レベルの高い人たちほど成功する可能性が高いのです。

第 11 問　お茶の水女子大学

得　点

／50

【解答】

問 1．**it seems fair to say that we possess**

問 2．アカシアの葉に有毒な物質が入っていることに気づいたキリンが，近くのアカシアを通り過ぎて遠く離れたところにあるアカシアの葉を食べること。

（別解）キリンが毒のあるアカシアの葉から100ヤードほど離れたところまで移動して別のアカシアの葉を食べ始めること。

問 3．**that were unaware of what was going on**

問 4．根に問題が生じた場合には，その情報は木全体に伝えられ，それによって葉が香りの化合物を放出するきっかけとなることができる。

問 5．木が自分に害を及ぼす虫の唾液と虫の種類を照合すること。

（別解）どの虫が自分に害を与えているかを，木が虫の唾液によって特定すること。

問 6．a ⑦　b ⑥　c ⑤　d ①　e ④　f ③　g ②

問 7．①

【配点と採点基準】（50点）

問 1．5 点　解答通り

問 2．7 点

・「アカシアの葉に有毒な物質が入っていることに気づいたキリンが」「キリンがアカシアの葉に毒があることに気づくと」などの内容…3 点

・「近くのアカシアの葉は食べない」「離れたところまで移動してアカシアの葉を食べる」「100ヤードほど離れたところまで移動して別のアカシアの葉を食べる」などの内容…4 点

問3． 5点　解答通り

問4． 8点

・If the roots find themselves in trouble, … 2点

・this information is broadcast throughout the tree, … 2点

・which can trigger the leaves to release scent compounds. … 4点

＊ which の指すもの（＝先行詞）を理解していないものは2点減

＊ trigger O to *do* の誤訳は2点減

＊ release scent compounds の誤訳は2点減

問5． 7点

・「害を及ぼす虫の唾液と虫の種類を木が照合する」「害を及ぼす虫の唾液から虫の種類を木が特定する」の内容… 7点

＊「木が」「樹木が」を記述していないものは4点減

問6． 14点（各2点×7）解答通り

問7． 4点　解答通り

【設問別解説】

問1．

・it seems fair to say that S V ...「…と言っても差し支えないように思われる」, to say that S V ... を受ける形式主語の it を用いた表現。

・we possess a secret language of scent「私たちが匂いという秘密の言語を持っている」

問2．

・第3段落第3文の It took the acacias mere minutes to start pumping toxic substances into their leaves ..., 同段落第4文の The giraffes got the message and moved on to other trees in the area. と，同段落最終文の they walked right by a few trees and resumed their meal only when they had moved about 100 yards away から必要な情報をまとめる。

問3．

・that を主格の関係代名詞として用いて，直前の名詞 trees を修飾する形容詞節を作る。

・be unaware of A「A に気づいていない，A を知らない」

・what is going on「今何が起こっているか，今の状況」

問4．

・root「根」, find *oneself* in trouble「厄介な状況に陥っている（のに気づく）」

・be broadcast「伝えられる，広められる」
・throughout the tree「木全体に」
・関係代名詞 which は直前のコンマの前の内容「そのこと（＝この情報が木全体に伝えられること)」を指す。
・trigger O to *do*「O が…する引き金となる，O が…するきっかけとなる」
・release scent compounds「匂いの化合物を放出する」

問 5．
・the match「その照合」の具体的内容は，直前の 2 つの文の中の，trees can accurately identify which bad guys they are up against. と The saliva of each species is different, and trees can match the saliva to the insect. から必要な情報をまとめる。

問 6．
a　be unfamiliar to A「A（人）には馴染みがない，A（人）に知られていない」
b　feed on A「A を餌にする，A を常食とする」
c　rid A of B「A から B を取り除く」，rid *oneself* of B「B から逃れる，B から抜け出す」
d　at work「働いている」
e　in milliseconds「ミリ秒で」，前置詞 in には「今から…で，…経つと」という「経過」を表す用法がある。
f　from the inside out「内側から外へ向かって」
g　evidence for A「A を裏づける証拠，A に有利な証拠」

問 7．
① **「どのようにして昆虫や動物が樹木に害を与えるか」**
② 「どのようにして樹木は匂いをコミュニケーションに利用しているか」
③ 「どのようにして樹木が互いにコミュニケーションを行っているか」
④ 「どのようにして樹木が昆虫や動物から身を守っているか」

【全訳】

辞書の定義によると，言語とは人間が互いと話すときに使うものだ。このように見ると，その概念が人間に限定されているわけだから，私たちは言語を使うことのできる唯一の存在であることになる。しかし，樹木もまた互いと話をすることができるかどうかを知ることは興味深いことではないだろうか。だが，どうやって？　樹木は絶対に音を出さないから，私たちは何も聞くことができない。枝どうしがこすれ合えばぎしぎし音を立てるし，葉はざわざわと音を立てるが，これらの音は風が立てるものであって，樹木はそれらをまったくコントロールしてない。つまり，樹木は完全に異なるコミュニケーションの方法を持っていることになる。樹木は香りを使うのだ。

コミュニケーションの手段としての香りとはどういうことだろうか。その概念は私たちにとってまったく馴染みがないわけでもない。そうでなければ，なぜ私たちは消臭剤や香水を使うだろうか。それに，私たちがそれらの製品を使用していないときでも，私たち自身の匂いは，意識的であれ潜在意識的であれ，他人に何かを伝えている。匂いがまったくないような人もいるが，私たちがその芳香によって強く引きつけられる人もいる。科学者たちは，汗に含まれるフェロモンが，私たちがパートナーを選ぶときの決定的な要因であると考えている。したがって，私たちは香りという秘密の言葉を持っていると言っても差し支えないように思われ，樹木もそれを行っているということを樹木は実証している。

例えば，40年前に，アフリカのサバンナで科学者たちがあることに気づいた。そこにいたキリンたちはサバンナアカシアを食べていたが，アカシアの方はこのことをとても嫌っていた。アカシアがこの動物を追い払うために有毒物質を葉に送り込み始めるのには，ほんの数分とかからなかった。キリンはそのメッセージを理解し，その地域の他の木へ移動した。ところで，キリンは近くの木に移動したのだろうか。そうではなかった。さしあたりキリンは数本の木のすぐそばを通り過ぎ，約100ヤード離れたところまで移動した後で食事を再開したのだった。

この行動の理由は驚くべきものだ。食べられていたアカシアの木は，危機が迫っていることを近隣の同じ種の木に知らせる警告ガスを放出したのだった。すぐに，前もって警告を受けたすべての木もまた葉に毒素を送り込んで準備を整えた。キリンはこのゲームには賢明に対処した。そこでキリンは，起こっていることに気づいていない木を見つけることができるサバンナの別の遠い場所に移動した。あるいは，キリンは風上に向かって移動した。というのも，香りのメッセージは微風に乗って近くの木々に運ばれるのであり，キリンが風上に向かって歩けば，キリンがそこにいることを知らないアカシアを近くで見つけることができるからだった。

私たちの近くにある森でも同様のプロセスが働いている。ブナやトウヒやオークはすべて，何かの動物に食べられ始めるとすぐに苦痛を表現する。イモムシが一枚の葉をガブリとかじると，損傷部の周辺の組織が変化する。それに加えて，人間の組織が傷ついたときに示す行動とまったく同様に，葉の組織が電気信号を発する。しかしながら，人間の信号の場合とは異なり，この信号はミリ秒単位では送信されない。そうではなく，植物の信号は毎分3分の1インチという遅い速度で伝わっていく。したがって，防御のための化合物が葉に到達して害虫の食事を台無しにするまでには，１時間ほどかかる。樹木は危険にさらされているときでさえ，実にゆっくりとしたテンポで生活を送るのだ。だが，このことは，木がその構造のさまざまな部分で起こっていることを管理できないということを意味しているわけではない。根に問題が生じた場合には，その情報は木全体に伝えられ，それによって葉が香りの化合物を放出するきっかけとなることができる。また，以前から利用している香りの化合物だけでなく，目の前の課題のために特別に配合された化合物を放出することもある。

さまざまに異なる化合物を生成するこの能力は，樹木がしばらくの間攻撃から逃れるのに役立つもう１つの特徴だ。一部の種の昆虫に関しては，樹木はどの悪党と対決しているのかを正確に識別することができる。種によって唾液が異なるため，樹木は唾液と昆虫の照合を行うことができるのだ。実際，その照合が非常に正確なので，樹木は特定の有益な捕食動物を招集するフェロモンを放出することができる。有益な捕食動物は，樹木を悩ませている昆虫をせっせと食べることによって樹木を助ける。例えば，ニレやマツは，葉を食べるイモムシの体内に卵を産む小さな寄生バチを招集する。ハチの幼虫は，発達するにつれ，内部から外へとより大きなイモムシを少しずつ食べ尽くしていく。いい死に方ではない。しかしながら，その結果，樹木は厄介な害虫から守られ，それ以上の被害を受けずに成長を続けることができる。樹木が唾液を認識できるという事実は，それに付随して，樹木が持っているに違いない別の能力を裏づける証拠にもなる。というのも，樹木が唾液を識別することができるのであれば，樹木は味覚も持っているに違いないことになるからだ。

【語句】

第１パラグラフ

- according to A「A によれば」
- definition「定義」
- being「存在」＝ existence
- concept「概念」
- limit A to B「A を B に制限する」
  ＝ restrict A to B
- species「種」
  ※単複同形
- definitely「絶対に，決して」
  ＝ absolutely
  ※否定文ではこの意味になる。
- produce「（音）を出す，…を生む」
- branch「枝」
- creak「ギシギシ音を立てる」
- rub against A「A にこすれる」
- leaf「葉」

※複数形は leaves。
・rustle「ざわざわと音を立てる」
・have no control over A「A を全くコントロールできない」
・It turns out (that) S V ...「(結果として) …ということになる，…ということがわかる」
・completely「完全に」= totally
・communicate「コミュニケーションを行う」
・scent「香り」

第2パラグラフ

・as a means of A「A の手段として」
・not (...) totally「全く…というわけではない」
※部分否定の表現。
・be unfamiliar to A「A（人）に知られていない」⇔ be familiar to A「A（人）に知られている」
・deodorant「消臭剤，防臭剤」
・perfume「香水，香料」
・product「製品」
・smell「匂い，香り」
・consciously「意識して，故意に」
・subconsciously「潜在意識的に」
・attract A to B「A を B に引きつける」
・because of A「A の理由で」
= owing to A
・aroma「芳香，香り」
※ smell よりも「芳しさ」の度合が強い。
・pheromone「フェロモン」
・decisive「決定的な」
・factor「要因，要素」
・partner「パートナー，連れ合い」
・It seems fair to say that S V ...「…と言っても差し支えないように思われる」
※ It は形式主語で，to say that S V ... を受ける。
・demonstrate that S V ...「…ということを実証する，…ということを示す」

第3パラグラフ

・decade「10年間」
・notice「…に気づく，…に注目する」
・giraffe「キリン」
・feed on A「A を餌にする，A を常食とする」
・not (...) one bit「少しも…ない」
= not (...) a bit
※否定の強調表現。
・It takes O_1 O_2 to *do*「O_1が…するのに O_2（時間）がかかる」
・pump A into B「A を B に送り込む，A を B に注入する」
・toxic「有毒な」
・substance「物質」
・rid A of B「A から B を取り除く」
※ rid *oneself* of B は「B から逃れる，B から抜け出す」の意味。
・message「メッセージ，伝えたいこと」
・move on to A「A に移動する」
・area「地域」

・close by「すぐ近くの［に］」
・for the time being「当分の間，さしあたり」= for the present
・resume「…を再び始める」
・meal「食事」

第4パラグラフ

・behavior「行動」
・astonishing「驚くべき，びっくりさせるような」= surprising
・give off A「Aを発する」
・warning gas「警告ガス」
・signal to A that S V ...「…だとAに合図する」
・neighboring「近隣の，近所の」
・crisis「危機，重大局面」
・at hand「差し迫った，近くに［の］」
・right away「すぐに，ただちに」
・prepare *oneself*「準備する，覚悟する」
・move farther away to A「より遠く離れたAまで移動する」
・be unaware of A「Aに気づいていない，Aを知らない」
　⇔ be aware of A「Aを知っている」
・go on「起こる」= happen
・upwind「風上に［の］」
　⇔ downwind「風下に［の］」
・carry A to B「AをBに運ぶ」
・nearby「近くの」
　⇔ distant「遠くの」
・breeze「微風，そよ風」
・have no idea (that) S V ...「…ということを全く知らない」

第5パラグラフ

・similar「よく似た，類似した」
・process「プロセス，過程」
・at work「働いている，活動している」
・register「…を表す，…を示す」
　= express
・pain「苦痛，痛み」
・as soon as S V ...「…するとすぐに」
・creature「動物，生き物」
・take a bite out of A「Aをひとかじりする，Aをひと口食べる」
・hearty「食欲旺盛な，元気な」
・tissue「（細胞の）組織」
・site「場所」= place
・damage「損傷」
・in addition「その上，さらに加えて」
　= besides, moreover
・send out A「Aを放つ」
・electrical signal「電気信号」
・just as S V ...「…とちょうど同じように」
・hurt「傷ついた，けがをした」
・transmit「…を伝える」
・in millisecond「ミリ秒で」
　※ in は「経過」を表す。
・instead「そうではなく，そうしないで」
・travel「伝わる」
・a third of A「Aの3分の1」
・inch「インチ」

・per minute「毎分，一分につき」
・accordingly「したがって，それゆえに」= therefore
・defensive「防御用の，防御的な」⇔ offensive「攻撃的な」
・compound「化合物」
・spoil「…を台無しにする」
・pest「害虫」
・slow lane「低速車線」
・be in danger「危険な状態にある」
・mean that S V ...「…ということを意味する」
・on top of A「A を完全に支配して」
・structure「構造」
・root「根」
・find *oneself* in trouble「厄介な状況に陥っている（のに気づく）」
・broadcast「…を伝える，…を伝わる」
・trigger O to *do*「O が…する引き金となる，O が…するきっかけとなる」
・release「…を放つ」
・not just A but (also) B「単に A だけでなく B も」
・specifically「特に，とりわけ」= particularly
・formulate「…を考案する」

第6パラグラフ

・feature「特徴」= characteristic
・help O (to) *do*「O が…するのに役立つ」
・avoid attack「攻撃から逃れる」
・for a while「しばらくの間」
・when it comes to A「A ということになると」
・insect「昆虫」
・accurately「正確に」
・identify「…を特定する，…を識別する」
・bad guy「悪いやつ，悪玉」
・up against A「A と対立して，A に直面して」
・match A to B「A を B とつり合わせる，A を B と照合して一致させる」
・match「つり合うもの，適合（すること），照合（すること）」
・precise「正確な，的確な」
・pheromone「フェロモン」
・summon「…を招集する，…を呼び出す」
・specific「特定の，はっきりした」
・beneficial「有益な，利益をもたらす」
・predator「捕食植物」
・eagerly「熱心に」
・eat up A「A を食べ尽くす」
・bother「…を悩ませる」= disturb, trouble
・call on A「A を招集する」= summon A
・parasitic「寄生性の，寄生的な」
・lay *one's* egg「卵を産む」
・bit by bit「少しずつ」
・from the inside out「内側から

外に向かって」
・die「死ぬ」
・The result is that S V ....「その結果…ということになる」
・save A from B「A を B から救う」
・bothersome「厄介な」
・keep *doing*「…し続ける」
・the fact (that) S V ...「…という事実」
・recognize「…を認識する，…を識別する」
・incidentally「付随的に，偶然に」
・evidence for A「A を裏づける証拠」
・a sense of taste「味覚」

《 Vocabulary Building Exercise 》

1. There is no general agreement on a standard **definition** of intelligence.
【a statement of the exact meaning of a word or phrase, especially in a dictionary】

1. 「知能の標準的な定義については，一般的な合意は存在しない」
【(特に辞書にあるような) 単語や語句の正確な意味を記したもの】

2. There was a **rustle** of paper as people turned the pages.
【a light dry sound like leaves or pieces of paper moving or rubbing against each other】

2. 「人々がページをめくると，紙がこすれ合う音がした」
【葉や紙片が揺れ動いたり互いに擦れ合ったりするときのような，かすかな乾いた音】

3. The air was filled with the **scent** of wild flowers.
【the pleasant smell that something has】

3. 「あたりには野の花の香りが漂っていた」
【何かが持っている心地よい匂い】

4. They didn't take into consideration the cost of cleaning up **toxic** waste.
【containing poison; poisonous】

4. 「彼らは，有毒廃棄物を処理する費用を考慮しなかった」
【毒のある／有毒な】

5. It will take at least 6 weeks before they are able to **resume** normal activities.
【to begin an activity again after an interruption】

5.「彼らが通常業務を再開することができるようになるまで，少なくとも6週間かかるだろう」
【中断の後で活動を再び始める】

6. Computers **transmit** the data in digital form.
【to send an electronic signal, radio or television broadcast, etc.】

6.「コンピューターは，データをデジタル形式で伝達する」
【電子的な信号，電波，テレビ放送などを送信する】

7. Water is a **compound** of hydrogen and oxygen.
【a substance formed from two or more elements】

7.「水は水素と酸素の化合物だ」
【2つ以上の要素［元素］から形成される物質】

8. Our boss would often **summon** us to his office.
【to order somebody to come to you】

8.「私たちの上司は，私たちをよく彼のオフィスに呼び出したものだった」
【誰かに自分のところに来るよう命じる】

9. I **definitely** remember sending the letter.
【without doubt】

9.「私は手紙を送ったことをはっきりと覚えています」
【疑いなく】

10. This is an example of the infection caused by a **parasite**.
【a small animal or plant that lives on or inside another animal or plant and gets its food from it; a person who always relies on or benefits from other people and gives nothing back】

10.「これは寄生虫によって引き起こされる感染症の例です」
【別の動物や植物の体の表面や内部に生息し，そこから栄養分を得る小さな動物や植物／いつも他人に頼ったり他人からの恩恵を得たりするが，何もお返しをしない人物】

《 Summary 》

Have you ever wondered if trees could communicate with each other? Of course, they can't talk using sound. But it turns out that they can use [scent] as a means of communication. Humans are affected by the way other people smell, both consciously and subconsciously. In fact, scientists believe that pheromones in [sweat] have a strong influence on how we choose partners. About 40 years ago, scientists discovered that acacia trees in Africa gave off a warning gas to signal to neighboring trees when their leaves were being eaten by giraffes. The [forewarned] trees then pumped toxic substances into their leaves to keep the giraffes from eating them. Leaf tissue sends out electrical signals like human tissue does when it is hurt. However, the [transmission] is very slow. It takes an hour or so before [defensive] compounds reach the leaves to protect the tree. The types of compounds trees produce can be very specific. For example, some trees can identify the saliva of insects and release pheromones that summon specific beneficial [predators] to get rid of the bothersome pests for them. (181 words)

【《Summary》の訳】

あなたは，樹木はお互いに意思を伝え合うことはできるのだろうかと思ったことはありませんか。もちろん，樹木は音を使って話すことはできません。しかし，樹木は香りをコミュニケーションの手段として使えることがわかりました。人間は，意識的であろうと潜在意識的であろうと，他人が持つにおいの影響を受けます。実際のところ，科学者は，汗に含まれるフェロモンが，私たちの配偶者の選び方に大きな影響を与えていると考えています。およそ40年前，科学者たちは，アフリカのアカシアの木がキリンに葉を食べられているときに，警告となる気体を放出して近くの木に合図を送っていることを発見しました。すると，前もって警告された木はキリンが葉を食べないように，葉に有毒物質を送り込みました。葉の組織は，傷つけられたときに人間の細胞組織がするのと同じように電気信号を出します。ただし，その伝達速度はとても遅いのです。防御用の化合物が木を守るために葉に到達するまでには，1時間ほどかかります。木が生成する化合物の種類はとても特殊なものです。たとえば，いくつかの樹木は昆虫の唾液を識別し，その厄介な害虫を駆除してくれる有益な捕食動物を招き寄せるフェロモンを放出することができるのです。

第12問　慶應義塾大学

得点
／50

【解答】

問１．cannot help but bring about
問２．③
問３．offer a fantasy which is no better
問４．③
問５．そうなれば，当然のことだが，地域住民は自分たちが望んでいた経済の盛況以外のものまで抱えることになってしまう。それは，家庭生活や子どもの安全に影響を及ぼすかもしれない社会不安だ。
問６．ケニアのサファリとビーチのツーリズムから得られる収入のうちでケニアに残るのは半分にも満たない。その主な理由は，パッケージツアーが外国企業によって企画され，その外国企業が外資系の航空会社やホテルに依存しているからだ。
問７．④
問８．②
問９．③

【配点と採点基準】（50点）

問１．４点　解答通り
問２．４点　解答通り
問３．４点　解答通り
問４．４点　解答通り
問５．10点
・Unsurprisingly, … 1 点
・then, … 1 点
・the locals get more than the economic boom they had hoped for … 4 点
＊ the locals の誤訳は 2 点減

＊ get more than A の誤訳は 2 点減
＊ the economic boom they had hoped for の誤訳は 2 点減
・social disturbances which can affect family life and the safety of children. … 4 点
＊ social disturbances の誤訳は 2 点減
＊ which ... 以下が social disturbances を修飾する形容詞節であることを理解していないものは 2 点減
＊ affect の誤訳は 2 点減
＊ family life and the safety of children の誤訳は 2 点減

問 6． 12点
・less than half of the income from safari and beach tourism in Kenya remains in Kenya, … 4 点
＊ less than half of A の誤訳は 2 点減
＊ the income from A の誤訳は 2 点減
＊ safari and beach tourism in Kenya の誤訳は 2 点減
＊ remains in Kenya の誤訳は 2 点減
・mainly because of package tours arranged by foreign companies, … 4 点
＊ mainly because of A の誤訳は 2 点減
＊ package tours の誤訳は 2 点減
＊ arranged by foreign companies の誤訳は 2 点減
・which rely on foreign-owned airlines and hotels. … 4 点
＊関係代名詞 which の先行詞を理解していないものは 2 点減
＊ rely on A の誤訳は 2 点減
＊ foreign-owned airlines and hotels の誤訳は 2 点減

問 7． 4 点　解答通り
問 8． 4 点　解答通り
問 9． 4 点　解答通り

【設問別解説】

問 1．
・cannot help but *do*「…せざるを得ない，どうしても～してしまう」
・bring about A「A をもたらす，A を引き起こす」（= cause A）

問 2．
・「観光客は観光スポットそのものに行くだけで，多くの場合，有意義な文化交

流がなされていない」というこのパラグラフ全体の主旨から判断する。
「(ここを訪れる年間1100万人の観光客は) しばしば，地元の文化を経験するのに劣らずツーリズムそのものを経験する」

① 「(彼らは) しばしば，地元の文化の経験が豊かであるのと同じくらいにツーリズムそのものの経験も豊かだ」
② 「(彼らは) しばしば，ツーリズム体験から以上に地元の文化から学ぶことのほうが多い」
③ 「(彼らは) しばしば，地元の魅力ではなく，ツーリズムそのものについて学ぶ」
④ 「(彼らは) 通常，ツーリズムを通して，地元の文化そのものを経験する」

問3.

・no better than A「A と同レベルに過ぎない，A 同然の」
・which を主格の関係代名詞として用いて，a fantasy を修飾する形容詞節 which is no better than ... を組み立てる。

問4.

(⑷) を含む第４段落では，ツーリズムが地元にもたらす恩恵が誇張されたものであることを，いくつかの根拠を列挙しながら説明している。(⑷) の直前の２つの文では，ツーリズムが地元に益する雇用を生み出すわけではないことが話題となっていて，(⑷) から始まる文では，ツーリズムによる収入が年間を通じて安定しているわけではないことが話題となっている。(⑷) には，箇条書きの目印となる③ Moreover「さらには，それに加えて」を補うのが適切。

問5.

・unsurprisingly「驚くことではないが，当然のことながら」
・then「その結果，したがって」
・the locals「地元の人々」
・get more than A「A 以外のものまで手に入れる，抱え込む」
・the economic boom they had hoped for「彼らが望んでいた経済の盛況[好景気]」，they had hoped for = which they had hoped for（名詞句 the economic boom を修飾する形容詞節）
・ダッシュの後の social disturbances which ... は，他動詞 get の目的語 more than the economic boom they had hoped for を具体的な内容に言い換えている。
・social disturbances「社会不安，社会の乱れ」
・which can ... children は，名詞句 social disturbances を修飾する形容詞節。
・can affect「…に影響を与える可能性がある」

問６.

・less than half of A「A の半分未満」
・income from A「A から得られる収入」
・remain in Kenya「ケニアにとどまる」
・mainly because of A「主として A という理由［原因］で」
・because of package tours arranged by foreign companies「外国企業によって企画されるパッケージツアーが原因で，パッケージツアーが外国企業によって企画されるから」
・which = the foreign companies
・rely on A「A に頼る，A に依存する」
・foreign-owned「外資系の，外国人［外国企業］が所有している」

問７.

（ ⑺ ）を含む文の文末の which are paid for by local taxpayers「それらは地元の納税者によって支払われている」に注目する。④pay fully for を補うと「ほとんどの観光客は自分が利用するサービスの対価を十分に支払っているわけではない」となり，自然な文脈になる。

問８.

（ ⑻ ）の直前の２つの文では，エコツーリズムはさまざまな問題を解決すると言われているが，エコツーリズムの規模が問題だと指摘している。（ ⑻ ）の直後の文では，mass eco-tourism というのは言語矛盾だと述べている。この文脈に当てはまるものを選ぶ。

① 「エコリゾートの巨大なネットワークを作れば，明らかに持続可能なものになる」
② **「エコツーリズム事業でさえ，環境へのマイナスの影響がある」**
③ 「経済的負担は，環境への影響をはるかに越えたものになるだろう」
④ 「エコリゾートによって生み出される環境への被害はほとんどないか，皆無だ」

問９.

（ ⑼ ）の直前に「こうしたことは，私たちの旅行に対する考え方に影響するだろうか」と問いかけている。（ ⑼ ）の直後の文では「私たちは旅行のやり方を変えなければならない」と訴えている。（ ⑼ ）には 反意表現の③ Who could doubt it?「誰が疑うことができようか，そうなることに疑いの余地はない」を補うのが最適。

【全訳】

2015年５月に，中国のある１つの企業が４日間の団体旅行のために6,400人の従業員をフランスに送り出した。この旅行のために，ルーブル美術館の貸し切り見学，パリ市内の140軒のホテルの予約，カンヌとモナコの4,700室以上が必要だった。しかし，私たちはこのような観光をこれ以上どれだけ受け入れることができるのだろうか。今日，私たちには，バルセロナ，フィレンツェ，ベニスといった人気都市からますます多くの不満の声を聞いているが，いずれの都市も観光客に圧倒されているのだ。さらには，観光客はサンゴ礁から熱帯雨林にいたる美しくも傷つきやすい多くの自然の景勝地をゆっくりと破壊している。ツーリズムは変化しなければならない，さもなくば，制限が課せられるようにならなければならない。

ツーリズムを制限することは，何にも増して第一に私たちの地球環境に対する責務だ。ガラパゴス諸島は最もよい実例だ。ガラパゴス諸島はダーウィンが進化論についての彼の考えを発展させる力となった隔絶した場所として有名だが，今ではそこに何万人もの観光客が訪れている。しかしながら，クルーズ船は，否応無しに多くの汚染を引き起こしてしまう。，石油やプラスチック，人間の排泄物や食品廃棄物，そして遠くの陸地から運ばれてくる外来生物などだ。もちろん，これは極端な一例だ。だが，行き先がどこであろうと，観光客は環境に負担をかける。彼らは，汚染や交通渋滞，ビーチや公園の大混雑を引き起こす。

史跡へのツーリズムは，こうした危険の影響を受けないように思われるかもしれない。観光客は，歴史遺産の鑑賞を通じて文化の違いを体験するためにやって来る。しかしながら，多くの場合は，そのようなツーリズムは有意義な文化交流を促進できていないのだ。フィレンツェを例にとってみよう。ここに魅かれて訪れる年間1100万人の観光客は，しばしば，地元の文化を経験するのに劣らずツーリズムそのものを経験する。観光客は長い行列に耐えるが，結局はそこで得られるのはそれぞれの名所での簡単な説明と非常に限られた滞在時間だけだ。ボッティチェッリの絵画を２分間だけ鑑賞するために１時間列に並ぶのは，ほとんど価値がないことのように思われる。確かに多くの観光スポットは「本物の文化体験」を約束しているのだが，結局は偽物を売ることを余儀なくされる。大人気の観光地は，しばしば偽りのように思われることがある。そうした場所は，地域の文化を正確に見せるのではなく，代わりにディズニーランドに行くのと大差ないファンタジーを提供するのだ。

ツーリズムを促進する側は，しばしばその経済的な利点を挙げる。しかしながら，それが地域にもたらすメリットは誇張されがちだ。ツーリズムが生み出す類の仕事は，多くの場合は，客室の清掃，小売り，輸送などの低賃金のサービス部門の仕事だ。そうした仕事は地元の若者にはほとんど魅力がなく，多くのホテルはその代わりにそのような仕事を行うのを安い移民労働者に任せる。それに加えて，ツーリズムの大部分は季節に左右される。自治体やリゾート地は，オフシーズンになると収入が減少するため，苦しむかもしれない。さらに悪いことに，ツーリズムは犯罪の増加をもたらす可能性がある。観光地の中には，美術館や文化的なイベントではなく，バーやストリップ劇場などで若者の要望に応じているところもある。そうなれば，当然のことだが，地域住民は自分たちが望んでいた経済の盛況以外のものまで抱えることになってしまう。それは，家庭生活や子どもの安全に影響を及ぼすかもしれない社会不安だ。

利潤の追求がツーリズムの急成長を推進してきた。ツーリズムは世界で最も規模が大きく最も急速に成長する産業になっている。1950年には，およそ2,500万人が外国旅行をした。一方で，国連世界観光機関（UNWTO）によると，2015年までに国際観光客到着数は12億人近くに達し，1.5兆ドルの輸出収入を生み出した。UNWTOの予測では，2030年までに，国際観光客到着数は18億人に達すると見込まれている。

それにもかかわらず，ツーリズムからの利益は単なる幻想であることが多い。得られたお金の多くは単に海外に戻っていくだけなのだ。例えば，研究者たちは，ケニアのサファリとビーチのツーリズムから得られる収入のうちでケニアに残るのは半分にも満たないことを発見したが，その主な理由は，パッケージツアーが外国企業によって企画され，その外国企業が外資系の航空会社やホテルに依存しているからだ。さらに悪いことに，ほとんどの観光客は自分が利用するサービスの対価を十分に支払っているわけではない。観光客の増加は，既存の水道設備，輸送システム，駐車場，そして警察や救急車などの他の公共サービスに過度の負担をかけるが，それらの対価は地元の納税者によって支払われているのだ。また，人気の観光地では，外部からの訪問者が不動産を買いあさることで住宅価格が上昇し，地元の人たちのための住居の供給を減らすことになるかもしれない。

持続可能性と小規模運営を重視するエコツーリズムは，しばしば，これらの問題への解決策として描かれる。しかし，それが役に立つことがあったとしても，規模の問題は残るだろう。エコツーリズム事業でさえ環境にマイナスの影響を及ぼす。大量のエコツーリズム事業，すなわち大衆エコツーリズムは，必然的に言語矛盾である。観光需要を減らすためには，私たちは社会的損失・環境的損失といったツーリズムの外部コストに取り組み，私たちが引き起こしている被害を回復させる資金を生み出すために世界中で何らかの形の観光税を導入する必要がある。

こうしたことのすべては，私たちが旅行をどのように見るべきかという問題に影響を及ぼすのだろうか。もちろん，そうなることに疑いの余地はない。私たちが旅行の習慣を変える必要があることは，あらゆる証拠が示している。アイザック・ディネーセンの言葉を借りれば，インターネットの時代にあって，私たちの誰もが「自分の頭の中での旅をする人」になることができる。私たちは自宅の居間から離れることなく，地球の隅々を探索することができる。自明のことだが，今日の旅行者のほとんどは科学者でも探検家でもない。現代の旅行の大部分は単なるツーリズムであり，現実から逃避するための娯楽の一形態なのだ。それは，他の余暇活動のほとんどがそうであるように，節度を保つのが一番なのだ。

【語句】

第１パラグラフ

・company「会社」
・employee「従業員」
⇔ employer「雇用者」
・vacation「（旅行などのための）休暇」
・require「…を必要とする」
・private viewing「貸し切り見学」
・booking「予約」＝ reservation
・tourism「観光産業，観光旅行」
・increasing「ますます増加する」
・complaint「不満」
・be overwhelmed with A「A に圧倒されている」
・tourist「観光客，旅行者」
・furthermore「その上，さらに」
＝ moreover, besides
・fragile「もろい，壊れやすい」
・natural site「自然の景勝地」
・coral reef「サンゴ礁」
・rainforest「熱帯雨林」
・place restrictions upon[on] A「A に制限を加える」

第２パラグラフ

・restrain「…を規制［制限］する」
・first and foremost「何よりもまず，いの一番に」
・duty「義務」
・the global environment「地球環境」
・illustration「実例，例」
・remote「遠く隔たった，遠い」
＝ distant
・location「場所，位置」
・help O (to) *do*「O が…するのに役立つ」
・develop「…を展開する，…を進展させる」
・view「考え方，見方」
・evolution「進化論，進化」
・tens of thousands of A「何万

ものA」
・cruise ship「クルーズ船，大型巡航客船」
・cannot help but *do*「…せざるを得ない」
= cannot help *doing*, cannot but *do*
・bring about A「Aをもたらす，Aを引き起こす」= cause A
・pollution「汚染，公害」
・human waste「人間の排泄物」
・food waste「食品廃棄物」
・non-native species「外来生物」
・distant「遠い」= remote
・shore「陸（地）」
・extreme example「極端な例」
・put a strain on A「Aに負担をかける」
・environment「環境」
・create「…を引き起こす」
= cause
・excess traffic「交通過多，交通渋滞」
・overcrowding「大混雑，過密状態」

第3パラグラフ
・historical site「史跡」
・immune「影響を受けない，免疫のある」
・experience「…を経験する」
・via A「Aの媒介で，Aを通じて」
・appreciation「鑑賞」
・heritage「文化的［歴史的］遺産」
・fail to *do*「（意志に反して）…しない」
・promote「…を促進する」
・meaningful cultural exchange「有意義な文化交流」
・attract「…を引きつける」
・endure「…に耐える」
・queue「列」= line
・only to *do*「だが結局…する」
・brief explanation「簡単な説明」
・limited「限られた，有限の」
・attraction「呼び物，アトラクション」
・in line「一列に並んで」
・worthwhile「価値がある，やり甲斐のある」
・magnet「人を引きつける場所」
・promise「…を約束する」
・authentic「本物の，真正の」
・be obliged to *do*「…せざるをえない，…することを余儀なくされる」
・ultimately「結局，最終的に」
・fake「偽物」
・mass「たくさんの，多数の」
・false「誤った，間違った」
・accurately「正確に」
・instead「そうではなく」
・offer a fantasy「ファンタジー［空想］を提供する」
・no better than A「Aと同じレベルに過ぎない，A同然の」

第4パラグラフ
・promoter「促進者，奨励者」
・cite「…を引き合いに出す，…を

引用する」
・economic advantage「経済的利点」
・benefit「利益」
・exaggerate「…を誇張する」
・low-paid service-sector job「低賃金のサービス部門の仕事」
・housekeeping「客室清掃」
・retail「小売り」
・transport「輸送」
・hold little attraction for A「Aにとってほとんど魅力がない」
・youth「若い人たち」= young people
・turn to A to *do*「Aに…することを頼る」
= depend[rely] on A to *do*
・immigrant labor「移民労働者」
・moreover「さらに，その上」
= furthermore, besides
・seasonal「ある季節だけに限った，季節的な」
・suffer「…を受ける，…に耐える[苦しむ]」
・off-season「閑散期，オフシーズン」
・due to A「Aが原因で」
= because of A
・the slowdown in income「収入の減少」
・worse still「さらに悪いことに」
・increase in A「Aの増加」
・crime「犯罪」
・cater for A「Aの要求を満たす，Aに応じる」
・bar「酒場，バー」
・strip club「ストリップ劇場」
・unsurprisingly「驚くことではないが，当然のことながら」
・the locals「地元の人々」
・economic boom「経済の盛況[急成長]」
・hope for A「Aを望む」
・disturbance「不安，心配，混乱」
・affect「…に影響する」

第5パラグラフ

・desire for profit「利潤の追求，利益の欲求」
・drive「…を促進する」
= promote
・rapid growth「急成長」
・fastest-growing「最も急速に成長する」
・industry「産業」
・according to A「Aによれば」
・the UN World Tourism Organization「国連世界観光機関」
・close to A「A近く，ほとんどA」
・billion「10億」
・generate「…を生み出す，…を発生させる」
・trillion「1兆」
・export earnings「輸出収入」
・forecast「…を予想する，…を予測する」

第6パラグラフ

・nevertheless「それにもかかわ

らず」
= nonetheless
・illusion「幻想，錯覚」
・researcher「研究者，調査員」
・less than half of A「Aの半分未満」
・income「収入」
・mainly because of A「主としてAという理由［原因］で」
・arrange「…を取り決める，…を企画［計画］する」
・rely on A「Aに依存する，Aに頼る」
= depend on A
・foreign-owned「外国人［外国企業］所有の，外資系の」
・airline「航空会社」
・pay for A「Aの代金を支払う」
・access「…を利用できる，…を入手できる」
・added「追加された，付け加えられた」
・excessive「過度の，度を越した」
・existing「既存の」
・water supply「水道設備」
・ambulance「救急車」
・taxpayer「納税者」
・housing price「住宅価格」
・the supply of accommodation「住居の供給」

第7パラグラフ

・eco-tourism「エコツーリズム，環境を意識した観光旅行」
・emphasis on A「Aの強調，Aの重視」
・sustainability「持続可能性」
・small-scale「小規模の」
⇔ large-scale「大規模の」
・operation「運営，運行」
・portray O as C「OをCであると描写する」
・issue「問題（点），争点」
・the problem of scale「規模の問題」
・negative「否定的な」
⇔ positive「肯定的な」
・environmental「環境上の」
・venture「ベンチャー事業」
・an abundance of A「豊富なA，Aの豊富さ」
・necessarily「必然的に」
・contradiction「矛盾，矛盾する言動」
・term「言語，用語」
・weaken「…を弱める」
⇔ strengthen「…を強める」
・tourist demand「観光需要」
・address「…に取り組む，…に立ち向かう」
・external「外的な」⇔ internal「内的な」
・employ「…を使用する，…を利用する」= use
・some version of A「何らかの形のA」
・tourism tax「観光税」
・worldwide「世界中で［に］」
・funds「資金」

第 8 パラグラフ

・doubt「…を疑う」
・evidence「証拠」
・suggest (that) S V ...「…だと示唆［暗示］する」
・in the age of the Internet「インターネットの時代において」
・as S put it「S が述べたように，S の言葉を借りれば」
・explore「…を探検する，…を探究する」
・corner「隅，隅の部分」
・the globe「地球」= the earth
・living room「居間」
・explorer「探検家」
・a form of A「A の一形態」
・entertainment「娯楽」
・leisure「余暇（活動）」
・moderation「節度」

《 Vocabulary Building Exercise 》

1．Seats go quickly, so it is essential to **book** in advance.

【to arrange to have or use something on a particular date in the future; to buy a ticket in advance】

1．「席はすぐに売り切れてしまうので，事前に予約することが必要です」
【未来の特定の日に何かを手に入れたり使ったりできるように手配をする／事前にチケットを購入する】

2．Be careful not to drop it; it's very **fragile**.

【easily broken or damaged】

2．「それを落とさないように注意してください。とても壊れやすいのです」
【壊れやすかったり傷がつきやすかったりする】

3．John managed to **restrain** his anger.
【to stop something that is growing or increasing from becoming too large】

3．「ジョンはようやくのことで怒りを抑えた」
【何かが大きくなったり増えたりし過ぎないように食い止める】

4. Many people are **immune** to this disease.
【able to resist catching or being affected by a particular disease or illness; not affected by something】

4. 「多くの人たちは，この病気に免疫がある」
【特定の疾患にかかったり症状が出たりすることに抵抗できる／何かの害の影響を受けない】

5. He tends to **exaggerate** the significance of his job.
【to make something seem larger, better, worse or more important than it really is】

5. 「彼には自分の仕事の重要性を誇張する傾向がある」
【何かを実際よりも大きく，よりよく，より悪く，あるいはより重要に見せかける】

6. During the **disturbance** which followed, three college students were hurt.
【a situation in which people behave violently in a public place】

6. 「その後に起きた騒動の中で，3人の大学生が負傷した」
【公共の場で人々が暴力的に振る舞うような状況】

7. It is difficult to **forecast** when the next earthquake will happen.
【to say what you expect to happen in the future, based on information that is available now】

7. 「次の地震がいつ起こるのか予測するのは難しい」
【現在入手可能な情報に基づいて，将来に起こると予想することを述べる】

8. The housing was to be used to provide temporary **accommodation** for the homeless.
【a place to live, work or stay】

8. 「その住宅は，ホームレスの人たちに一時的な宿泊場所を提供するために使われる予定だった」
【住んだり働いたり滞在したりするための場所】

9. His public speeches are in direct **contradiction** to his personal lifestyle.
【a lack of agreement between facts, opinions or actions】

9.「彼の演説は，彼の個人的なライフスタイルと完全に矛盾している」
【いくつかの事実，意見，あるいは行動の間に整合性が欠けていること】

10. Patients are commonly advised to drink alcohol in **moderation** and to avoid overeating.
【the quality of being reasonable and not extreme】

10.「患者は，たいていお酒を飲むのを控えめにし，食べすぎないよう忠告される」
【妥当で極端ではないという性質】

《 Summary 》

Tourism has grown so much in recent years that it is starting to destroy many fragile but beautiful natural sites and put stress on famous cities such as Florence and Venice, which are overwhelmed with tourists. When too many tourists visit remote locations like The Galapagos Islands, they put strains on the environment. Even historical sites which people supposedly visit to appreciate cultural heritage fail to offer an authentic experience because places are too crowded and people spend more time standing in queues than viewing art. Tourism does not really help local people economically because it only creates low-paid service-sector jobs. Instead, they have to deal with social disturbances and pay high taxes for public services, such as police and ambulance. Eco-tourism places emphasis on sustainability, but this is impossible when the scale becomes too large. In the end, it may be best for us and the environment to stay home and become “travelers in our minds,” using the Internet. (160 words)

【《Summary》の訳】

近年観光業が急速に成長したため，傷つきやすいけれど美しい数多くの自然景勝地が損なわれ始め，観光客であふれるフィレンツェやベニスなどの有名な都市に大きな負荷をかけています。あまりにも多くの観光客がガラパゴス諸島のような遠隔地を訪れると，その環境に負荷がかかります。人が文化遺産を鑑賞するために訪れるとされる史跡でさえ，混雑しすぎて人は芸術作品を見るよりも列に並んでいる時間の方が長くなるので，本物の体験を提供することができません。観光業は，低賃金のサービス部門の仕事しか生み出さないので，実際に地元の住民を経済的に助けることはありません。それどころか，住民は社会生活の混乱に対処したり，警察や救急車などの公共サービスに高額の税金を支払ったりしなければなりません。エコツーリズムは持続可能性を重視するものの，規模が大きくなりすぎるとそれも不可能となります。結局，私たちは自宅にとどまり，インターネットを使って「空想の世界の旅人」になることが，私たちと環境にとって最善なことなのかもしれません。

第13問　早稲田大学

得　点

/50

【解答】

問1．⑤

問2．②

問3．不平等が動機となるはずだったスーパースター選手たちに対して，不平等を増したことがマイナスの影響を及ぼしたようだったが，そのようなことは，不平等な報酬の主な影響が協調性とチームの団結を弱めることだと考えていれば想定できることだ。

問4．２つの国の所得の分布を描いた国名が示されていないグラフを見せられて，アメリカ人の92パーセントが，スウェーデンに見られる不平等が少ない状態で暮らす方がいいと言った。

問5．**rather than the way it is**

問6．A　③　　B　④　　C　②

【配点と採点基準】（50点）

問1．6点　解答通り

問2．5点　解答通り

問3．12点

・Higher inequality seemed to have a negative effect on the superstar players … 3点

＊ higher inequality の誤訳は2点減

＊ have a negative effect on A の誤訳は2点減

・it was meant to motivate, … 2点

＊直前の the superstar players を修飾する形容詞節であることを理解していないものは2点減

・which is what you would expect … 3点

・if you believed that … 1点

・the chief effect of pay inequality was to reduce cooperation and team unity … 3点

問4．8点

・Presented with unlabeled charts … 2点

・depicting income distributions of two countries, … 2点

＊直前の charts を修飾する形容詞句であることを理解していないものは2点減

・92 percent of Americans said … 1点

・they would prefer to live with the modest inequality … 2点

・that exists in Sweden. … 1点

問5． 4点　解答通り

問6． 15点（各5点×3）解答通り

【設問別解説】

問1．

ファーストクラスの客室がある機内でエコノミークラスの乗客が自分の座席に着くまでの2つのパターンを示して，「エア・レイジ」の発生率を比較している。選択肢(a)の中の however や，選択肢(b)の中の those two scenarios などは特にわかりやすいヒントになる。エコノミークラスの乗客がファーストクラスの客室を通る場合の(c)が最初に来る。次に，ファーストクラスの客室を通らない場合の(a)が来る。最後に，2つの場合を比較した(b)が続くことになる。

(a)「また一方で，一部の便では乗客は航空機の中央部から乗り込む」

(b)「それらの2つの状況を調べたところ，エコノミークラスでの『エア・レイジ』事案は，乗客がファーストクラスを通らなかった場合と比べて，ファーストクラスを通らなければならなかった場合には3倍発生しやすいということを研究者たちは発見した」

(c)「ファーストクラスのセクションがある場合には飛行機の前方にあるので，エコノミークラスの乗客は一般的にその客室を通り抜けて自分の座席にたどり着く」

問2．

（ (2) ）の直前の「報酬の格差が優れたパフォーマンスと勝利への動機を生むと思われるかもしれない」という内容の文と，（ (2) ）の直後の「平等が保たれたチームの方が成績が良かった」という内容の文を自然な流れでつなぐものを選ぶ。

①「(経済学者たちは) オーナーたちが正しいことを発見した」

②「(経済学者たちは) その逆が真実であることを発見した」

③「(経済学者たちは) このことが報酬を上げるのに役立つことを明らかにした」

④「(経済学者たちは) 彼らの発見にほとんど価値を見出さなかった」

問3.

・higher inequality「不平等が大きくなること，格差がより大きいこと」

・have a negative effect on A「Aにマイナスの影響を与える」「Aに悪影響を及ぼす」

・the superstar players it was meant to motivate「格差を大きくすることが動機づけになるはずだったスーパースターたち」，it was meant to motivate（= whom it was meant to motivate）は，it（= higher inequality）was meant to motivate the superstar players「それ（=格差を大きくすること）はスーパースターの選手たちに動機を与えることを目的としていた」の文を前提とした形容詞節。

・which is what you would expect「そのことはあなたが想定するだろうと思われることだ」，関係代名詞 which の先行詞は直前のコンマの前の内容。

・what you would expect if you believed that S V ...「あなたが…だと信じていたとしたらあなたが想定すると思われること」，仮定法過去を用いている。

・pay inequality「賃金の格差，報酬の不平等」，cooperation「協調(性)」，team unity「チームの団結」

問4.

・presented with A「Aを示されて」「Aを見せられた時に」，過去分詞を用いた分詞構文。

・unlabeled charts「国名が示されていないグラフ［図表］」

・charts depicting income distributions of two countries「2か国の収入の分布を表したグラフ［図表］」，depicting income distributions of two countries「2つの国の所得の分布を描いた」の部分は，直前の unlabeled charts を修飾する形容詞句。

・prefer to *do*「…する方を好む」

・live with A「Aを持って生きる，Aを受け入れる」

・modest inequality「少ない不平等」

・that exists in Sweden の部分は，直前の名詞句 the modest inequality を修飾する形容詞節。that は主格の関係代名詞。

問5.

・B rather than A「AというよりもむしろB」(= not so much A as B)

・the way it(= the world) is「世界のありのままに」

問6.

A「スライスしたキュウリを研究者に投げ返したサルたちは，(　　)」

①「与えられている種類のキュウリを嫌っていた」

②「公平の重要性を理解できなかった」

③ **「他のサルがもっといい扱いを受けていたことに気分を害した」**→第３段落第２～３文および第４段落の内容に一致する。

④ 「研究者に投げることのできるそれ以上の石を持たなかった」

B 「キース･ペインは，私たちが（　　）と考えるのは間違いだと示唆している」

① 「不平等の問題に関するデータが実情を正確に反映している」

② 「最低限の賃金を稼ぐことが家族の関係を強化するだろう」

③ 「人間は社会的な生き物だという言い表し方が一番いい」

④ **「貧困が社会の絆を弱める理由だ」**→第９段落以下の内容に一致する。

C 「筆者は，彼が説明する問題に対処するためには私たちが（　　）必要があると結論づけている」

① 「不幸の原因と兆候を区別する」

② **「アメリカ社会がいかに不平等になっているかに焦点を絞る」**→本文全体の主旨に一致する。

③ 「社会の最下層部の人々の収入を増やす」

④ 「アメリカにおける人種間の緊張の重要性を理解する」

【全訳】

ある実験で，数匹のサルがキュウリの輪切りと引き換えに小石を渡すように教え込まれた。そのサルたちは，この取引を喜んでいた。

次に，研究者たちは無作為に選んだ１匹のサルに，別のサルに見えるところで，前よりもはるかに良い条件の取引を持ちかけた。それは１個の石を１粒のブドウと交換することだった。ブドウはサルの大好物なので，このサルはわくわくしていた。

その後，研究者はもう１匹のサルのところに戻ったが，小石との交換に差し出したのはキュウリだけだった。今度はこの申し出が侮辱的なものとなっていた。何匹かのサルは，怒りと反感で研究者に向けてキュウリを投げ返した。

言い換えれば，サルたちは公平性をとても気にしていたのだった。そのサルたちにとって大事だったのは，自分が何を受け取るかだけではなく，他のサルが何を手に入れるかということもだった。

不平等な扱いに腹を立てるのはサルだけではない。例えば，２人の学者は，乗客が腹を立てたり暴力を振るったりすることさえある「エア・レイジ」事件を引き起こす要因が何であるかを特定するために，何百万もの飛行のデータを調べた。その大きな１つの要因は，ファーストクラスの客室の存在だった。

エコノミークラスのセクションで事案が起こる可能性は，その航空機にファーストクラスの客室もあった場合には４倍の高さだった。ファーストクラスのセクションがあると，騒動が起きる可能性は，9時間の遅延が発生したときと同じくらいの高さになった。ファーストクラスのセクションがある場合には飛行機の前方にあるので，エコノミークラスの乗客は一般的にその客室を通り抜けて自分の座席にたどり着く。また一方で，一部の便では乗客は航空機の中央部から乗り込む。それらの2つの状況を調べたところ，エコノミークラスでの「エア・レイジ」事案は，乗客がファーストクラスを通らなかった場合と比べて，ファーストクラスを通らなければならなかった場合には3倍発生しやすいということを研究者たちは発見した。

ノースカロライナ大学チャペルヒル校の心理学教授，キース・ペインは，不平等が社会をどのように不安定化させるかをテーマにした才気あふれる新刊 *The Broken Ladder* の中で，この調査に言及している。これは，不平等がアメリカで公衆衛生上の危機を生み出すと主張した重要で興味深い著作だ。

不平等に関するデータは，衝撃的な真実を明らかにした。アメリカの最上位1パーセントの人たちが，下位90パーセントの人たちよりも多くの資産を保有しているのである。政策研究所によると，ウォール街で支払われる1年間のボーナスの総額だけでも，1時間あたり7.25ドルという最低賃金でフルタイムで働いているすべてのアメリカ人の年収を上回っている。そして，明らかになりつつあるのは，社会をまとめる絆が弱まっていっているということだ。

ペインは，本当の問題は不平等ではなく貧困であるという世間の考えに異議を唱えているが，社会は底辺層の不利な状況だけでなく社会階層全体に広がる不平等によっても形が決められるという彼の主張には説得力がある。不平等に取り組むことが優先事項でなければならないのだ。というのも，私たち人間は社会的な生き物なので，ブドウを受け取る人がいたりキュウリを受け取る人がいたりするのを私たちが見ると，社会が崩壊し始めるからだ。

社会の崩壊の影響は底辺層の人々だけでなく，最上位の幸運に恵まれた人々にも及ぶ。野球を例に考えてみよう。一部のチームのオーナーたちが，他のオーナーたちよりも，上下差の幅がはるかに大きい額の報酬を選手たちに支払うとすると，報酬の格差が動機となってパフォーマンスが高まり，勝利数も増えると思われるかもしれない。

実際は，経済学者たちがデータを分析したところ，その逆が真実であることがわかった。より多くの平等が保たれたチームの方がはるかに良い成績を上げたのだったが，これはおそらく，選手たちがお互いにより親密な絆を感じたためだろう。

さらには，スター選手でさえも，報酬の差が小さいチームに所属している方が成績が良いことがわかった。「不平等が動機となるはずだったスーパースター選手たちに対して，不平等を増したことがマイナスの影響を及ぼしたようだったが，そのようなことは，不平等な報酬の主な影響が協調性とチームの団結を弱めることだと考えていれば想定できることだ」とペインは指摘した。

同様のことが国の統計にも現れている。米国を含め所得格差が最も大きい国々は，一般的に，人々の健康状態がより悪く，殺人がより多く，より幅広い社会問題を抱えている。

人々は直感的にこの事実を理解しているように思われる。というのも，人々は不平等が現状よりもずっと少ないことを望んでいるからだ。40か国の人々を対象にした調査では，リベラルな人たちは会社の社長には平均的な労働者の４倍の報酬を支払うのが妥当だと言い，保守的な人たちは５倍が妥当だと言った。実際には，アメリカで最大手の株式公開会社の平均的な社長は，平均的な労働者のおよそ350倍も稼いでいるのだ。

２つの国の所得の分布を描いた国名が示されていないグラフを見せられて，アメリカ人の92パーセントが，スウェーデンに見られる不平等が少ない状態で暮らす方がいいと言った。共和党員も民主党員も，富裕層も貧困層も，誰もが同じような差でスウェーデンを選んだ。

「不平等のレベルが無視できないほど大きくなると，誰もが奇妙な行動を取り始める」とペインは指摘する。「不平等は私たちの行動や感情に，体系的で予測可能な形で繰り返し同一の影響を及ぼすのだ」

「不平等によって，私たちは奇妙なことを信じ，ありのままの世界ではなく，むしろ自分が望む形の世界に迷信的に執着するようになる」と彼は言う。「収入だけでなくイデオロギーや人種ごとのグループに分割し，互いへの信頼感をむしばむことで，不平等は私たちを分断する。不平等はストレスを生み出し，私たちすべてを不健康にし不幸にすることになる」

この言葉を今の政治の背景の中で考えてみよう。「ストレス」「分断」「不幸」などの言葉は，よく耳にする言葉ではないだろうか。

国について話されることの多くはドナルド・トランプのような個人の話題に集中している。その理由もよくわかる。しかし，このような人たちは原因であるとともに兆候でもあって，これらの問題の根源を明らかにするためには，私たちは政治の奥まで，貧困の奥まで，人種の奥まで進んで行って，今日のアメリカの現状である不平等と対峙しなければならないのではないかと私は思う。

【語句】

第１パラグラフ
・experiment「実験」
・hand over A「A を手渡す」
・in exchange for A「A と交換に」
・cucumber「キュウリ」
・deal「取引」

第２パラグラフ
・researcher「研究者，調査員」
・randomly「無作為に，でたらめに」
・within sight of A「A の見えるところで」
・fellow「仲間，（一対のものの）片方」
・thrilled「ぞくぞくして，興奮して」

第３パラグラフ
・present「…を進呈する，…を贈呈する」
・pebble「小石」
・insulting「侮辱的な，無礼な」
・throw A back at B「A を B めがけて投げ返す」
・in anger and disgust「怒りと反感で」

第４パラグラフ
・in other words「言い換えれば」
・care about A「A を気にする，A に関心がある」
・fairness「公平（性），公正」
・matter「重要である」＝ count
・not just A but also B「単に A だけでなく B も」
＝ not only A but also B

第５パラグラフ
・offend「…に不快感を与える」
・inequality「不平等」
⇔ equality「平等」
・scholar「学者」
・examine「…を調べる，…を検査する」
・data「データ」
※ datum の複数形。
・flight「飛行，フライト」
・identify「…を特定する」
・factor「要素，要因」
・result in A「A に終わる，A の結果となる」
＝ end in A
・air rage「エア・レイジ，旅客機内の迷惑行為」
・incident「事件，出来事」
・passenger「乗客」
・first-class cabin「ファーストクラスの客室」

第６パラグラフ
・economy section「エコノミークラスのセクション［部門］」
・be four times as likely「起こる可能性が４倍ある」
・the risk of A「A の危険性［リスク］」
・disturbance「騒動，混乱」

・delay「遅延，延期」
・typically「概して，一般的に」
・walk through A「(歩いて) A を通り抜ける」
・get on「乗る」⇔ get off「降りる」
・in the middle of A「A の中央部で，A の真ん中で」
・scenario「(考えられる) 状況，一連の事柄」
・compared with A「A と比較すると」
・bypass「…を回避する，…を迂回する」

第7パラグラフ

・psychology「心理学」
・research「研究，調査」
・brilliant「すばらしい，見事な，異彩を放つ」
・destabilize「…を不安定にする」
⇔ stabilize「…を安定させる」
・fascinating「魅力的な」
= attractive
・work「著作，作品」
・argue that S V ...「…だと主張する」
・create「…を引き起こす」
= cause
・public-health crisis「公衆衛生上の危機」

第8パラグラフ

・reveal「…を明らかにする」
・annual「年１回の，毎年の」
・bonus「ボーナス，賞与」
・pool「(配当金などの) 総額」
・year-round「年間を通じて (の)」
・earnings「所得」= income
・work full time「フルタイムで働く」
⇔ work part time「パートで働く」
・minimum「最小限の」
⇔ maximum「最大限の」
・wage「賃金」
・an hour「１時間につき」
= per hour
・according to A「A によれば」
・the Institute for Policy Studies「政策研究所」
・weaken「…を弱める」
⇔ strengthen「…を強める」
・tie「絆」
・hold A together「A を団結させる」

第9パラグラフ

・challenge「…に異議を唱える」
・common「共通の，共有の」
・perception that S V ...「…という認識」
・not A but B「A ではなく B」
= B, not A
・poverty「貧困」
・be persuasive that S V ...「…ということに説得力がある」
・shape「…を形作る」
・disadvantage「不利 (な状況)」
⇔ advantage「有利 (な状況)」
・spectrum「領域，範囲」

・address「…に取り組む，…に立ち向かう」
・priority「優先事項」
・humans「人間，人類」
= human beings
・social creature「社会的な生き物」

第10パラグラフ
・breakdown「崩壊」
・affect「…に影響する」
・those at the bottom「底辺層の人々」
= the people at the bottom
・pay O_1 O_2「O_1にO_2を支払う」
・a much wider range of A「はるかに広範囲に及ぶA」
・salary「給料，給与」
・incentive「動機」
= motive, motivation

第11パラグラフ
・economist「経済学者」
・analyze「…を分析する」
・opposite「正反対なこと［もの］」
・bond「絆」= tie

第12パラグラフ
・what is more「さらには」
・It turns out that S V ...「…であることがわかる」
・flat「平らな，均一の，一律の」
・pay「報酬，給料」
・have a negative effect on A「Aにマイナスの影響を与える」
・be meant to *do*「…することになっている，…するために意図されている」
・expect「…を予想する」
・reduce「…を弱める」
= weaken
・cooperation「協調性，協力」
・team unity「チームの団結［結束］」

第13パラグラフ
・similar「類似した，よく似た」
・emerge「現れる，出現する」
・statistics「統計」
・gap「格差，隔たり」
・including A「Aを含めて」
・killing「殺害，殺すこと」

第14パラグラフ
・instinctively「本能的に」
・liberal「リベラル派の人」
・company president「会社の社長」
・average「平均的な」
・conservative「保守派の人」
・public company「株式公開会社」

第15パラグラフ
・be presented with A「Aを示される，Aを提示される」
・unlabeled「ラベルのついていない，分類されていない」
・chart「グラフ，図表」
・depict「…を描く，…を描写する」
・income distribution「所得の分

布」
・prefer to *do*「…する方を好む」
・modest「控えめな」
・Republican「共和党員」
・Democrat「民主党員」
・A and B alike「A も B も同様に」
・by similar margins「同じような差で」

第16パラグラフ

・ignore「…を無視する」
・act strange「奇妙な行動を取る」
・in the same fashion「同じやり方で」
　= in the same way
・systematic「体系的な」
・predictable「予測可能な」
・again and again「何度も何度も」

第17パラグラフ

・make O *do*「O に…させる」
・odd thing「奇妙なこと」
・superstitiously「迷信的に」
・cling to A「A に執着する，A にしがみつく」
・the world as we want it to be「私たちがそうあって欲しいと望む世界」
・B rather than A「A というよりむしろ B」
　= not so much A as B
・the way S is「ありのままの S」
・divide「…を分ける，…を引き離す」
・split A into B「A を B に分割する」
・camp「同志，仲間，グループ」
・not only A but also B「A だけでなく B も」
　= B as well as A
・ideology「イデオロギー，観念形態」
・race「人種」
・eat away at A「A を侵食する，A をむしばむ」
・trust「信頼」
　= confidence, reliance
・one another「お互い」
　= each other
・generate「…を生み出す，…を発生させる」
・stress「ストレス」

第18パラグラフ

・in the context of A「A の背景の中で，A の文脈の中で」
・politics「政治」
・term「言葉，用語」
・division「分断」
・unhappiness「不幸」
・sound familiar「聞き覚えがある」

第19パラグラフ

・the national conversation「国について話されること」
・get focused on A「A に集中する」
・individual「個人」

・B such as A「A のような B」
・understandable「理解できる」
・suspect that S V ...「…ではないかと思う」
・cause「原因」⇔ result「結果」
・uncover「…を明らかにする，…を暴く」
・root「根，根源」
・go deeper「より深くまで進む，より奥まで行く」
・confront「…と向かい合う，…と対峙する」

《 Vocabulary Building Exercise 》

1. After extended discussion, the **deal** was made.
【an agreement, especially in business, on particular conditions for buying or doing something】

1.「長引いた議論の末に，取引が成立した」
【(特にビジネスで) 何かを購入したり実行したりするための特定の条件に関する合意】

2. I find it **insulting** to be spoken to in that way.
【causing or intending to cause somebody to feel offended】

2.「そのように話しかけられるのは侮辱的だと感じます」
【人の気分を害するような，あるいはそのような意図を持った】

3. His decision can only be understood in **context**.
【the situation or set of circumstances in which something happens and that helps you to understand it】

3.「彼の決定は文脈の中でしか理解できない」
【起こったことを理解するのに役立つような状況や一連の事情】

4. Neil did not mean to **offend** anybody with his joke.
【to make somebody feel upset because of something you say or do that is rude or embarrassing】

4.「ニールは，自分の冗談で誰かの気分を害するつもりはなかった」
【無作法なことや当惑させるようなことを言ったり，したりして人を怒らせる】

5. The messages were **persuasive** enough to encourage hundreds of people to join.
【able to persuade somebody to do or believe something】

5. 「そのメッセージは，数百人の人たちを参加する気にさせるほど説得力がありました」
【人に何かをしたり信じたりするように説得することができる】

6. The policy fails to **address** the needs of the poor.
【to think about a problem or a situation and decide how you are going to deal with it】

6. 「その政策は貧しい人たちのニーズに対処することができていない」
【ある問題や状況について考え，それにどう対処するのか決断する】

7. This programme has provided a great **incentive** for students to continue their studies.
【something that encourages you to do something】

7. 「このプログラムは，学生が勉強を続けるための大きな動機を与えている」
【人にやる気を起こさせるもの】

8. These films **depict** life in Tokyo in 1960s.
【to show or describe something; to show an image of somebody / something in a picture】

8. 「これらの映画は1960年代の東京での生活を描いている」
【何かを示したり描写したりする／絵で誰か，あるいは何かのイメージを示す】

9. She beat the other runners by a **margin** of ten seconds.
【the difference between two amounts】

9. 「彼女は，ほかの走者に10秒の差をつけて勝った」
【2つの数量の間にある差】

10. I think this is just one **symptom** of the poor state of the economy.
【a change in your body or mind that shows that you are not healthy; a sign that something has been caused by something else】

10.「これは悪い経済状態を示す兆候のほんの一例でしかないと思います」
【人が健康でないことを示す体や心の変化/何かがほかの何かによって引き起こされたという兆候】

《 Summary 》

An experiment showed that monkeys care about fairness. When some monkeys saw other monkeys offered grapes instead of cucumbers in exchange for stones, they reacted with anger and disgust. Humans also care deeply about fairness. When scholars examined data from "air rage" incidents, they discovered that a feeling of inequality was as likely to increase the risk of a disturbance as a long delay. In other words, inequality destabilizes societies. Keith Payne challenges the idea that poverty is the real problem. He claims that society begins to break down when some people are paid much more than others. Even professional baseball teams perform worse if superstars are paid much higher salaries than the other players because bonds between teammates are weaker. National statistics show that countries with large wealth gaps have a greater range of social problems. People seem to understand this instinctively. Inequality affects our actions and feelings in a predictable fashion. It divides us into separate groups and makes us stressed, unhealthy and unhappy. (166 words)

【《Summary》の訳】

ある実験で，サルは公平さを気にかけていることがわかりました。一部のサルたちは，ほかのサルたちが石と引き換えにキュウリではなくブドウをもらっているのを見ると，怒りと不快感を示しました。人間も公平さに強い関心を持っています。学者が「エア・レイジ」事例のデータを調べたところ，不公平感は長時間の遅延と同じくらい騒動が起きるリスクを高める可能性があることを発見しました。つまり，不公平感は社会を不安定にするのです。キース・ペインは，貧困が本当の問題であるという考えに異議を唱えています。彼は，一部の人々がほかの人々よりもかなり多くの給与を得るようになると，社会が崩壊し始めると主張しています。プロ野球チームでさえ，スーパースターに他の選手たちよりも非常に高額の報酬が支払われると，チームメート間の絆が弱くなるために成績が下がります。国家統計でも，富の格差が大きい国ほど，より広範な社会問題を抱えていることを示しています。人はこうしたことを直感的に理解しているようです。不公平さは，私たちの行動や感情に予測可能な形で影響を与えます。それは私たちを異なる集団に分断するとともに，ストレスにさらし，不健康で不幸にするのです。

第 14 問　名古屋大学

得 点
/50

【解答】

問 1．オランダの大学の学費が予想外に安かったこと。(22字)
(別解) オランダの大学の学費がアメリカよりもはるかに安かったこと。(29字)

問 2．人文系の科目の基礎がなければ，学生たちと，その学生たちが知識人として入っていく民主社会の両方が，文明を努力に値するものにする，遺産の全貌に対する視野と批判的思考習慣を奪われてしまうことになる。

問 3．①・②（順不同）

問 4．④

問 5．大学生時代は知的・道徳的・精神的に成長できるまたとない機会だと知りながら，就職活動もしなければならないということ。

問 6．a ④　b ⑦　c ⑤　d ⑥　e ③　f ②

【配点と採点基準】(50点)

問 1．6 点
・「オランダの大学の学費が予想外に安かった」「オランダの大学の学費がアメリカよりも安かった」の内容 … 6 点

問 2．14点
・Without a base in humanities, … 2 点
・both the students and the democratic society these students must enter as informed citizens … 4 点
　＊ these students must enter as informed citizens が the democratic society を修飾する形容詞節であることを理解していないものは 2 点減
　＊ as informed citizens の誤訳は 2 点減
・are denied … 3 点
・a full view of the heritage and critical habits of mind … 3 点
　＊ a full view of the heritage の誤訳は 2 点減

＊ critical habits of mind の誤訳は 2 点減

＊ a full view of the heritage and critical habits of mind の併置関係を理解していないものは 1 点減

・that make civilization worth the effort. … 2 点

＊ that make civilization worth the effort が a full view of the heritage and critical habits of mind を修飾する形容詞節であることを理解していないものは 1 点減

＊ make civilization worth the effort の誤訳は 2 点減

問3．6点（各3点×2）解答通り

問4．6点　解答通り

問5．6点

・「大学生時代は知的・道徳的・精神的に成長できる時期であるのに，同時に職を見つけなければならない時期でもある」の内容 … 6点

問6．12点（各2点×6）解答通り

【設問別解説】

問1．

直後の段落で，オランダの大学生が支払う学費をドルに換算した総額と，アメリカの大学生が支払う学費の総額を対比していることから判断する。

問2．

・without a base in A「A の基礎がなければ」

・these students must enter as informed citizens の部分は，直前の名詞句 the democratic society を修飾する形容詞節。these students must enter as informed citizens = which these students must enter as informed citizens（目的格の関係代名詞の省略）

・be denied O_2「O_2を与えられない，O_2を奪われる」は deny O_1 O_2「O_1にO_2を与えない，O_1からO_2（機会など）を奪う」の受動態の形。

・a full view of the heritage「遺産[伝統]の全景，遺産の全体像をとらえること」

・critical habits of mind「批判的な思考習慣」

・make civilization worth the effort「文明を努力する価値のあるものにする」，make O C「O を C にする」

・that make civilization worth the effort は，名詞句 a full view of the heritage and critical habits of mind を修飾する形容詞節。that は主格の関係代名詞。

問3.

・直前の段落の内容から判断すると，these answers「これらの回答」とは「科学・工学ではなくて，人文・教養教育の価値を重視するという立場からの回答」を指していることがわかる。

・筆者は科学者だが，人文系の科目を重視しない教育に異議を唱えているという点と，大学をある種の高等職業訓練の場だと見なすことにも強く反対している点を前半のパラグラフから読みとる。

問4.

・直後の段落で，「今の学生は科学・工学と人文・教養教育のどちらかを重視するだけでは不十分だ」「今の学生は生きていく中で，今の時点では想定していない能力が求められる可能性がある」ということが述べられている。

① 「学校の格と職業対策とのバランス」

② 「大学のステータスと大学が学生に与える機会とのバランス」

③ 「情報の流れのスピードと一般教養教育の発達とのバランス」

④ 「科学・工学で得られる知識や技能と人文・教養科目で得られる知識や技能とのバランス」

問5.

「このジレンマ」とは，直前の文の中の students must find a balance between the real pressure to find a job and the understanding that they will not get this chance to grow intellectually, morally and spiritually again の内容を指している。

問6.

a in preparation for A「A に備えて」

b contrast A with B「A を B と対比させる」

c turn A into B「A を B に変える」

d put a high value on A「A に重きを置く」

e hope for A「A を望む」

f by all means「何としてでも」

【全訳】

オランダ人の友人と最近スカイプで話したとき，私たちは彼女の子どもたちのことや，その子どもたちのオランダの大学での経験について話した。どうやら，費用と支払いについてキャンパスでは抗議が起こっていたようだった。「彼らは，今はいくら払っているの？」と私は尋ねたが，返ってくる答えに備えて歯ぎしりをしていた。「そうねえ。今は年に1,800ユーロくらいかしらね」と彼女は言った。

何だって！

友人の子どもたちは世界最高の大学に通っていて，結局はその教育に8,000ドルもかからないことになるのだ。米国と比べてみるがいい。米国では高等教育の平均費用は私立学校で128,000ドルを上回り，公立大学に通う州外居住者は96,000ドル，同じ公立大学に通う州内居住者は約40,000ドルだ。

これらの数字は，私が先週「一般教養教育の価値」と題した講演で親と学生たちのグループを相手に講演を行った時に念頭にあった重要なデータポイントだった。一般教養科目とは一部の科学を含むと定義されてはいるが，この用語は人文系科目（英語，歴史，哲学など）に重点を置く教育と，工学などの技術系科目に重点を置く教育を対比させるために使われることが時々ある。

自分が科学者であるにもかかわらず，私は人文系の科目を重視しない教育は機会の逸失であると固く信じている。人文系の科目の基礎がなければ，学生たちと，その学生たちが知識人として入っていく民主社会の両方が，文明を努力に値するものにする，遺産の全貌に対する視野と批判的思考習慣を奪われてしまうことになるのだ。

もちろん，一般教養教育が価値を持つかどうかという疑問には別の見方もある。それは，その疑問の代わりに，大学がある種の高等職業訓練，すなわち，特定の仕事のための特定の資格を取るために通う場所と見なされるべきかどうかと問うことだ。

それにもまた，私は強く反対したい。

私たち大学に進学する者にとって，そこで過ごす４年間は，しばしば，世界の中での自分の位置について私たちが深く広く考えるために私たちが自分自身に与えられる唯一の機会となるのだ。（給料のよい仕事のみを重視して）大学を単なる職業訓練にしてしまうことは，学生たちと，彼らを必要とする社会にとっては，もう１つ別の機会の逸失を意味するのだ。

だから，科学・工学の価値に対する人文・教養教育の価値に関するお決まりの疑問に対する，私のお決まりの答えはこうだ。私は，学者としての観点から人文・教養教育を支持し，それらが意味することを最後まで擁護するつもりだ。

だが世界は変化したわけで，私が思うに，もはやこれらの答えでは十分ではないのだ。

均衡を破るのは大学の学費高騰だけではない。それは，情報（すなわち，データ）に基づいて動く世界の到来とともに社会全体に広がった巨大な変化でもあるのだ。そこで，それを念頭に置くと，教育における人文系科目の価値に対する私の更新版の，お決まりの答えを超える答えは，要はバランスだということだ。

学生が科学・工学系あるいは人文・教養系の「いずれか」に焦点を絞るだけでは，もはや十分ではない。今日の学生たちは，人生を生きていく中で，幅広いスキルを要する複数の職業の諸段階を通っていくことだろう。映画のシナリオを書きたいと思う若者が，映画に関連したアプリのためのウェブ・コンテンツの作り方を習得しなければならない状況に身を置くことになるかもしれない。その仕事には，プロトコルとシステム構築の技術に手を染めることが含まれる可能性も高い。同様に，プログラミングでスタートした若者が，ストーリー・テリングに重きを置くテレビゲーム会社で働く状況に身を置くことになるかもしれない。彼は仕事をうまくやるために，北欧神話が人間界と動物界の関係をどのように表しているかをさらに深く理解しなければならなくなるかもしれないのだ。

こうした変化は，高騰し続ける大学の学費と相まって，学生たちとその親たちが自らの選択を行う際に明確な考えを持った自分に正直な選択ができるための努力をしなければならないということを意味している。学生は，自分の望む成長の機会を与えてくれるのは「名門」校だけだろうなどと考えて，教育消費主義の安易な罠に落ちてはならない。世の中には優れた学校はいくらでも，たくさん存在する。学生は借金を負うことにはとても慎重になるべきであり，自分の選択によって想定される結果がどのようなものになるかについて明確にわかっていなければならない。あなたが，詩人になりたいとか，ローマ史を勉強したいとかいう望みを持っているのであれば，何が何でもそうした情熱を追い求めなさい。だが，卒業するときにどうなるかについては，現実的でありなさい。準備を整えておきなさい。教育費が問題であれば，そうした費用について，そして，どの学校が自分に適しているかについて，賢明に選択しなさい。

このことが意味するのは，職を見つけるという現実のプレッシャーと，知的，道徳的，精神的に成長するこの機会は二度と得られないという理解との間で，学生がバランスを見つけなければならないということだ。このジレンマに対処する上で，誰もが第２のプランを持つべきだと私は主張したい。現実味のある代替プランへの１つの道は，C・P・スノーが「２つの文化」と呼んだものの隔たりの橋渡しをする２つの専攻科目，または少なくとも１つの副専攻科目を持つことだ。

【語句】

第１パラグラフ
・recent「最近の」
・the Netherlands「オランダ」
・apparently「見たところでは（…らしい）」
・protest「抗議」
・cost「費用」
・payment「支払い」
・grit *one's* teeth「歯ぎしりをする，歯をくいしばる」
・in preparation for A「A に 備えて」
・a year「一年につき」

第２パラグラフ
・wow「うわあ」
※「驚き・喜び」などを表す表現。

第３パラグラフ
・kid「子ども」＝ child
・university「大学」
・in the end「結局は，最終的に」
・cost O_1 O_2「O_1 に O_2（お金）がかかる」
・less than A「A 未満」
⇔ more than A「A 以上」
・compare A to B「A を B と 比較する」
・higher education「高等教育」
・private school「私立学校」
・out-of-state resident「州外居住者」
⇔ in-state resident「州内居住者」
・attend「…に通う」

第４パラグラフ
・key data point「重要なデータ上のポイント」
・hold A in *one's* mind「A を 心に抱く」
・address「…に講演をする，…に演説する」
・talk「講演，講話」
・title O C「O に C と名称を与える」
・define A to B「A を B と定義する」
・include「（全体の一部として）…を含む」
・term「用語，言葉」
・be used to *do*「…するために用いられる」
・contrast A with B「A を B と対比させる」
・focus on A「A に集中する」
・philosophy「哲学」
・technical subject「技術系科目」
・B such as A「A のような B」
・engineering「工学」

第５パラグラフ
・in spite of A「A にもかかわらず」
＝ despite A
・fail to *do*「（意志に反して）…しない」
・place a heavy emphasis on A「A をとても重視する」
・missed opportunity「機会の逸失」

・without A「Aがなければ」
・base「基礎，基盤」
・democratic society「民主社会」
・informed citizen「知識人，知識のある市民」
・deny O_1 O_2「O_1にO_2を与えない」
⇔ allow O_1 O_2「O_1にO_2を与える」
・a full view of the heritage「遺産の全景，遺産の全体像をとらえること」
・critical habits of mind「批判的な思考習慣」
・make civilization worth the effect「文明を努力する価値あるものにする」

第6パラグラフ

・the question of whether S V ...「…であるかどうかという疑問」
・value「価値，重要性」
・question whether S V ...「…であるかどうかを問う」
・see A as B「AをBだと見なす」
= regard A as B
・higher vocational training「高等職業訓練」
・specific「特有の，特定的な」
・certification「資格」

第7パラグラフ

・push back「反対する，抵抗する」

第8パラグラフ

・sole「唯一の，ただひとつの」
・chance「機会」= opportunity
・think deeply and broadly about A「Aについて深く広く考える」
・turn A into B「AをBに変える」
= change A into B
・nothing more than A「Aにすぎない，まさにA」
・job training「職業訓練」
・emphasize「…を強調する，…を重視する」
・pay well「給料が良い，十分割に合う」
・represent「…を表す，…を表現する」

第9パラグラフ

・traditional「伝統的な，従来の」
・vs.「…に対して，…対」
= versus
・standpoint「観点，見地」
・scholar「学者」
・stand by A「Aを支持する」
・defend「…を擁護する」
・to the last breath「最後まで，死ぬまで」

第10パラグラフ

・no longer「もはや（…）ない」

第11パラグラフ

・alter「…を変える，…を改める」
・equation「均衡，平衡」

・vast change「巨大な変化」
・sweep through A「A に急速に広まる」
・with the advent of A「A の到来とともに」
・run「…を動かす」
・information「情報」
・i.e.「すなわち，言い換えれば」＝ that is (to say)
・data「データ，資料」
※ datum の複数形。
・with O in mind「O を考えて，O を念頭に置くと」
※ with O C の形。
・updated「更新した，最新の」
・response to A「A に対する返答」

第12パラグラフ

・during the course of *one's* life「人生を生きていく中で」
・expect to *do*「…するつもりである，…すると思っている」
・multiple「多数の，複数の」
・career「経歴」
・phase「段階，時期」
・a wide range of A「広範囲に及ぶ［さまざまな］A」
・screenplay「（映画の）シナリオ」
・Web content「ウェブ・コンテンツ」
・movie-related「映画に関連した」
・app「（コンピューター）アプリケーション」＝ application
・effort「取り組み，試み」
・get *one's* hands dirty「汚れ仕事［過酷な仕事］をする」
・protocol「プロトコル，通信規約」
・system architecture「システム構築」
・likewise「同様に」＝ similarly
・start up「立ち上がる」
・program「プログラムを作る」
・video game company「テレビゲーム会社」
・put a high value on A「A に重きを置く」
・storytelling「物語を書くこと［話すこと］，ストーリー・テリング」
・require O to *do*「O に…することを要求する」
・the relationship between A and B「A と B の関係」
・realm「領域，分野，界」

第13パラグラフ

・combined with A「A と相まって」
・ever-spiraling「絶えず急上昇する」
・mean that S V ...「…ということを意味する」
・strive for A「A を目指して努力する」
・clarity「明快さ，明確さ」
・choice「選択」
・fall into A「A（罠など）に落ちる」
・trap「罠，策略」
・educational consumerism「教育消費主義」

・status「高い立場，ステータス」
・opportunity「機会」= chance
・hope for A「A を望む」
・excellent「非常にすぐれた，優秀な」
・out there「世の中には，外には」
・get into debt「借金を負う」
・expected「想定された，予期された」
・outcome「結果」= result
・long to *do*「…することを切望する」
・poet「詩人」
・Roman history「ローマ史」
・by all means「何としてでも，ぜひとも」
・pursue「…を追求する」
・passion「情熱」
・realistic「現実的な，実際的な」
・graduate「卒業する」
・be prepared「備える，準備する」
・issue「問題（点）」
・wisely「賢明に」

第14パラグラフ

・find a balance between A and B「A と B の間でバランスを見つける」
・the real pressure to *do*「…せよという現実のプレッシャー［圧力］」
・the understanding that S V ...「…という理解」
・intellectually「知的に」
・morally「道徳的に」
・spiritually「精神的に」
・deal with A「A に対処する，A に対応する」
・dilemma「ジレンマ，板ばさみ」
・argue that S V ...「…だと主張する」
・path「たどる道，方針，方向」
・viable「実現可能な，実行可能な」
・alternative plan「代替プラン，代わりの計画」
・double major「２つの専攻科目」
・span「…に橋をかける」
・divide「隔たり」
・culture「文化」

《 Vocabulary Building Exercise 》

1. The use of animals in experiments has for long been the focus of political **protest**.
【the act of saying or showing publicly that you object to something】

1.「実験に動物を使うことは，長い間にわたって政治的な抗議活動の焦点となってきた」
【何かに反対であることを公に発言したり，表現したりする行為】

2. He is due to **address** a conference on human rights next week.
【to make a formal speech to a group of people】

2.「彼は来週，人権に関する会議で演説をすることになっている」
【多数の人たちに向けて正式な演説をする】

3. Many countries want to develop stronger forms of **vocational** education.
【connected with the skills, knowledge, etc. that you need to have in order to do a particular job】

3.「多くの国々が，より強固な職業教育の形式を築こうとしている」
【特定の業務を行うために必要なスキルや知識などに関連した】

4. They didn't **certify** the safety of those foods.
【to state officially, especially in writing, that something is true; to give somebody an official document proving that they are qualified to work in a particular profession】

4.「彼らは，それらの食品の安全性を認定していなかった」
【あることが本当であると公式に（特に書面で）述べる／人に特定の職業で働く資格があることを証明する公式な文書を与える】

5. The leap forward in communication was made possible by the **advent** of the mobile phone.
【the coming of an important event, person, invention, etc.】

5.「携帯電話の登場によって，コミュニケーションにおける飛躍的な発展が可能となった」
【重要な出来事，人物，発明などが世に現れること】

6. By the end of that conflict, Europe was entering a new **phase** of historical development.
【a stage in a process of change or development】

6.「その紛争が終結するまでには，ヨーロッパは歴史的な発展の新たな段階に入りつつあった」
【変化または発展の過程における一段階】

7. Questions of consciousness lie outside the **realm** of physics.
【an area of activity, interest or knowledge】

7. 「意識に関するいくつかの疑問は，物理学の分野の範囲外にある」
【活動や関心，知識などの領域】

8. Her parents **strive** hard to keep themselves very fit.
【to try very hard to achieve something】

8. 「彼女の両親は，自分たちの健康を万全に保つために懸命に努力している」
【何かを達成するために一生懸命に努力する】

9. It is not clear whether the television debates actually influenced the **outcome** of the elections.
【the result or effect of an action or event】

9. 「そのテレビ討論が実際に，その選挙結果に影響を与えたかどうかは明らかではない」
【ある行動や出来事がもたらす結果や影響】

10. If there was any delay, then the rescue plan would cease to be **viable**.
【that can be done; that will be successful】

10. 「少しでも遅れがあれば，その救出計画は実行可能ではなくなるだろう」
【行うことができる／成功するであろう】

《 Summary 》

Unlike Europe, where the cost of a university education may be less than $8,000, higher education in America is extremely expensive. This means that students have to think carefully about whether to study [liberal] arts. Some people say that students should focus on technical subjects, such as engineering, in order to get a high-paying job. But the writer doesn't think that college should be a kind of [vocational] training for a specific job. Instead, he strongly believes that it is important to have a base in the [humanities] to have a full view of our heritage and critical ways of thinking. College is often students' [sole] chance to think deeply and broadly about things. As a [scholar], he defends the value of a traditional education, but he realizes that the world has changed. He believes students need a balance between technical skills and skills like storytelling. Students and their parents must think realistically about the expected [outcomes] of their choices. They must consider the importance of finding a job, but also find ways to grow intellectually, morally and spiritually. (179 words)

【《Summary》の訳】

大学教育の費用が8,000ドル未満の場合もあるヨーロッパとは異なり，アメリカの高等教育は非常に高額です。このことは，学生が文科系の科目を専攻するかどうか慎重に考えなければならないことを意味します。報酬の高い仕事に就くためには，学生は工学などの技術系の科目に専念すべきだと言う人もいます。しかし，筆者は，大学教育は特定の仕事のための一種の職業訓練であるべきだとは考えていません。むしろ彼は，私たちが受け継いだ遺産の全体像を把握し，批判的な考え方を身につけるには，人文科学に基盤を置くことが大切だと固く信じています。大学は多くの場合，学生が物事について深く広く考える唯一の機会です。一人の学者として，彼は伝統的な教育の価値を擁護していますが，世界が変わったことにも気づいています。彼の考えでは，学生には技術的な能力と話術のような能力とのバランスが必要です。学生とその保護者は，自らの選択がもたらすと思われる結果を現実的に検討しなければなりません。就職先を見つけることの大切さを考慮する必要がありますが，知的，道徳的，そして精神的に成長する方法も見つけなければなりません。

第 15 問　慶應義塾大学

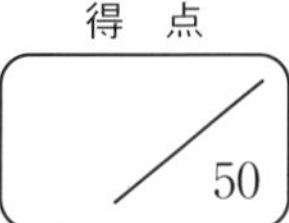

【解答】

問 1．③

問 2．博物館や図書館は非営利の文化機関なので，政府の助成金による支援がなければ，設備を維持して質の高いサービスを提供することは困難だ。

問 3．①

問 4．政府が芸術や文化活動に資金を提供すると，観光客を引き寄せることによって経済的な利益がもたらされるということ。

問 5．それに続いて，一般の人々が芸術と文化に触れる機会を拡大し，都市の再生を促し社会的排除［社会的疎外］と戦うのに役立つような芸術政策が立てられた。

問 6．a ②　b ②　c ①　d ④

【配点と採点基準】（50点）

問 1．4 点　解答通り

問 2．10点

・since museums and libraries are non-profit cultural organizations, … 2 点
  ＊ since の誤訳は 2 点減
  ＊ non-profit cultural organizations の誤訳は 2 点減

・it is difficult for them to *do* … 2 点

・maintain their facilities and offer a high quality of services … 4 点
  ＊ maintain their facilities の誤訳は 2 点減
  ＊ offer a high quality of services の誤訳は 2 点減
  ＊等位接続詞 and による maintain their facilities と offer a high quality of services の並置関係を理解していないものは 2 点減

・without support from government grants … 2 点

問 3．4 点　解答通り

問４．６点
・「政府が芸術を支援すると経済的な利益がある」の内容 … ３点
・「観光客を引き寄せるから」の内容 … ３点
問５．10点
・Subsequently, … １点
・an art policy was developed … ２点
・to widen public access to art and culture … ３点
＊ widen public access to art and culture の誤訳は２点減
・and to help drive urban rebirth and fight social exclusion. … ４点
＊等位接続詞 and による to widen public access to art and culture と to help ... の並置関係を理解していないものは２点減
＊ help *do* の誤訳は２点減
＊ drive urban rebirth の誤訳は２点減
＊ fight social exclusion の誤訳は２点減
＊等位接続詞 and による drive urban rebirth と fight social exclusion の並置関係を理解していないものは２点減
問６．16点（各４点×４）解答通り

【設問別解説】

問１．

第２段落第３文の中で，博物館・アートギャラリーの見学，合唱団への参加，音楽家の演奏の鑑賞，詩を読むこと，ストリート・パフォーマンスの見物が挙げられているが，映画を見ることについての言及はない。

問２．

・since S V ... は「理由」を表す副詞節として用いられている。
・non-profit cultural organizations「非営利の文化機関」
・it is difficult for them to maintain ...「それら（＝博物館や図書館）が…を維持することは困難だ」という意味の形式主語構文。
・maintain their facilities「設備を維持する」
・offer a high quality of services「質の高いサービスを提供する」
・without support from government grants「政府の助成金による支援なしに」

問３．

only go so far「そこまでしか行けない，限界がある」

① **「限界がある」**　② 「野放し状態だ」
③ 「実現することはない」　④ 「変わらないままだ」

問4.

「このこと」とは，直前の文 Government funding of the arts and cultural activities brings economic benefits by attracting tourists. の内容を指している。

問5.

・subsequently「その後に，それに続いて」
・an art policy was developed「芸術政策が立てられた，芸術方針が練り上げられた」
・to widen ... 以下は，名詞句 an art policy を修飾する形容詞句。to widen public access to art and culture と to help drive urban rebirth and fight social exclusion を等位接続詞 and がつないでいる。受動態を用いた文や，第１文型（S V）の文では，しばしば主語の名詞を修飾する要素が述部の後で示される。
・widen public access to art and culture「一般の人々が芸術と文化に触れる機会を拡大する」, access to A「A を利用［入手］する機会，A に触れる機会」
・help drive urban rebirth and fight social exclusion「都市の再生を推進し社会的排除［社会的疎外］と戦うのに役立つ」, help (to) *do*「…するのに役立つ，…するのを助ける」，ここでは，等位接続詞 and が drive urban rebirth と fight social exclusion をつないでいる。

問6.

a　far from *doing*「…するどころか」の表現を補うと，「国からの資金を打ち切るどころか，芸術への政府の資金提供を保護し，増やすことさえ必要だ」と自然な文意の流れができる。

b　第３段落では「国民の歴史やアイデンティティを示す遺産としての美術と文化の価値」が話題となっていることを理解する。また，直後の文の中で使われている代名詞 them は，選択肢②の中の museums を指していると考えるのが妥当。

① 「明らかに，多くの作家が私たちの遺産のコンテンツを忙しく創作している」
② **「実際のところ，博物館は遺産に関連したこのような事業のまさに中心にある」**
③ 「明らかに，遺産は国民のプライドの意識と強固に結びついている」
④ 「結局のところ，大部分の現代国家にとってナショナリズムの意識が不可欠だ」

c　第６段落では，国が資金を提供することによって一般人が芸術や文化を楽しむことが可能になることを説明している。直前の文の「政府からの助成金は，すべての国民が安い出費で芸術や文化に触れ，日常生活の不可欠の一部にすることを可能にする」という内容を受けて，それによって何が可能になるかを考える。

① **「(それは,）所得の不平等があってもすべての一般市民が共通の基盤を見つけること（を可能にする)」**

② 「(それは,）芸術への資金提供を通じて政府が所得の不平等を解決すること（を可能にする)」

③ 「(それは,）少数集団の者たちが自分たちの芸術への資金提供を通じて迷惑がられていると感じること（を可能にする)」

④ 「(それは,）裕福な国民だけが芸術を鑑賞すること（を可能にする)」

d　直前の文の「個人がどんなに貢献するとしても一般市民に芸術を提供することは政府の責務だ」という内容から，どのような support が不可欠なのかを考える。

①「財政的な」　②「相互の」　③「民間の」　④ **「国家の」**

【全訳】

多くの国々で長い歴史を持つ政府機関が芸術への資金を提供している。例えば，英国芸術評議会や米国の全米芸術基金（NEA）がある。どちらも，絵画，彫刻，音楽，舞踏，民芸などのさまざまな芸術分野だけでなく，図書館，劇場，博物館などの文化施設にも支援を行っている。加えて，これらの組織は，人々が芸術や文化イベントを楽しむことを促す一連のプログラムにも資金を提供している。この種の支援は，特に経済的に景気が後退している時期には重要である。私たちは，国からの資金を打ち切るどころか，芸術への政府の資金提供を保護し，さらには増やすことさえ必要だ。

まず第一に，芸術と文化は人々の生活を豊かにする。ロンドンの国立肖像画美術館の元館長であるサンディ・ネアーンが言ったように，「文化と芸術は，個人としての人間にとっても共同体の一員としての人間にとっても必要不可欠なものだ。博物館やアートギャラリーに出かけるのを楽しむにしても，合唱団で歌うにしても，並はずれた音楽家の演奏を聴くにしても，詩を読むにしても，ストリート・パフォーマンスの興奮に加わるにしても，それは生活を価値あるものにする一部」なのだ。さらには，人の移動や社会の変化が激しい時代にあって，人々を結びつけ，国民に共通の経験を与えるのを助け，互いの相違を調整する手段を見つけるといったことにおいて，芸術は重要な役割を果たす。

芸術と文化は，一国民の歴史とアイデンティティが深く根づいている遺産を象徴するものだ。この遺産は，国のさまざまな文化施設に保存されている。小説家のマイケル・ローゼンによれば，「図書館や博物館や公文書館の感嘆すべき点は，私たちが自分を他者と —— しばしば数百年もしくは数千年もさかのぼって —— 関係づけることができるというところだ。これは，私たちが人類の歴史と姿を発見し，私たちがそのどこに，どのように位置づけられるかを知るための手段の一つ」なのだ。実際のところ，博物館はこの遺産に関連した事業のまさに中心にある。したがって，博物館を維持し，支援し，振興することは私たちの義務なのだ。

にもかかわらず，芸術の分野の中には独立して自ら維持することができず，継続するために常に政府からの資金提供を必要とするものがある。ロンドンやニューヨークなどの大都市で商業的に成功している大劇場とは対照的に，小さな都市や町にある地方劇場はチケットの売り上げが必然的に限られるため安定性を欠くのが普通だ。また，博物館や図書館は非営利の文化機関なので，政府の助成金による支援がなければ，設備を維持して質の高いサービスを提供することは困難だ。さらに，資金の提供によって芸術家がリスクを冒しながら芸術そのもののための実験を行うことが可能になるので，そのような資金提供は芸術の革新のためにも必要だ。

可能な場合にはいつでも，民間からの寄付金が政府の助成金に取って代わることができるし，そうすべきだと主張する人がいるかもしれない。米国では芸術や文化に対する民間の支援は比較的安定して確保できているが，他の多くの国々では芸術への寄付は当然のこととは思われていない。今日では，非常に裕福な個人や企業が世界経済を支配しているので，彼らにもっと負担を求めることができるのは明らかだ。しかしながら，民間部門からの慈善的な寄付には限界があるだろう。私たちの芸術活動を民間企業の政治的または経済的な需要に「過度に」依存させることは賢明ではないだろう。不況の時には，民間からの資金提供は常に危険にさらされるだろう。

対照的に，安定した政府の資金提供は，できるだけ多くの人々が芸術と文化を楽しむことを可能にする。政府の助成金により「誰も」が芸術や文化に手頃な出費で触れることが可能になり，その結果として芸術や文化が日常生活の欠かせない一部となるのだ。それは，所得の不平等とは関係なしにすべての国民が共通の立場を見つけることを可能にしてくれる。さらには，美術館ツアーや文化プログラムは，裕福な大人たちだけでなく，貧しい人々や子どもたちにも芸術に触れる機会を与えてくれる。それらのプログラムを通じて，人々は芸術の大切さと，未来の世代のために文化遺産を保護する必要性を理解することができるのだ。

芸術や文化活動への政府の資金提供は，観光客を引き寄せることによって経済的な利益をもたらす。それが次に，郊外の再開発を促し，観光関連サービスの成長を促進するかもしれない。1980年代に，英国の政治家たちには，芸術と文化が国内の脱工業化都市の再生に役割を果たせる貴重な資源であることがわかっていた。当時，英国の政治家クリス・スミスは，芸術が「創造産業」の一つであるという考えを取り上げた。それに続いて，一般の人々が芸術と文化に触れる機会を拡大し，都市の再生を促し社会的排除［社会的疎外］と戦うのに役立つような芸術政策が立てられた。この変化は今日にまで重要な意味を持っている。今日，英国芸術評議会の概算によれば，英国は芸術への資金提供の１ドルの投資に対して４ドルを上回る利益を得ているのだ。

芸術は生活の質の向上のために不可欠なものだ。英国芸術評議会は，ウェブサイトでこの点を強調し，「偉大な芸術と文化は私たちを触発し，私たちを結びつけ，私たち自身と周囲の世界について私たちに教えてくれる」と断言している。個人の貢献がどんなに大きくても，国民に芸術を提供することは常に政府の責任である。だからこそ，国が継続的に芸術を支援することが大切であり，確実に実行されなければならないのだ。

【語句】

第１パラグラフ

・long-established「長い歴史を持つ」

・government organization「政府機関」

・fund「…に資金を提供する」

・nation「国，国家」

・the Arts Council England「英国芸術評議会」

・the National Endowment for the Arts「全米芸術基金」

・support「…を支援する，…を援助する」

・not only A but also B「Ａだけでなく Ｂも」＝ B as well as A

・a variety of A「さまざまなＡ」

・including A「Ａを含めて」

・painting「絵画」

・sculpture「彫刻」

・folk art「民芸（品）」

・cultural institution「文化施設」

・B such as A「ＡのようなＢ」

・library「図書館」

・theater「劇場」

・museum「博物館」

・in addition「その上，さらに」
＝ besides, moreover

・an array of A「ずらりと並んだＡ，一連のＡ」
※ array は「列挙，一続き」の

意味。
・encourage O to *do*「O に…するように励ます［勧める］」
・critical「重大な，決定的に重要な」
・especially「とりわけ，特に」
・during economic recessions「経済的な景気後退の時期に」
・far from *doing*「…するどころか」
・withdraw「…を取り消す，…を撤回する」
・state money「国からの資金」
・protect「…を守る」
・increase「…を増やす」
⇔ decrease「…を減らす」
・government funding「政府の資金提供」
＝ governmental funding

第2パラグラフ

・to begin with「まず第一に」
・enrich「…を豊かにする」
・former「以前の」
・director「館長」
・the National Portrait Gallery「国立肖像画美術館」
・necessity「必要不可欠なもの，必需品」
・individual「個人」
・community「共同体，地域社会」
・choir「合唱団，聖歌隊」
・extraordinary「並はずれた，普通でない」⇔ ordinary「普通の」
・poetry「詩」
※不可算名詞。poem「詩」は可算名詞。
・share in A「A を分かち合う，A を共有する」
・excitement「興奮」
・street performance「ストリート・パフォーマンス，路上演技」
・worthwhile「価値がある」
・furthermore「さらに，その上」
＝ in addition, moreover
・in an age of A「A の時代に」
・migration「移住，移動」
・serve an important role in A「A において重要な役割を果たす」
＝ play an important role[part] in A
・bring A together「A をまとめる」
・citizen「国民」
・common experience「共通の経験」
・accommodate「…を調整する」
・difference「相違，違い」

第3パラグラフ

・represent「…を象徴する，…を表す」
・heritage「遺産」
・identity「独自性，アイデンティティ」
・firmly「しっかりと，堅く」
・root「…を根付かせる」
・preserve「…を保存する」
・various「さまざまな」

・according to A「Aによれば」
・novelist「小説家」
・wonder「驚異，驚嘆」
・archive「公文書館，公文書保管所」
・relate A with B「AをBと関連づける」
　= connect A with B
・stretch back A「Aをさかのぼる」
・shape「形，姿」
・humanity「人類」
　= humans, human beings
・fit into A「Aにはまる，Aに合う」
・indeed「実際は」
・at the very heart of A「まさにAの中心部に」
・heritage-related「遺産に関連した」
・industry「事業，産業」
・therefore「それゆえに，したがって」
　= thus, hence
・duty「義務」

第4パラグラフ

・nevertheless「それにもかかわらず」
　= nonetheless
・field「分野」
・sustain「…を維持する」
・independently「独立して」
・require「…を要求する」
・constant「絶えず続く，不変の」
・continue「継続する」
・in contrast to A「Aとは対照的に，Aとは違って」
・commercially「商業的に」
・grand「堂々たる，立派な」
・lack stability「安定性を欠く」
・ticket sales「チケットの売り上げ，チケットの販売数」
・limit「…を制限する」
　= restrict
・non-profit「非営利の」
・organization「機関，団体，組織体」
・maintain「…を維持する」
　= sustain
・facility「施設，設備」
・offer「…を提供する」
・a high quality of services「質の高いサービス」
・support「援助，支援」
・grant「補助金，助成金」
・moreover「さらに，その上」
　= in addition, besides, furthermore
・artistic innovation「芸術の革新」
・enable O to *do*「Oが…するのを可能にする」
　= allow［permit］O to *do*
・take a risk「リスクを冒す」
・experiment「実験する」
・for the sake of art itself「芸術そのもののために」

第5パラグラフ

・argue that S V ...「…だと主張

する」
・wherever possible「可能な場合はどこでも」
・private donation「民間からの寄付金」
・replace「…に取って代わる」
・relatively「比較的」
・secure「確実な，確保された」
・take A for granted「A を当然のことだと見なす」
・extremely「極度に，きわめて」
・wealthy「裕福な」
・corporation「(民間) 企業」
・dominate「…を支配している」
・the global economy「世界経済」
・ask A of B「B に A をくれと頼む」
・charitable「慈善的な」
・sector「部門」
・only go so far「そこまでしか行けない，限界がある」
・unwise「賢明でない」
・make A dependent on B「A を B に依存させる」
・overly「過度に，あまりにも」
・political「政治的な，政治に関する」
・economic「経済（上）の」
・demand「需要」⇔ supply「供給」
・private enterprise「民間企業」
・difficulty「困難」
・be at risk「危険にさらされている」

第6パラグラフ

・by contrast「対照的に」
・stable「安定した」
⇔ unstable「不安定な」
・as many (A) as possible「できるだけ多く（の A)」
・ensure「…を確実にする，…を保証する」
・affordable「手頃な，手の届く範囲の」
・access to A「A を利用［入手］する機会，A に触れる機会」
・an integral part of daily life「日常生活の欠かせない一部」
・allow O to *do*「O が…するのを可能にする」＝ enable O to *do*
・common ground「共通の立場」
・despite A「A にもかかわらず」
＝ in spite of A
・income inequality「所得の不平等」
・gallery tour「美術館ツアー」
・well-to-do「裕福な」
・gain an understanding of A「A を理解する」
・future generation「未来の世代」

第7パラグラフ

・activity「活動」
・benefit「利益」
・attract「…を引きつける」
・in turn「今度は，次に」
・promote「…を促進する」
・redevelopment「再開発」
・suburb「郊外」

・tourism-related「観光関連の」
・politician「政治家」
・recognize A as B「A を B だと認める」
・valuable「貴重な，価値のある」
⇔ valueless「価値のない」
・resources「資源」
・play a part in A「A において役割を果たす，A に役立つ」
・renewal「再生，再開発」
・post-industrial「脱工業化の，脱工業化時代の」
・take up the idea of A as B「A が B だという考えを取り上げる」
・creative「創造的な」
・subsequently「その後に，それに続いて」
・art policy「芸術政策」
・develop「…を練り上げる，…を進展させる」
・widen「…を拡大する」
⇔ narrow「…を狭くする」
・help (to) *do*「…するのに役立つ，…するのを助ける」
・drive「…を推し進める，…を推進する」= promote
・urban rebirth「都会の再生」
・fight「…と戦う」
・social exclusion「社会的排除，社会的疎外」
・estimate that S V ...「…だと推定［概算］する」
・benefit「利益を得る」
・investment「投資」

第 8 パラグラフ

・vital「きわめて重要な，不可欠な」
= essential
・a better quality of life「よりよい生活の質」
・make this point「この点を強調する」
・website「ウェブサイト」
・declare that S V ...「…だと断言する，…だと宣言する」
・inspire「…を鼓舞する，…を激励する」
・contribute「貢献する」
・provide B for A「A に B を供給する」
= provide A with B
・responsibility「責任」
・continued「継続的な」

《 Vocabulary Building Exercise 》

1. Drug companies and the government will jointly **fund** the necessary medical research.
【to provide money for something, usually something official】

1. 「製薬会社と政府は，必要な医学研究に共同で資金を提供することにしている」
【(たいていは公的な）何かのために資金を提供する】

2. He has been singing in his church **choir** since he was six.
【a group of people who sing together, for example in a church or school】

2. 「彼は６歳の頃から自分が通う教会の合唱団で歌っている」
【例えば教会や学校などで合唱をする人たちのグループ】

3. These were measures intended to pull the economy out of **recession**.
【a difficult time for the economy of a country, lasting months or years, during which trade and industrial activity are reduced, and more people are unemployed】

3. 「これらは経済を不況から脱出させることを目的とする措置だった」
【数か月または数年間にわたって続く貿易や産業活動が停滞して失業者が増えたりするような，国の経済にとって困難な時期】

4. She decided to **withdraw** her resignation.
【to no longer provide or offer something; to stop taking part in something】

4. 「彼女は辞任を取り下げることにした」
【もうこれ以上何かを与えたり提供したりしない／あることに参加するのをやめる】

5. She modified her views so as to **accommodate** the objections of American feminists.
【to consider something such as somebody's opinion or a fact and be influenced by it when you are deciding what to do or explaining something】

5.「彼女は，アメリカのフェミニストたちからの異議に配慮して自分の見解を修正した」
【取るべき行動を決定したり何かを説明したりするときに，他人の意見や事実を検討して，それに影響される】

6. The study was supported by a **grant** from the government.
【a sum of money given by a government or other organization for a particular purpose】

6.「その研究は，政府からの助成金によって支援された」
【特定の目的のために，政府やそのほかの組織から提供される資金】

7. The project is funded by public **donation**.
【something that is given to a person or an organization such as a charity, in order to help them; the act of giving something in this way】

7.「そのプロジェクトは，一般からの寄付によって資金を得ている」
【個人や慈善団体などの団体を支援するために提供されるもの／そのようにして何かを提供する行為】

8. We offer quality products at **affordable** prices.
【cheap enough that people can buy it】

8.「当店は，高品質の製品をお手頃な価格でご提供しています」
【人が購入できるくらい安価な】

9. Music is an **integral** part of the school's curriculum.
【being an essential part of something】

9.「音楽は学校のカリキュラムの中でも不可欠な部分だ」
【何かの欠かせない部分となっている】

10. **Subsequently**, new guidelines were issued to all employees. 【afterwards; after something else has happened】	**10.**「その後，新たな方針がすべての従業員に伝えられた」 【後で／何か別のことが起こった後で】

《 Summary 》

It is important for government organizations to fund the arts, especially during times of economic recessions. Art and culture enrich public life and help citizens find common experiences in age of migration and social change. Each people's history and identity are firmly rooted in its art and culture. This heritage is preserved in cultural institutions like libraries, museums and archives, which allow us to relate to people who lived hundreds or thousands of years ago. These institutions need governmental funding to continue, especially in small cities and towns. Extremely wealthy individuals and corporations can provide private donations, but the freedom of artists to take risks and experiment would be lost if artists had to depend on the demands of private enterprise. Government funding ensures that all people can enjoy art and culture. It brings economic benefits by attracting tourists. Since the arts are vital for a better quality of life, continued state support of the arts is critical. (158 words)

【《Summary》の訳】

政府機関が芸術に対して資金を提供することは，特に景気後退の時期には重要なことです。芸術と文化は，人々の生活を豊かにし，人の移動や社会の変化が激しい時代に市民が共通の経験に気づくことに役立ちます。それぞれの民族の歴史とアイデンティティは，その民族の芸術と文化に深く根ざしています。このような遺産は，図書館，博物館，公文書館などの文化施設に保管されていて，そこで私たちは数百年前や数千年前に生きていた人々に自分たちを関連づけることができます。これらの施設は，特に小規模な都市や町では，継続するために政府からの資金を必要としています。非常に裕福な個人や企業であれば，個別の寄付をすることができますが，芸術家が民間企業からの要望に依存しなければならなくなると，芸術家がリスクを冒して新しいことを試す自由が失われます。政府による資金提供によって，あらゆる人たちが芸術と文化を楽しむことが保証されます。観光客を引き寄せることで，経済的な恩恵がもたらされます。芸術はより良い生活の質のために必要不可欠なものなので，芸術に対する国の継続的な支援が不可欠です。

第16問　東北大学

得　点

/50

【解答】

問1．私が週末に向けて，とんでもない量の仕事を，つまり，とうてい読み切れないほどの学生の小論文を家に持ち帰ることは知れ渡っている。

問2．⑵a　②　⑵b　④

問3．自分が行う仕事に要する時間の予測を立てても，実際にはもっと多くの時間がかかってしまうこと。

(別解) 自分がこれから行う仕事に要する時間を少なく見積もってしまうこと。

問4．私は自分のすべての論文を書くのにどれだけの時間がかかったかがわかっているのに，今後の執筆にかかる時間に関しては後になって愚かだったとわかる予測をしてしまう。

問5．A　②　B　⑥　C　⑤　D　④　E　①　F　③

【配点と採点基準】（50点）

問1．8点

・I've been known to *do* … 2点

・bring home ridiculous amounts of work for weekends … 3点

・more student essays than I can possibly read. … 3点

問2．4点（完答）解答通り

問3．6点

・「仕事をするのに予定していたよりも多くの時間がかかる」「仕事に要する時間を少なく見積もってしまう」などの内容 … 6点

問4．8点

・I know how long all of my articles have taken me to write, … 3点

・but I make what turn out to be silly predictions … 3点

・of my future writing time. … 2点

問5．24点（各4点×6）解答通り

【設問別解説】

問１.

・be known to *do*「…することが知られている」

・bring home A（= bring A home）「A を家に持ち帰る」，目的語の A が長いので副詞 home の後に移動している。

・ridiculous amounts of work「とんでもない量の仕事」「ばかばかしいほど多くの仕事」

・for weekends「週末用に，週末に向けて」

・more student essays than I can possibly read「私が読めるのよりも多くの枚数の学生のエッセイ[小論文，作文]」「とうてい読み切れないほどの学生のエッセイ[小論文，作文]」

・ダッシュの後の名詞句 more student essays than I can possibly read は，ダッシュの直前の名詞句 ridiculous amounts of work for weekends を同格的に言い換えている。

問２.

直前の文に書かれた First, make your best estimate, then double that, and finally increase your unit of measurement. という計算の指示に当てはめる。（ (2)a ）には，one hour を２倍にした two hours が入り，（ (2)b ）には two hours の単位を上げた two days が入る。

問３.

直後の文から planning fallacy という語句が planning failures「計画の失敗」を意味することがわかる。第１段落第４～５文から，これは「いつ仕事が完成するかを予測するが，後になってその予測よりも多くの時間がかかったことを知る」ことだと判断できる。「これから行う仕事に要する時間を少なく見積もってしまう」などと表現することもできる。

問４.

・how long all of my articles have taken me to write「私のすべての論文が，書くのにどれだけの時間がかかったか」，他動詞 know の目的語となる間接疑問文。

・what turn out to be silly predictions「(後になって[やってみて]) 愚かな予測だったとわかるもの，後になって愚かだったとわかる予測」

・make predictions「予測を立てる」，turn out to be C「C だとわかる，結局 C になる」

・predictions of my future writing time「今後の執筆にかかる時間についての予測」

問5.

A　空所の直前の2つの文の「悲観的な見積もりは48日かかるというものだった」「実際には56日かかった」という内容から判断すると②を補うのが適切。

B　空所の直前の「1週間で課題を仕上げるように求められた学生たちが，1週間後に課題を半分も終えていなかった」という内容に対して，具体的なデータを紹介している⑥を補うのが適切。選択肢⑥の中の they は the students を指している。

C　空所の直前の「税金の払戻しを期待できる者たちでも，税金についての書類を仕上げるのが少しも早くなかった」という内容から判断すると⑤を補うのが適切。選択肢⑤の中の even when money was sitting on the table「お金がテーブルの上に置かれている時でも」とは，「払戻し金が手に入ることが期待できる時でも」という意味を表している。また，選択肢⑤の中の they は those expecting refunds「払い戻しが期待できる人々」を指している。

D　空所の直前の「人々は，未来に起こる問題のことについてはめったに考えない」に対して，even less frequently という頻度の比較を行っている④を補うのが適切。なお，選択肢④の中の they は people を指している。

E　空所の直前の2つの文の「私たちは，過去の失敗は稀なことであって今行っている予測とは関係がないものと考える」「私たちは，ある程度は正しい」という内容に対して，「私たちが正しい」ことを裏づけている内容の①を補うのが適切。

F　筆者が今後の抱負をユーモラスに語っている最終段落の文脈から判断すると，③を補うのが適切。

【全訳】

　私は，自分がどれくらいの量の仕事を仕上げられるかという点について相変わらず絶望的に楽観的だ。期間は問題ではない。私は，今日，今週，今学期，そして実際のところ生涯のうちに自分がどのくらい仕上げられるかに対して楽観的な予測をしている。私が週末に向けて，とんでもない量の仕事を，つまり，とうてい読み切れないほどの学生の小論文を家に持ち帰ることは知れ渡っている。私は自分がある計画をいつ仕上げられるかに対して，自分では妥当だと思う見積もりを立てる。ずっと，ずっと後になって，自分の見積もりがとんでもなく楽観的であって，実際にその仕事を仕上げるには3倍の時間がかかったことがわかるのだ。

　私は，ある計画にどれくらいの時間が必要となるかを適切に予測するにはどうすればよいかについて，以前に受けたことのあるいくつかの助言を思い出す。まず，あなたの最善の見積もりをして，次にそれを２倍にして，最後に測定の単位を上げるのだ。もしあなたの目算が１時間であれば，次にそれを２時間にして，最後に２日にするというわけだ。私たちは，見積もりをするのがなぜこんなに下手なのだろうか。

この失敗はとてもよく知られていて，プランニング・ファラシー［計画錯誤］という呼び名があるくらいだ。この種の計画の失敗はまた，信じられないほど厄介で高くつくこともある。実にすばらしいところは，私たちはみな，自分が過去に間違ってきたことをわかっているという点だ。私は自分が先週末に仕上げた仕事がどれほど少なかったかわかっているのに，にもかかわらず，今週末になればあまりに多くの仕事を持ち帰るだろう。私は自分のすべての論文を書くのにどれだけの時間がかかったかがわかっているのに，今後の執筆にかかる時間に関しては後になって愚かだったとわかる予測をしてしまう。過去のことは思い出せるのに，どうしてもそれを繰り返す運命にあるのだ。

プランニング・ファラシー［計画錯誤］に関して私が気に入っている研究は，1994年のビューラーとグリフィンズとロスによる一連の研究だ。彼らは，大学生たちに，大きく重要な課題，つまり卒業論文を仕上げるための計画について尋ねた。学生たちは，いつ仕上げられるかについて最善の場合の見積もりを立て，その次に悲観的な見積もり（うまくいかない可能性のあることがすべてうまくいかないと想定した見積もり）を立てた。学生たちの最善の場合の見積もりは平均して34日で仕上がるだろうというもので，悲観的な見積もりは平均48日だった。実際には，学生たちは56日間で仕上げた。悲観的な見積もりでさえ，楽観的だったのだ！　おそらく，うまくいかない可能性のあることがすべてうまくいかず，うまくいかないことがさらにいくつかあったのだろう。

その研究者たちは，もっと期間を短くして同様の実験を行った。彼らは，学生たちに学業課題（小論文を書くことと宿題をやること）と，個人的課題（アパートの掃除と自転車の修理）の両方をいつ仕上げられるかを見積もるように求めた。その学生たちは，１週間以内で仕上げられるだろうと思うものを選ぶように求められた。翌週に研究者たちが再び戻った時に，彼らはその研究を終了することができなかった。なぜならば，学生たちは実は課題の約半分も仕上げていなかったからだ。平均すると，彼らはその課題を５日以内に仕上げるだろうと思っていたのだが，最終的に10日かかったのだった。とんでもなく楽観的な見積もりだったのだ。

別の調査では，研究者たちは人々に，税金に関する書類を仕上げて提出することを求めた。一部の人々にとっては，払戻しが期待できるわけだから，これを仕上げることは嬉しいことだろう。払戻しが期待できる人々は，払戻しが期待できない人々よりも早く仕上げる見積もりを立てた。(冗談じゃない。(税金を) 払わなければいけないのなら，そんなことするわけないじゃない！) だが，もちろん，払戻しが期待できる人々は，少しも早く仕上げなかった。お金がテーブルの上に置かれていても，絶望的に楽観的だったのだ。

人はどうして，課題を仕上げることに関してこんなに楽観的なのだろうか。問題は，人が判断を下すのにどんな情報を利用するかによる。人々は一般的に今後のことに焦点を絞る。人々は，どれだけの仕事があるか，仕事のさまざまな部分のこと，仕事する時間がいつ持てるか，その仕事がどれくらい重要なものかなど，自分の計画について考える。人々は，未来に起こる問題のことについてはめったに考えない。過去に締め切りに間に合わなかったことについて考えることはさらに少ない。だから，まず問題なのは，人々が，自分が以前に期限通りに仕上げられなかったことがあるとわかっていても，新しい見積もりを立てる際にはその情報を利用しないのかもしれないということだ。

だが，たとえ人が過去のことを実際に考えたとしても，自分たちが以前に目標を達成できなかったことは退けてしまうのかもしれない。たしかに前回はうまくいかないことがあったが，そんなことは二度と起こらないだろう。ある大学生は，先週末にジョンのパーティーに行ったために勉強しなかったことはわかっているのかもしれないが，今週末にはジョンはパーティーを開かないこともわかっているのだ（もちろん，ジムがパーティーを開くかもしれないのに，そのことは頭に浮かばない)。私は，以前に原稿を書いたときに他の用事に邪魔されたことは知っているが，その用事が一度限りのことで再び現れることはないということも知っているのだ。もちろん，別の一度限りの用事は必ず生じるが，その関連性を私はわかっていないのだ。私たちは，過去の失敗は稀なことであって今行っている予測とは関係がないものと考える。私たちは，ある程度は正しい。同じ問題がもう一度起こる可能性は低いわけだから。私たちの失敗は，別の問題が必ず生じるということがわかっていないということだ。

そこで私はこのことを，仕事を仕上げる時期について私自身が立てた見積もりを私が守れなかったことが何度もあったことを，共著者の皆様に謝罪する機会として利用したいと思う。今度は私の予測がずっと上手くなっていると私は十分に確信している。

【語句】

第1パラグラフ
・remain C「C のままである」
・hopelessly「絶望的に」
・optimistic「楽観的な」
⇔ pessimistic「悲観的な」
・accomplish「…を成し遂げる」
・frame「枠組，枠」
・matter「重要である」＝ count
・prediction「予測，予想」
・academic term「(学校の) 学期」
・be known to *do*「…することが知られている」
・bring home A「A を家に持ち帰る」
＝ bring A home
※目的語の A が長いので副詞の home の後に移動している。
・ridiculous amount of work「とんでもない量の仕事，ばかばかしいほど多くの仕事」
・for weekends「週末用に，週末に向けて」
・essay「エッセイ，小論文，作文」
・reasonable「妥当な，無理のない」
・estimate「見積もり，概算」
・project「計画，企画」
・wildly「とても，極めて」
・It takes O_1 O_2 to *do*.「O_1 が…するのに O_2 (時間) がかかる」

第2パラグラフ
・advice「忠告」
・receive「…を受け取る」
・appropriate「適切な，ふさわしい」
・the amount of A「A の総計［総数 / 総量］」
・require「…を要求する」
・double「…を 2 倍にする」
・increase「…を大きくする，…を上げる」
・unit「単位」
・measurement「測定，計量」
・be poor at *doing*「…するのが下手である」
⇔ be good at *doing*「…するのが上手である」

第3パラグラフ
・failure「失敗」⇔ success「成功」
・be well known「よく知られている」
・fallacy「誤り，間違い」
＝ error
・sort「種類」＝ kind
・incredibly「信じられないほど」
・troublesome「厄介な，面倒な」
・expensive「高価な，費用のかかる」
⇔ inexpensive「安価な」
・cool「すてきな，すばらしい」
・wrong「間違って，誤って」
・in the past「過去に」
・nonetheless「それにもかかわらず」
＝ nevertheless
・article「論文，記事」

・turn out to be C「C だとわかる，結局 C になる」
・silly「愚かな，ばかな」
= foolish
・future writing time「今後の執筆にかかる時間」
・be doomed to *do*「…する運命にある」
・repeat「…を繰り返す」

第 4 パラグラフ

・favorite「お気に入りの，大好きな」
・research「研究，調査」
・a set of A「一連の A」
・task「課題，仕事」
・pessimistic「悲観的な」
⇔ optimistic「楽観的な」
・assume that S V ...「…だと想定する」
・go wrong「うまくいかない」
・on average「平均して」
・average「…を平均する，平均が…となる」
・in reality「実際は，実は」
・guess（that）S V ...「…だと推測する」
・as well「同様に」

第 5 パラグラフ

・researcher「研究員，調査員」
・replicate「…を再現する，…をやり直す」
・on a shorter time period「もっと短い期間で，期間をもっと短くして」
・estimate「…を見積もる」
・assignment「宿題」
・clean an apartment「アパートを掃除する」
・fix a bike「自転車を修理する」
・choose「…を選ぶ」= select
・call back「再び戻る」
・end up *doing*「結局…することになる」

第 6 パラグラフ

・submit「…を提出する」
= present
・document「書類」
・regarding A「A に関して（の）」
= concerning A
・tax「税金」
・anticipate *doing*「…することを予想する」
・refund「払い戻し（金）」
・No kidding.「冗談じゃありません，いい加減にしてよ」
・those expecting refunds「払い戻しが期待できる人々」
・not（...）any sooner「少しも早く（…）ない」
・sit on the table「テーブルの上においてある」
※ sit は「（…に）ある，（…に）存在する」の意味。

第 7 パラグラフ

・depend on A「A によって決まる，A にかかっている」

・information「情報」
・judgement「判断」
・typically「一般的に，概して」
・focus on A「A に焦点を当てる，A に集中する」
・various「さまざまな」
・failure to *do*「（意志に反して）…しないこと」
・meet a deadline「締め切りに間に合う」
・frequently「頻繁に，しばしば」
・on time「時間通りに」

第８パラグラフ

・dismiss「…を退ける，…を捨てる」
・previous「以前の」
・meet a goal「目標をかなえる」
・last time「前回」
・college student「大学生」
・come to mind「心［頭］に浮かぶ」
・manuscript「原稿」
・disrupt「…を中断させる，…の継続を断つ」
・demand「要求（されること），用件，用事」
・one-time「１回限りの」
・be bound to *do*「必ず…する」
・occur「生じる，起こる」
＝ happen
・realize「…をはっきり理解する，…を悟る」
・see A as B「A を B だと見なす」
＝ regard A as B
・unrelated to A「A に無関係な」
・current「今の，現在の」
・to some extent「ある程度」
＝ in some degree
・be unlikely to *do*「…する可能性は低い」
⇔ be likely to *do*「…する可能性は高い」

第９パラグラフ

・opportunity to *do*「…する機会」
＝ chance to *do*
・apologize to A「A に謝る」
・co-author「共著者」
・completely「すっかり，十分に」
＝ totally

《 Vocabulary Building Exercise 》

1. The report expresses an **optimistic** view about reducing US dependence on foreign oil.
【expecting good things to happen or something to be successful; showing this feeling】

1. 「その報告書は，米国の外国産石油への依存度を減らすことについて楽観的な見方を示している」
【よいことが起こったり何かが成功したりすることを期待するような／そのような気持ちを表している】

2. Not everyone is so **pessimistic** about the future as you are.
【expecting bad things to happen or something not to be successful】

2. 「誰もがあなたほど未来に悲観的であるわけではありません」
【悪いことが起こったり何かがうまくいかなかったりすると予期している】

3. Mothers **typically** worry about their children.
【in a way that shows the usual qualities or features of a particular type of person, thing or group】

3. 「母親というものは普通，子どものことを心配する」
【特定の種類の人，物，または集団が普通持っている資質や特徴を表して】

4. You've done so much work—you're **bound** to pass the exam.
【certain or likely to happen, or to do or be something】

4. 「あなたはとても頑張ったのだから，きっとその試験に合格するでしょう」
【起こること，何かをすること，何かになることが確実な，あるいはその可能性が高い】

5. She was unwilling to make a **prediction** about which books would sell in the coming year.
【a statement that says what you think will happen; the act of making such a statement】

5.「彼女は，翌年にどの本が売れるのか予測をしたくなかった」
【これから起こると思うことを伝える言葉／そのような発言をする行為】

6. He invited her to his laboratory to see if she could **replicate** the experiment.
【to copy something exactly】

6.「彼は彼女を自分の実験室に招き，彼女がその実験を再現することができるかどうか確認しようとした」
【何かを正確にまねる】

7. Candidates for the degree are required to **submit** a 30,000-word thesis.
【to give a document, proposal, etc. to somebody in authority so that they can study or consider it】

7.「学位の取得希望者は，30,000語の論文を提出する必要がある」
【審査や検討をしてもらうために，書類や提案書などを権限のある人に手渡す】

8. We **anticipate** that sales will rise next year.
【to expect or predict something】

8.「当社は，来年は売上が増えると予想している」
【何かを期待したり予測したりする】

9. They warned that climate change could **disrupt** economic activity.
【to make it difficult for something to act or continue in the normal way】

9.「彼らは，気候変動が経済活動を混乱させる可能性があると警告した」
【何かにいつもどおりの動作や継続を困難にさせる】

10. If there is a delay of 12 hours or more, you will receive a full **refund** of the price of your trip.
【a sum of money that is paid back to you, especially because you paid too much or because you returned goods to a shop】

10. 「もし12時間以上の遅延が発生したら，旅行代金の全額を返金いたします」

【特に過払いがあった場合や店に商品を返品した場合に払い戻される金額】

《 Summary 》

The author says that he is hopelessly optimistic about how much work he can accomplish. He always makes unreasonable estimates, so he cannot make appropriate predictions. He explains that this failure is called "the planning fallacy." A set of studies about this asked college students to estimate how much time they thought they would need to finish their graduation thesis. Everyone took even longer to finish them than their most pessimistic estimates. Researchers replicated these results using tasks that took less time. Even when people anticipated getting tax refunds, they took longer than they expected to submit their tax documents. Why does this happen? People tend to believe that nothing will go wrong, even though delays are bound to occur. We think that past failures are unusual and this time everything will go smoothly. But that is almost never the case. (141 words)

【《Summary》の訳】

筆者は，自分がどれだけの仕事を成し遂げられるかについて，あきれるほど楽観的だと言う。彼はいつも不合理な見積もりをするので，適切な予測をすることはできません。彼は，この失敗は「計画錯誤」と呼ばれるものだと説明しています。このことに関する一連の研究では，大学生に卒業論文を完成させるのにどれだけの時間が必要なのか見積もるよう頼みました。全員が，論文を書き終えるのに，最も悲観的な見積もりよりもずっと長い時間がかかりました。研究者たちは，これよりも短い時間で完了する作業を使って，この結果を再現しました。人々は税金の還付が期待できる場合でも，税金関連の書類の提出には予想以上に時間がかかりました。どうしてこのようなことが起こるのでしょうか。遅れは必ず発生しますが，人は問題など起こらないと思い込みたがるのです。私たちは，過去の失敗は珍しいことで，今回はすべてが順調に進むと考えるのです。しかし，そのようなことは，ほとんど事実無根なのです。

第１問の【語句】リスト

第１パラグラフ

・make a point「主張する」
・look A in the eye「Aの目を見る」
・the other person「相手」
・spouse「配偶者」
・boss「上司」
・politician「政治家」
・gaze「凝視，注視」
・convince A that S V ...「Aに…ということを確信させる」
・position「立場，見解」
・valid「正当な，有効な」
・It turns out that S V ...「…ということがわかる」
・cast one's glance「視線を向ける」
・in a different direction「違う方向に」

第２パラグラフ

・psychologist「心理学者」
・assistant professor「准教授」
・government「政治，行政，政府」
・negotiation「交渉」
・longtime「長年の，長期にわたる」
・collaborator「協同研究者，協力者」
・realize that S V ...「…だと（はっきりと）理解する」
・this piece of A「この１つのA」
・conventional「月並みな，平凡な，従来型の」
・wisdom「（先人の）知恵，賢明な教え」
・stare at A「Aをじっと見る」
・(be) likely to do「…する可能性が高い」
・academic work「学術研究」
・focus on A「Aに集中する，Aに焦点を当てる」
・what S call C「SがCと呼ぶもの」
・context「状況，文脈」
・gaze at A「Aをじっと見つめる」
・strengthen「…を強くする，…を強化する」
・bond「絆」
・potential「潜在的な，（…に）なる可能性のある」
・mate「配偶者，連れ合い」
・improve「…を向上させる」
・connection「つながり，関係（性）」
・when it comes to A「Aということになると」
・persuasion「説得」
・interaction「やりとり，相互作用」
・from the perspective of A「Aの視点［観点］から」
・get A across「Aを理解させる，Aをわからせる」
・make eye contact「アイコンタクトを行う」

第３パラグラフ

・paper「（学術）論文，（研究）論文」
・publish「…を発表する，…を公表する」
・proposition「意見，命題」
・win over A「Aを説き伏せる，Aを味方に引き入れる」
・disagree with A「Aに同意しない」
・conduct「（調査など）を行う」
・respond to A「Aに反応する」
・favorably「好意的に，好意を持って」
・opposing「反対の，相反する」
・argument「主張，論拠」
・at an angle「斜めに，傾いて」

・*recipient*「受け取り手，聞き手」
・*focus A on B*「Aの焦点をBに合わせる，AをBに集中させる」
・*counterpart*「対応［相当］するもの，対の片方」

第4パラグラフ

・*totally*「まったく，すっかり」
・*prove that S V ...*「…ということを証明［立証］する」
・*stare A down*「Aをにらみつけて目をそらさせる」
・*attack*「攻撃する」
・*intuition*「直感」
・*drive*「…を推進する」
・*prolonged*「長期の，長引く」
・*dominate*「…を支配する」
・*reaction*「反応，反動」
・*instinctive*「本能的な，直感的な」

第5パラグラフ

・*run a study*「調査［研究］を行う」
・*observe*「…を観察する」
・*controversial*「賛否両論のある，異論の多い」
・*subject*「話題，問題，主題」
・*assisted suicide*「自殺幇助」
・*nuclear power phase-out*「原子力発電の段階的廃止」
・*including A*「Aを含めて」
・*instance*「実例，例」
・*a tendency to do*「…する傾向」
・*agree with A*「Aに同意する」
・*measure whether S V ...*「…かどうかを測定する」
・*at the outset*「最初は，最初に」
・*change one's mind*「決心を変える，考えを変える」
・*participant*「被験者，参加者」
・*persuade*「…を説得する」

第6パラグラフ

・*rely on A*「Aに頼る，Aに依存する」
・*farming practice*「農業のやり方，農業の実践」
・*direct O to do*「Oに…するように指示する」
・*those who S V ...*「…する人々」
・*B rather than A*「AではなくB」

第7パラグラフ

・*consistent*「一貫した，矛盾がない」
・*go back and forth*「行ったり来たりする」
・*note*「…と指摘する」
・*wander around*「（うろうろと）さまよう」
・*force oneself to do*「無理に…しようとする」
・*look into A*「Aの中をのぞく」
・*advise that S V ...*「…ということを忠告する」

第8パラグラフ

・*the same as A*「Aと同じもの［こと］」
・*face-to-face*「対面して，向き合って」
・*go on*「起こる」
・*lean in*「身を乗り出す」
・*in other ways*「別のやり方で」
・*attractive*「魅力的な」
・*at least*「少なくとも」
・*isolate*「…を分離［隔離］する」

第9パラグラフ

・*next time S V ...*「今度…するときは」
・*let O do*「Oを…するままにしておく」

第２問の【語句】リスト

第１パラグラフ

- *citizen*「市民」
- *set about doing*「…することにとりかかる」
- *put A to death*「Aを殺す」
- *the number of civilian deaths*「民間人の死者数」
- *bombing*「爆撃」
- *entire*「全体の，全部の」
- *calm*「穏やかな」
- *orderly*「整然とした，秩序のある」
- *shelter*「避難所，収容所」
- *stretch*「広がる，伸びている」
- *turn A over*「Aを引き渡す」
- *animal welfare society*「動物福祉協会」
- *run out of A*「Aを切らす，Aを使い果たす」
- *burial ground*「埋葬地」
- *local hospital*「地方病院」
- *body*「遺体，死体」
- *bury*「…を埋葬する，…を埋める」

第２パラグラフ

- *out of necessity*「必要に迫られて，必要から」
- *food supply*「食料供給」
- *scarce*「乏しい，少ない」
- *following*「次の，次に来る」
- *Nor did S do ...*「Sはまた…しなかった」
- *issue*「…を発する，…を出す」
- *instruction*「指示，命令」
- *tell O to do*「Oに…するように命じる」
- *for the good of A*「Aの（利益の）ために」
- *rather*「むしろ」
- *mass action*「集団行動，大衆行動」
- *arise*「起こる」
- *apparently*「見たところ（は）…らしい，どうやら…らしい」
- *voluntarily*「自発的に，任意に」
- *population*「住人，人々」
- *terrify*「…をひどく怖がらせる，…をぞっとさせる」
- *reality*「現実」

第３パラグラフ

- *immediately*「すぐに，直ちに」
- *realize*「…をはっきり理解する，…を悟る」
- *complain that S V ...*「…だと不満［不平］を言う」
- *evidence*「証拠」
- *daily*「毎日の，日単位の」
- *large numbers of A*「非常に多くのA」
- *for no better reason than that S V ...*「…という理由だけで」
- *inconvenient*「不便な」
- *keep O alive*「Oを生かしておく」
- *likewise*「同様に」
- *argue against A*「Aに反する結論を下す」
- *faithful*「忠実な，献身的な」
- *There is no need to do*「…する必要がない」
- *let O do*「Oに…させる，Oを…するままにしておく」
- *creep into A*「Aの中に忍び込む」
- *mass killing*「大量殺処分」
- *lessen*「減る，少なくなる」
- *survive*「…を切り抜ける，生き残る」

・last「持ちこたえる，生き延びる」

第4パラグラフ

・have a great deal to do with A「A と大いに関係がある」
・the relationship of A to B「A と B の関係」
・human「人間，人類」
・cattle「ウシ」
・be useful to A「A に役立つ」
・security「警備，防護，安全」
・hunting「狩猟」
・status「地位，身分」
・companion animal「伴侶動物，連れ合いとしての動物」
・initially「最初に，初めに」
・side benefit「副次的な恩恵」
・with urbanization「都会化とともに」
・less and less「ますます（…）ない」
・no longer「もはや（…）ない」
・in the traditional sense「従来の意味で」

第5パラグラフ

・attitude「態度，姿勢」
・(all) well and good「よろしい，しかたない」
・peacetime「平時，平和時」
・significant「かなりの，相当数の，重大な」
・portion「部分，割り当て」
・treatment「待遇」
・run an image「画像を掲載する」
・silk pillow「シルクのクッション」
・note that S V ...「…だと指摘する」
・make a comment「コメントをする，批評する」
・no doubt「疑いなく，確かに」
・widespread「広範囲に及ぶ」
・luxury item「ぜいたく品」
・compete with A「A と競争する，A と張り合う」

第6パラグラフ

・memory「記憶」
・determine「…を決定する」
・fate「運命」
・wander「さまよう，歩き回る」
・despite A「A にもかかわらず」
・attention「注目，注意」
・all but「ほとんど」
・write A out of history「歴史から A を削除する［消す］」
・researcher「研究者，調査員」
・ask A for B「A に B を（くれるよう）頼む」
・despite the fact that S V...「…だけれども」
・report that S V ...「…だと報告する」
・continue「（間断なく）続く」
・day and night「昼も夜も，昼夜の別なく」

第7パラグラフ

・It makes sense that S V ...「…は理屈に合う，…は理解できる」
・chapter「章」
・reveal「…をさらけ出す，…を明らかにする」
・a deep-rooted tendency toward A「A への根深い傾向」
・needless panic「不必要なパニック」

- pride oneself on A「Aを誇る」
- self-control「自制，克己」
- in the face of A「Aに直面して（の）」
- legacy「遺産」
- phrase「フレーズ，言い回し」
- carry on「（仕事などを）続ける」
- odd「奇妙な，変わった」
- weaken「…を弱くする」
- suggest「…を示唆［提案］する」
- terror「恐怖」
- the lack of reason「理性の欠如」

第３問の【語句】リスト

第１パラグラフ

・grandparents「祖父母」
・unlike A「Aと違って」
・selection「品ぞろえ」
・magazine「雑誌」
・flip through A「Aをすばやくめくる，Aをざっと読む」
・pass the time「時間をつぶす」
・other than A「A以外に」
・slightly odd「少し変わっている」
・object「物，物体」
・warrant「…を保証する」
・attention「注意，注目」
・entitle O C「OにCという題を付ける」
・crazed「熱狂的な」
・as a kid「子どもの頃（の）」
・quote book「名言集，格言集」
・one hundred times over「100回以上」
・stick「（心に）とどまる，（心から）離れない」
・crowed「混み合った」
・It ain't over「それは終わらない」
・saying「格言，ことわざ，言い習わし」
・stand out「きわ出つ，傑出している」

第２パラグラフ

・mental「精神の」
・the other half「残りの半分」

第３パラグラフ

・add up「計算が合う，（数字が）一致する」
・attempt to do「…しようと試みる」
・unpack「…の意味を解明する」
・philosophy「哲学」
・make a point「主張する」
・mentality「精神力，精神構造」
・suggest that S V ...「…ということを示唆［暗示］する」
・concept「概念，考え」
・mathematically「数学的に」
・erroneous「誤った，間違った」
・phrase「表現，言い回し，フレーズ」
・retain「…を保つ，…を保持する」
・the idea that S V ...「…だという考え」
・strength「強さ」
・have a role in A「Aにおいて役割を果たす」
・common knowledge「常識，共通の知識」
・find one's way into A「Aにたどりつく，Aに入り込む」
・cliché「（陳腐な）決まり文句」
・universally accepted truth「広く受け入れられている事実」
・there is more to A than B「AにはB以上のものがある，AはBだけがすべてではない」
・pure physical talent「純粋な身体的才能」
・psychology「心理学」
・broad study「幅広い研究」
・mind「精神」
・affect「…に影響する」
・performance「パフォーマンス，出来ばえ」
・participation「参加，加入」
・silly「愚かな」
・assume that S V ...「…だと思い込む，…だと決めてかかる」

・consider O separate「O を別物だと考える」
・athletic body「運動を行う肉体」
・scientifically「科学的に」
・the link between the two「その 2 つの関連（性）」
・obstacle「障害（物）」
・current「今の，現在の」
・technological innovation「技術革新」

第 4 パラグラフ

・despite A「A にもかかわらず」
・the absence of A「A がないこと」
・method「方法，手段」
・the distinction between A and B「A と B の区別」
・athletic competition「運動競技」
・trace A back to B「A を B までさかのぼらせる」
・ancient「古代の，太古の」
・soon after S V ...「…したあとすぐに」
・be held「開催される，行われる」
・fable「寓話，たとえ話」
・moral「教訓」
・Slow and steady wins the race「遅くても着実な者が勝つ」
・message「伝えたいこと，メッセージ」
・hold true「有効である，当てはまる」
・physically equipped「身体能力が備わって」
・skilled「技術を身につけて」
・approach「取り組み（方）」
・enhance「…を高める」
・chance「可能性」
・level「…を平等にする，…を平らにする」
・playing field「競技場，運動場」
・regardless of A「A とは関係なく」
・skill「技能」

第 5 パラグラフ

・remarkable「注目に値する，驚くべき」
・athlete「運動選手」
・What does it mean to do?「…するということはどういう意味なのか」
・thrive「栄える，繁栄する」
・era「時代，時期」
・exploding「爆発的に増加している」
・statistic「統計」
・analysis「分析」

第 6 パラグラフ

・vital「極めて重要な」
・utilize「…を利用する，…を役立たせる」
・ridiculous「馬鹿げた，おかしな」
・take A for granted「A を当然のことと思う」
・cast A aside「A を脇に置く，A を捨てる」
・implication「含意，意味すること」
・intricacy「複雑（さ），込み入っていること」
・dogma「定説，教義」
・at face value「額面通りに」
・including A「A を含めて」
・significance「重要性」
・see A as B「A を B だと見なす」
・make-or-break「成否を左右する」
・whereas S V ...「（～），だが一方で…」
・athleticism「運動能力」
・defining「決定的な，典型的な」
・feature「特徴」
・consistently「一貫して，常に」

・bat「…の打率を上げる」
・drive「(ボール) を強く打つ，飛ばす」
・over A「A 以上」
・perform「やってのける，成果を出す」
・under pressure「プレッシャーのもとで」
・undermine「…を弱体化させる，…をひそかに傷つける」
・constantly「絶えず」
・appearance「外見」
・alternative to A「A に取って替わるもの，A に代わる選択肢」
・bias「偏見」
・surround「…を取り巻く，…を囲む」
・shed light on A「A に光を投げかける，A を解明する」
・overlook「…を見過ごす，…を見落とす」
・investigate「…を調査する，…を調べる」
・commonsense「常識に富む，常識的な」
・seemingly「一見 (…) のように思える，見かけは」

第4問の【語句】リスト

第1パラグラフ

・*grandmother*「祖母，おばあちゃん」
・*darling*「あなた，お前」
・*nod*「うなづく」
・*Danish*「デンマーク人の，デンマーク語（の）」
・*be eager to do*「しきりに…したがる，…することを切望する」
・*bring up A*「A を育てる」
・*bilingually*「二カ国語を話せるように」
・*come to do*「…するようになる」
・*accept that S V ...*「…であることを認める」
・*reply*「返事をする，答える」

第2パラグラフ

・*painful*「苦痛を与える，痛ましい」
・*share*「…を共有する，…を分かち合う」
・*loved ones*「最愛の［身内の］人たち」
・*pass A on to B*「A を B に伝える」
・*tough*「骨の折れる，難しい」
・*immigrant*「移民（の）」
・*feel a sense of failure*「挫折感を味わう」
・*wring one's hands*「両手を固く握りしめる」
・*parenting*「子育て，育児」
・*nurture*「…を育てる」
・*successfully*「首尾よく，うまく」

第3パラグラフ

・*linguistic*「言語の，言葉の」
・*sponge*「吸収する人［物］，スポンジ」
・*mean that S V ...*「…ということを意味する」
・*exposure*「（身を）さらすこと，さらされること」
・*quite a bit*「かなり」
・*comfortably*「気楽に，心地よく」
・*mental work*「頭を使う作業」
・*have a motive to do*「…する動機を持つ」
・*either A or B*「A であれ B であれ」
・*avoid*「…を避ける」

第4パラグラフ

・*wither*「衰える，しぼむ」
・*move abroad*「国外に移動［移住］する」
・*foreign-born*「海外で生まれた」
・*share*「割り当て，割合」
・*accumulate*「積もる，増える」
・*That is because S V ...*「それは…だからだ」
・*typically*「一般的に，主として」
・*monolingual*「単一言語の，一言語使用の」
・*struggle to do*「…するのに苦労する」

第5パラグラフ

・*in the past*「過去には」
・*discourage A from doing*「A に…するのを思いとどまらせる」
・*valuable resource*「貴重な資源」
・*factor*「要因，要素」
・*conspire*「共謀する，（悪い方向に）重なる」
・*ensure that S V ...*「確実に…するようにする」

第6パラグラフ

- *institutional pressure*「制度的な圧力」
- *lack prestige*「威信を欠く」
- *reluctantly*「しぶしぶ」
- *comply*「(規則などに) 従う」
- *offspring*「子，子孫」
- *shame*「残念なこと，遺憾なこと」
- *suggest that S V …*「…ということを示唆[暗示] する」
- *vocabulary*「語彙」
- *somewhat*「いくぶん，多少」
- *for a while*「しばらくの間」
- *hint at A*「A をほのめかす，A をそれとなく言う」
- *cognitive advantage*「認知能力に関する利点」
- *be skillful at A*「A がうまい，A が上手だ」
- *complex task*「複雑な仕事[課題]」
- *be good at A*「A が得意だ」
- *maintain attention*「注意力を維持する」
- *at the other end of life*「晩年になって」
- *suffer*「…を受ける，…をこうむる」
- *onset*「(通例よくないことの) 開始，(病気の) 発症」

第7パラグラフ

- *even without A*「A がなかったとしても」
- *side-effect*「副次的な効果，副作用」
- *though*「しかしながら」
- *A's connection to B*「A と B とのつながり」
- *in itself*「それ自体」
- *bring A about*「A を生み出す，A をもたらす」
- *heritage language*「継承言語」
- *strategy*「戦略，方針」
- *national language*「(その) 国の言語」
- *the most common approach*「最も一般的な取り組み[アプローチ]」
- *linguist*「言語学者」
- *emphasize*「…を強調する」
- *necessity*「必要性」
- *recommend doing*「…することを勧める」
- *reserve*「…を取っておく」
- *occasion on which S V …*「…する機会」

第8パラグラフ

- *emphasis*「重点，強調」
- *impose*「…を課す」
- *lead to A*「A につなげる，A を引き起こす」
- *rejection*「拒絶，却下」
- *argue that S V …*「…だと主張する」
- *let O do*「(望み通り) O に…させる」
- *emotional*「感情的な」
- *give up on A*「A に見切りをつける」
- *return to A*「A に戻る」
- *determine when S V …*「いつ…かを決める」
- *decide on A*「A に決定する」
- *trip to A*「A への移動」
- *after-school activity*「放課後の活動」
- *exclude*「…を除外する，…を排除する」
- *joke about A*「A について冗談を言う」
- *incorporate A into B*「A を B に組み入れる」
- *youngster*「若者，子ども」
- *restrict*「…を制限する」
- *allow O_1 O_2*「O_1 に O_2 を許す」

・entertainment「娯楽」

第9パラグラフ

・intimate「個人的な，私的な」
・identity「自分であること」
・fail to do「（意志に反して）…しない［できない］」
・drill A into B「AをBに徹底的に教え込む」
・young mind「子どもの頭脳［知力］」
・a matter of A「Aの問題」

第5問の【語句】リスト

第1パラグラフ

・polar exploration「極地探検」
・Arctic「北極の」
・Antarctic「南極の」
・continent「大陸」
・region「地域，地方」
・defy「…に従わない，…を寄せ付けない」
・explorer「探検家」
・adventurer「冒険家」
・lure「魅力」
・commercial「商業（上）の」
・imperial「帝国の」
・ambition「野望，野心」
・disappearance「消滅，消えること」
・expedition「探検，遠征隊」
・famous case「有名な事件」
・initiate「…を開始する，…を始める」
・a dozen A「十数（回）の A」
・rescue「救助（の）」
・as many (as) A「同数の A」
・disturbing「心を掻き乱すような」
・ice-bound「氷に閉ざされた」
・while *doing*「…しながら」
・trek「（徒歩で）骨の折れる旅をする」
・overland「陸上［陸路］で」
・seek aid「助けを求める」
・succumb to A「A に屈する」
・helplessly「無力に」
・environment「環境」
・dwell「住む，居住する」
・permanently「永久に，恒久的に」
・flourish「栄える，繁栄する」
・widow「未亡人」
・proclaim that S V ...「…だと宣言［公言］する」
・lay down *one's* life「命を捧げる」
・in the service of A「A の役に立つために，A に奉仕するために」
・as truly as if S V ...「…かのように忠実に」
・perish「死滅する」
・naval「海軍の」
・claim A for B「B に対して A があると主張する」
・myth「神話」
・motive「動機」
・drive to *do*「…したいという衝動」
・appropriate「…を占有する，…を自分のものにする」
・psychologically「心理的に」
・B if not A「A でなくとも B」
・politically「政治的に」
・remote「遠い，遠方の」

第2パラグラフ

・be true of A「A に当てはまる」
・unique「独特な，唯一の」
・featureless「特徴［特色］のない」
・geographical「地理的な，地理学上の」
・the planet「地球」
・inaccessibility「近づきにくいこと」
・generations of A「数世代の A」
・endurance「忍耐力」
・declare that S V ...「…だと宣言する」
・mankind「人類」
・master of A「A の支配者」
・establish「…を立証する，…をはっきりさせる」

- *officer*「士官，武官」
- *the Norwegian*「ノルウェー人」
- *survive*「…を（切り抜けて）生き残る」
- *extraordinary*「異常な，普通でない」
- *lock*「…を閉じ込める」
- *drift*「漂流する，漂う」
- *demonstrate that S V …*「…ということを証明する」
- *not A but B*「AではなくB」
- *land-mass*「大陸，広大な土地」
- *ice cap*「氷冠」
- *narrative*「物語，記述」
- *wilderness*「荒野，未開［無人］の地」
- *remarkably*「著しく，際立って」
- *sane*「正気な」
- *good-tempered*「温厚な，気立ての良い」
- *humorous*「ユーモアのある」
- *transform A into B*「AをBに変形させる，AをBに変質させる」
- *filthy*「汚れた，不潔な」
- *savage*「野蛮人」
- *fat*「脂肪，脂身」

第3パラグラフ

- *produce*「…を生み出す」
- *literature*「文献，文学（作品）」
- *bleak*「暗い，わびしい」
- *face to face with A*「Aに直面して」
- *intense physical suffering*「激しい肉体的苦痛」
- *philosophical question*「哲学的疑問」
- *fatal*「致命的な，命取りになる」
- *body*「死体」
- *entry*「記載，記入」
- *factual*「事実に基づく」
- *rationalise*「…を合理的に説明する」
- *fate*「運命」
- *bold spirit*「大胆な精神」
- *slip away*「消える，なくなる」
- *confront*「…に直面する」
- *solely*「単に」
- *vanity*「虚栄心」
- *day-dream*「空想，白昼夢」
- *awful*「恐ろしい，すさまじい」

第4パラグラフ

- *all the* + 比較級「（ある理由によって）それだけ…」
- *unbearable*「耐えられない」
- *beat*「…を打ち負かす」
- *additionally*「その上，さらに」
- *torment*「…をひどく苦しめる」
- *including A*「Aを含めて」
- *sympathise*「同情する」
- *drive A on*「Aを駆り立てる」
- *see (to it) that S V …*「…するように取り計らう［気をつける］」
- *be dependent on[upon] A*「Aに頼っている」
- *provide for A*「Aを養う」
- *ache*「心を痛める，悲しむ」
- *a sense of personal guilt*「自責の念」
- *for God's sake*「お願いだから」
- *look after A*「Aの世話をする」
- *need not have done*「…する必要はなかった」
- *fear*「心配する，恐れる」
- *securely*「確実に，安心して」
- *force O to do*「Oに…することを強いる」
- *re-examine*「…を再検証する，…を見直す」

・pursue「…を追求する」
・vision「理想像」
・the ultimate end「究極の目標」
・idealism「理想主義」
・see A as B「A を B だと見なす」
・essential「不可欠の，絶対必要な」
・process「過程，プロセス」
・sacrifice「犠牲」
・individual「個人の」
・self「自己，自分自身」
・noble cause「崇高な大義」
・come to *do*「…するようになる」
・symbolise「…を象徴する」
・destiny「運命」
・mythology「神話」
・Britishness「英国人気質」
・call on[upon] O to *do*「O に…するように求める」
・embrace「…を受け入れる」
・reject「…を拒絶する」

第6問の【語句】リスト

第1パラグラフ

- *the United Nations*「国際連合（国連）」
- *estimate that S V ...*「…だと概算する」
- *human beings*「人類，人間」
- *high percentage*「高い比率」
- *comparatively*「比較的」
- *development*「進展，発展」
- *modern humans*「現生人類」
- *that is*「つまり，すなわち」
- *recognize A as B*「AをBだと認める[認識する]」
- *anatomically*「解剖学的に」
- *(be) similar to A*「Aと似て（いる）」
- *be around*「(人が）生きている，存在している，活動している」
- *the vast majority of A*「Aの大部分，Aの大半」
- *hunter-gatherer*「狩猟採集民」
- *existence*「生活」

第2パラグラフ

- *follow*「…の後に来る，…に続く」
- *agricultural revolution*「農業革命」
- *take place*「起こる，生ずる」
- *fundamental*「基本的な，根本的な」
- *involved in A*「Aに伴う，Aに関係している」
- *rather than doing*「…するのではなく」
- *wander*「歩き回る，さまよう」
- *from place to place*「あちこちに[を]」
- *in search of A*「Aを捜して」
- *animal migration*「動物の移動」
- *fertility pattern*「豊作[繁殖]のパターン」
- *plant*「植物」
- *crop*「作物」
- *breed*「…を飼育する」
- *particular location*「特定の場所」
- *separate family*「別個の家族，独立した家族」
- *B rather than A*「AではなくB」
- *tribal*「種族の，部族の」

第3パラグラフ

- *adapt to A*「Aに順応する」
- *instinct*「本能」
- *be suited to A*「Aに適している」
- *settled*「安定した，落ち着いた，定着した」
- *agricultural-industrial*「農工業の」
- *material advantage*「物質的な利点」
- *ready*「素早い，迅速な」
- *supply*「供給」
- *access to A*「Aの利用[入手]の権利，Aへのアクセス」
- *a large range of A*「広範囲に及ぶ[さまざまな] A」
- *medical service*「医療（サービス）」
- *convenient*「便利な」
- *transport system*「輸送システム」
- *urban condition*「都市環境」
- *produce*「…を生み出す，…を生じさせる」
- *emotional*「感情的な」
- *ancestor*「祖先，先祖」
- *be less likely to do*「…する可能性がそれほど高くない」
- *depression*「憂うつ，意気消沈」
- *loneliness*「孤独」

・overcrowded environment「過密環境」
・have regular contact with A「A と定期的に接触する」

第4パラグラフ
・judge「…を判断する」
・compare A with B「A と B を比較する」
・city-dweller「都市居住者」
・describe「…を記述する, …を描写する」
・be free to do「自由に…する(ことができる)」
・household chore「家事」
・bill「勘定, 請求書」
・boss「上司」
・scold「…をしかる」
・pollution「汚染, 公害」
・varied「さまざまな, 変化に富んだ」
・diet「食事」
・infectious disease「感染病」
・common「普通の, よく起こる」
・skilled「熟練した, 技術を身につけた」
・physically「肉体的に」
・fit「体調がよい」
・given that S V ...「…ということを考慮すると」
・extremely「とても, きわめて」
・imagine if S V ...「もし…だったらと想像する」
・strand「(人を) 立ち往生させる」
・panic「うろたえる, パニックになる」
・survive「生き残る」
・situation「状況, 事態」
・consider O C「O を C だと考える [見なす]」
・emergency「緊急事態」
・daily reality「日常的な現実」

第5パラグラフ
・exchange A for B「A を B と交換する」
・relate「…を述べる, …を物語る」
・walk the same route「同じ道を歩いて行く」
・subway train「地下鉄の列車」
・perform the same process「同じ作業を行う」
・peacefully「安らかに, 穏やかに」

第6パラグラフ
・disadvantage「不利」
・period「期間, 時期」
・infant mortality「乳幼児の死亡率」
・medical care「医療」
・develop「…を発展 [発達] させる」
・mental health「精神的健康」
・satisfaction「満足 (感)」
・jealousy「嫉妬 (心)」
・tribe「種族, 部族」
・depend on A「A に依存する, A に頼る」
・achieve「…を獲得する, …を勝ち取る」
・stranger「見知らぬ人」

第７問の【語句】リスト

第１パラグラフ

- *conduct research on A*「Aを研究する」
- *emotion*「感情，情緒」
- *facial expression*「（顔の）表情」
- *psychologist*「心理学者」
- *startling*「びっくりさせる，仰天させる」
- *photograph*「写真」
- *fear*「恐怖感，おびえ」
- *wide-eyed*「目を大きく開いた」
- *identify*「…を特定する，…を見分ける」
- *frightened face*「おびえた顔」
- *indication*「表示，徴候」
- *threat*「おどし，威嚇」
- *in other words*「言い換えれば」
- *think of A as B*「AをBだと考える［見なす］」
- *universal*「普遍的な，一般的な」
- *interpretation*「解釈」
- *emerging*「新生の，新興の」
- *increasingly*「ますます，だんだん」
- *support*「…を支持する」
- *reflect*「…を反映する」
- *instead of A*「Aではなくて」
- *reliable*「信頼できる」
- *display*「表示，示すもの」
- *state*「状態，様子」
- *intention*「意図，意志」

第２パラグラフ

- *act like A*「Aのように行動する」
- *road sign*「道路標識」
- *affect*「…に影響する」
- *psychology professor*「心理学教授」
- *direct the course of A*「Aを方向づける」
- *social interaction*「対人的なやりとり，社会的相互作用」
- *That is not to say that S V ...*「そうだからといって…ということではない」
- *actively*「積極的に，活発に」
- *manipulate*「…を操作する，…をたくみに扱う」
- *frown*「しかめっ面，渋い顔」
- *may well be C*「たぶんCだろう」
- *unconscious*「無意識の，意図していない」
- *less A than B*「AというよりむしろB」
- *a mirror of A*「Aを映し出すもの［鏡］」
- *go on*「起こる」
- *signal*「合図」
- *disgusted face*「うんざりした顔」
- *disgust*「…に嫌気を起こさせる」
- *conversation*「会話」

第３パラグラフ

- *sensible*「賢明な，分別のある」
- *fundamental*「根源的な，基本となる」
- *instinctive*「本能的な」
- *fix*「…を定着［固定］させる」
- *viewpoint*「見地，見方」
- *criticize*「…を批判する」
- *challenge*「…に異議を唱える」
- *share*「…を分かち合う，…を共有する」
- *recognize*「…を認識する」
- *reflection*「反映，反映するもの」

第４パラグラフ

- *include*「（全体の一部として）…を含む」
- *recent work*「最近の研究」
- *B as well as A*「Aと同様Bも」

・native「原住民の」
・study participant「被験者，研究の参加者」
・attribute A to B「A（性質など）がBにあると考える」
・in the same way S V ...「…するのと同じように」
・declare that S V ...「…だと明言［断言］する」
・describe「…を説明［表現］する」
・deal with A「Aを扱う，Aに関係がある」
・B, not A「AではなくB」
・evidence that S V ...「…という証拠」

第5パラグラフ

・exhibit「…を表す，…を見せる」
・analysis「分析」
・a minority of A「Aの少数（の者）」

第6パラグラフ

・enormous「非常に大きい，莫大な」
・consequence「影響，帰結」
・field「分野」
・artificial intelligence「人工知能」
・specifically「特に，とりわけ」
・robotics「ロボット工学」
・a good number of A「かなりの数のA，非常にたくさんのA」
・example face「顔の実例」
・frown「しかめっ面をする，まゆをひそめる」
・signal「…に合図を送る，…に信号を送る」
・B other than A「A以外のB」
・unhappiness「不機嫌，不幸，不運」
・respond to A「Aに反応する，Aに応答する」
・incorrectly「不正確に，不適切に」

第7パラグラフ

・though「しかしながら」
・have most of an effect on A「Aに大いなる影響を与える」
・interpret「…を解釈する」
・It turns out that S V ...「…ということがわかる，（結果的に）…ということになる」
・communicate「コミュニケーションを行う」
・see A as B「AをBだと見なす」
・mirror「…を映し出す」
・not A but rather B「Aではなく（むしろ）B」
・hidden「隠れた，隠された」
・kind of like A「Aのようなもの」
・railroad track「鉄道線路」
・agree with A「Aに同意する」
・one's point of view「自分の見方」

第8パラグラフ

・take laughter「笑いを例にとる」
・absolutely「絶対的に，完全に」
・crucial「決定的な，きわめて重大な」
・poorly-timed「タイミングの悪い」
・reveal「（隠されていること）を明らかにする」
・inner joy「心の中の喜び」
・pay close attention to A「Aに細心の注意を払う」
・hostility「敵意」

第9パラグラフ

・calculating「打算的な，抜け目のない」

- compare A to B「AをBに例える」
- invisible「目に見えない」
- the other「相手」
- right back「まったく逆に」
- social creature「社会的な生き物」
- after all「結局」

第8問の【語句】リスト

第1パラグラフ

- psychologist「心理学者」
- experiment「実験」
- invite A into B「AをBに招き入れる」
- tiny「小さな」
- contain「(中味の全体として)…を含む」
- treat「おやつ，ご馳走」
- tray「お皿，お盆」
- marshmallow「マシュマロ」
- offer「提案，申し出」
- right away「すぐに，ただちに」
- be willing to do「…するのをいとわない，進んで…する」
- step out「外出する，席をはずす」
- not surprisingly「驚くことではないが，当然のことながら」

第2パラグラフ

- assume that S V ...「…だと思い込む」
- delay「…を遅らせる」
- gratification「満足」
- depend on A「Aによって決まる，Aにかかっている」
- willpower「意志力」
- allow O to do「Oが…するのを可能にする」
- resist「…に抵抗する」
- tempting「魅力的な，誘惑する」
- save money「貯金する」
- retirement「退職，隠居」
- participate in A「Aに参加する」
- conclude that S V ...「…だと結論づける」
- come to realize that S V ...「…ということがわかるようになる」
- inherently「本質的に，もともと」
- postpone「…を先延ばしにする」
- grit *one's* teeth「歯をくいしばる」
- in the face of A「Aにもかかわらず」
- temptation「誘惑」

第3パラグラフ

- without exception「例外なく」
- high delayer「先延ばしが上手な人」
- rely on A「Aに頼る」
- mental strategy「精神的戦略」
- find a way to do「…する方法を見つける」
- keep oneself from doing「…しないようにしておく」
- direct *one's* gaze away from A「Aから目を背ける，Aから視線を逸らす」
- delicious「(とても) おいしい」
- cover *one's* eyes「目を覆い隠す」
- hide-and-seek「かくれんぼ」
- tie *one's* shoelaces「靴ひもを結ぶ」
- pretend to do「…するフリをする」
- take a nap「昼寝をする」
- defeat「…を打ち負かす」

第4パラグラフ

- refer to A as B「AをBと呼ぶ」
- strategic「戦略的な，戦略上の」
- allocation「配分」
- attention「注意 (力)」
- argue that S V ...「…だと主張する」
- underline「…の根底にある，…の基礎となる」
- self-control「自制，克己」
- be about doing「…するということだ，

…することに関係している」
・*properly*「適切に」
・*direct*「…を方向づける，…を向ける」
・*spotlight*「スポットライト，注目」
・*look away*「目を逸らす」

第5パラグラフ

・*cognitive skill*「認知能力」
・*dieter*「ダイエットをする人」
・*core part*「核心部分」
・*follow up (with A)*「(A について) 追跡調査をする」
・*initial*「最初の」
・*subject*「被験者」
・*high school senior*「高校の最上級生」
・*task*「(課された) 作業 [仕事]，課題」
・*predictive*「予言的な」
・*a vast range of A*「非常に広範囲にわたる A」
・*struggle to do*「…しようともがく，…するのに悪戦苦闘する」
・*be likely to do*「…する可能性が高い」
・*behavioral problem*「行動上の問題」
・*stressful situation*「ストレスの多い状況」
・*have trouble doing*「…するのに苦労する」
・*pay attention*「注意を払う」
・*maintain*「…を維持する」
・*impressive*「印象的な」
・*academic number*「学業成績の数字」
・*score*「得点，点数」
・*on average*「平均して」

第6パラグラフ

・*correlation*「相関関係」
・*demonstrate*「…を実証する，…を示す」
・*strategically*「戦略的に」
・*allocate*「…を配分する」
・*resist*「…に抵抗する」
・*negative*「否定的な」
・*improve odds against A*「A に勝つ可能性を高める」
・*addiction*「中毒」
・*drive*「…を駆りたてる，…の原動力となる」
・*bounce*「弾む，活発に動く」
・*process*「過程」
・*consciously*「意識的に」
・*select*「…を選ぶ」

第7パラグラフ

・*furthermore*「さらに，その上に」
・*mental skill*「精神的能力」
・*valuable*「貴重な，価値のある」
・*the age of information*「情報 (化) の時代」
・*focus on A*「A に集中する，A に焦点を当てる」
・*incredibly*「信じられないほど」
・*a wealth of A*「豊富な A」
・*create*「…を生む，…を引き起こす」
・*poverty*「貧困，貧しさ」
・*bounded*「限界のある」
・*confusing*「困惑させる，混乱させる」
・*be full of A*「A でいっぱいである」
・*distraction*「気を散らすもの」
・*intelligence*「知性」
・*parse*「…を分析する」
・*make sense*「道理にかなう，意味をなす」

第８パラグラフ

・in recent decades「この数十年に」
・psychology「心理学」
・neuroscience「神経科学」
・severely「著しく，激しく」
・erode「…を侵食する」
・classical notion「伝統的な概念」
・free will「自由意志」
・unconscious mind「無意識の精神」
・It turns out that S V ...「(結果として) …ということになる」
・help O (to) do「O が…するのに役立つ」
・in the end「結局は，つまるところ」

第９問の【語句】リスト

第１パラグラフ

・*decades ago*「数十年前」
・*major source*「主要な源」
・*invite A to B*「AをBに招く」
・*colleague*「同僚」
・*efficient*「効率的な，能率的な」
・*form a friendship*「友人関係を築く」
・*productive*「生産的な，利益をもたらす」
・*meaningful relationship*「有意義な人間関係」

第２パラグラフ

・*national survey*「全国調査」
・*graduating*「卒業を控えている」
・*proportion*「比率，割合」
・*drop from A to B*「AからBに下がる」
・*start a company*「会社を起こす，起業する」
・*co-worker*「同僚」
・*increasingly*「ますます，だんだん」
・*focus A on B*「AをBに集中させる」
・*outside of work*「職場の外で」
・*norm*「標準，基準」
・*report doing*「…したことを報告する」
・*whereas S V ...*「(～)，だが一方…」

第３パラグラフ

・*be determined to do*「…することを決心している」
・*get down to A*「Aに本気で取りかかる」

第４パラグラフ

・*economic explanation*「経済的要因」
・*long-term employment*「長期雇用」
・*lifetime employment*「終身雇用」
・*disappear*「消える」
・*instead of doing*「…するのではなく」
・*career*「経歴，キャリア」
・*expect to do*「…するつもりである，…すると思っている」
・*move on*「(よい仕事に) 移る」
・*every few years*「数年ごとに」
・*forever*「永久に」
・*view A as B*「AをBだと見なす」
・*temporary*「一時的な」
・*presence*「存在」
・*greet*「…にあいさつをする」
・*arm's-length*「親密でない」
・*reserve*「…を取っておく」
・*treat*「…を扱う」
・*the way S V ...*「…するように」
・*stranger*「見知らぬ人」
・*sit next to A*「Aの隣に座る」
・*have a conversation with A*「Aと会話する」
・*on a long-distance train*「長距離列車で」
・*single-serving*「一回限りの」

第５パラグラフ

・*observer*「評論家」
・*blame*「…のせいにする，…の責任にする」
・*flexible working hours*「フレックスタイム制」
・*working from home*「在宅勤務」
・*remotely*「離れて，遠くで」
・*face-to-face*「向かい合って (の)」
・*encounter*「出会い，遭遇」
・*be critical to A*「Aにとって極めて重要である」

・as long as S V …「…する限り」
・per week「一週間につき」
・have an effect on A「Aに影響を及ぼす」
・quality「質，性質」
・workplace「職場，仕事場」
・affect「…に影響する」
・be constantly in touch with A「Aと絶えず連絡を取り合う」
・bother doing「わざわざ…する」
・connect A to B「AをBにつなぐ，AをBに接続する」
・round the clock「24時間ぶっ通しで」
・face「…に直面する」
・shortage「不足」
・the pressure to do「…せよという圧力［重圧］」
・get work done「仕事を終えてしまう」
・outweigh「…よりも重要だ，…を上回る」
・the desire to socialize「人付き合いをしたいという欲求」
・slave「奴隷」

第6パラグラフ

・sociologist「社会学者」
・argue that S V …「…だと主張する」
・peculiar「独特の，特有の」
・demand「…を要求する」
・go even further「さらにその先まで行く，それだけにとどまらない」
・avoid doing「…することを避ける」
・attention to A「Aに注意を向けること」
・emotion「感情」
・distract O doing「…することからOの注意を逸らす，Oの気を紛らわせて…できなくする」
・do God's will「神の意志を実践する」
・over time「やがて，時と共に」
・influence「…に影響を及ぼす」
・come to do「…するようになる」
・productivity「生産性」
・in particular「とりわけ，特に」
・mix A with B「AをBと混ぜる［混合する］」
・design「…を考案する」
・noticeably「著しく，目立って」
・fall from A to B「AからBに下がる」
・the number of A「Aの数」
・racial and gender diversity「人種や性別の多様性」
・common「ふつうの，ありふれた」
・take A for granted「Aを当然だと見なす」
・work ethic「職業倫理」
・persist「根強く持続する」

第7パラグラフ

・regardless of A「Aとは関係なく」
・race「人種」
・religion「宗教」
・generational shift「世代交代」
・reinforce「…をより強力にする，…を強化する」
・the idea that S V …「…という考え」
・place a value on A「Aに価値を置く」
・leisure time「余暇，自由時間」
・steadily「着実に」
・more than A「A以上」
・less than A「A未満，A足らず」
・see A as B「AをBだと見なす」
・primarily「主に，第1に」
・means to A「Aの手段」

・convince *oneself* that S V ...「…だと思い込む，…だと自分に言い聞かせる」
・efficiency「効率性」

第8パラグラフ

・underestimate「…を過小評価する」
・the impact of A on B「AがBに及ぼす影響」
・effectiveness「能率性」
・satisfying「満足のいく，納得のいく」
・provide「…を提供する」
・opportunity to *do*「…する機会」
・trusting「信じやすい，信頼する」
・be committed to A「Aに専心する，Aに献身する」
・facilities「施設，設備」
・employee「従業員」
・share「…を分かち合う，…を共有する」
・suggest that S V ...「…ということを示唆［暗示］する」
・promote「…を促進する」
・cooperation「協力（すること）」

第10問の【語句】リスト

第1パラグラフ

・the civil rights movement「公民権運動」
・benefit「…に利益を与える」
・not only A but (also) B「AだけではなくBも」
・minority「少数派，少数民族」
・Hispanic「ヒスパニック，ラテンアメリカ系の人」
・racial discrimination「人種差別」
・employment「雇用」
・housing「住宅（供給）」
・forbid「…を禁ずる」
・advance「…を前進させる，…を進める」
・reinforce「…を強化する，…をより強力にする」
・the ideal of equality of opportunity「機会の平等という理想」

第2パラグラフ

・paradox「パラドックス，逆説」
・the amount of diversity「多様性の総量，多様性の全体的な規模」
・continue to do「…し続ける」
・with each census「国勢調査のたびに」
・reveal that S V ...「…ということを明らかにする」
・segregation「隔離，分離」
・according to A「Aに応じて，Aによれば」
・race「人種」
・ethnicity「民族性，民族的背景」
・persist「根強く存在［存続］する，固執する」
・realize「…を（はっきり）理解する」
・on the one hand「一方で」
・be friends with A「Aと友人である」
・marry「…と結婚する」
・ethnic background「民族的背景」
・poll「世論調査」
・the (vast) majority of A「大多数のA，Aの大多数」
・on the other hand「他方で」
・segregate「…を隔離する，…を分離する」
・community「地域社会，コミュニティ」
・trend「傾向」
・move into A「A（の中）に移動する」
・suburb「郊外，都市の周辺部」
・ethnically「民族的に（見て）」
・diverse「異なった，多様な」
・neighborhood「地区，区域」
・do exist「実際に存在する」
・a number of A「たくさんのA」
・exception「例外」
・B rather than A「AというよりはむしろB」
・the rule「普通のこと，常態」

第3パラグラフ

・sociology「社会学」
・phenomenon「現象」
・report that S V ...「…だと報告する」
・separate A from B「AをBから分離する」
・Latino「米国在住のラテンアメリカ人」
・descent「血統，家系」
・in fact「いや実際は，それどころか」
・dominate「…を支配する，…を牛耳る」

- urban「都市の」
- decade「10年間」
- spread to A「A まで広がる」
- fast-growing「成長の早い，急成長している」
- people of color「有色人種」
- housing development「（低所得者向けの）住宅（団）地」
- B apart from A「A から離れた B」
- continue into future「未来へ続く」

第4パラグラフ

- choose to *do*「…する方を選ぶ」
- individual「個人」
- have the freedom to *do*「…する自由を持つ」
- provide「…を提供する」
- valuable support「貴重な支援」
- immigrant「移民」
- grocery store「食料品店」
- particularly「とりわけ，特に」
- participate in A「A に参加する」
- cultural festival「文化的なお祭りイベント」
- see A as B「A を B だと見なす」
- enrich「…を豊かにする」

第5パラグラフ

- negative side「マイナス面」
- this picture「この状況」
- gulf「大きな隔たり，格差」
- represent「…に相当する」
- grossly「大いに，極めて，著しく」
- under-represented「十分に代表されていない」
- Congress「（米国の）連邦議会」
- be true of A「A に当てはまる」
- medium「中間の，中位の」
- income「収入」
- married「既婚の」
- significantly「著しく，かなり」
- be against the law「法律に違反している」
- residential pattern「居住のパターン」
- create「…を生み出す」
- be likely to *do*「…する可能性が高い」
- condition「状況，状態」
- education「教育」
- trap A in B「A を B に閉じ込める」
- cycle「循環」
- poverty「貧困」
- unemployment「失業」
- violence「暴力」
- despair「絶望」
- frequent「頻繁な，常習的な」
- victim「犠牲者」
- violent crime「暴力犯罪」
- as many as A「A も」
- criminal record「犯罪歴」

第6パラグラフ

- believe in A「A を（正しいと）信じる」
- search for A「A を探し求める」
- chance「機会」
- attract「…を引きつける，…を魅了する」
- inspire「…を鼓舞する，…を激励する」
- in reality「現実には」
- financial resources「経済的資産」
- educational background「学歴」
- skill「技能」
- the Middle East「中東」

・socioeconomic level「社会経済的レベル」
・experience「経験」
・the Vietnamese「ベトナムの人々」
・the educated elite「教育を受けたエリート層」
・farmer「農民」
・fisherman「漁師」
・Cuban「キューバ人」
・wealth「富，財産」

第11問の【語句】リスト

第1パラグラフ

- according to A「Aによれば」
- definition「定義」
- being「存在」
- concept「概念」
- limit A to B「AをBに制限する」
- species「種」
- definitely「絶対に，決して」
- produce「（音）を出す，…を生む」
- branch「枝」
- creak「ギシギシ音を立てる」
- rub against A「Aにこすれる」
- leaf「葉」
- rustle「ざわざわと音を立てる」
- have no control over A「Aを全くコントロールできない」
- It turns out (that) S V ...「（結果として）…ということになる，…ということがわかる」
- completely「完全に」
- communicate「コミュニケーションを行う」
- scent「香り」

第2パラグラフ

- as a means of A「Aの手段として」
- not (...) totally「全く…というわけではない」
- be unfamiliar to A「A（人）に知られていない」
- deodorant「消臭剤，防臭剤」
- perfume「香水，香料」
- product「製品」
- smell「匂い，香り」
- consciously「意識して，故意に」
- subconsciously「潜在意識的に」
- attract A to B「AをBに引きつける」
- because of A「Aの理由で」
- aroma「芳香，香り」
- pheromone「フェロモン」
- decisive「決定的な」
- factor「要因，要素」
- It seems fair to say that S V ...「…と言っても差し支えないように思われる」
- demonstrate that S V ...「…ということを実証する，…ということを示す」

第3パラグラフ

- decade「10年間」
- notice「…に気づく，…に注目する」
- giraffe「キリン」
- feed on A「Aを餌にする，Aを常食とする」
- not (...) one bit「少しも…ない」
- It takes O_1 O_2 *to do*「O_1が…するのにO_2（時間）がかかる」
- pump A into B「AをBに送り込む，AをBに注入する」
- toxic「有毒な」
- substance「物質」
- rid A of B「AからBを取り除く」
- rid *oneself* of B「Bから逃れる，Bから抜け出す」
- move on to A「Aに移動する」
- area「地域」
- close by「すぐ近くの［に］」
- for the time being「当分の間，さしあたり」
- resume「…を再び始める」

・meal「食事」

第4パラグラフ

・behavior「行動」
・astonishing「驚くべき，びっくりさせるような」
・give off A「Aを発する」
・warning gas「警告ガス」
・signal to A that S V ...「…だとAに合図する」
・neighboring「近隣の，近所の」
・crisis「危機，重大局面」
・at hand「差し迫った，近くに［の］」
・right away「すぐに，ただちに」
・prepare *oneself*「準備する，覚悟する」
・move farther away to A「より遠く離れたAまで移動する」
・be unaware of A「Aに気づいていない，Aを知らない」
・go on「起こる」
・upwind「風上に［の］」
・carry A to B「AをBに運ぶ」
・nearby「近くの」
・breeze「微風，そよ風」
・have no idea (that) S V ...「…ということを全く知らない」

第5パラグラフ

・similar「よく似た，類似した」
・process「プロセス，過程」
・at work「働いている，活動している」
・register「…を表す，…を示す」
・pain「苦痛，痛み」
・as soon as S V ...「…するとすぐに」
・creature「動物，生き物」
・take a bite out of A「Aをひとかじりする，Aをひと口食べる」
・hearty「食欲旺盛な，元気な」
・tissue「（細胞の）組織」
・site「場所」
・damage「損傷」
・in addition「その上，さらに加えて」
・send out A「Aを放つ」
・electrical signal「電気信号」
・just as S V ...「…とちょうど同じように」
・hurt「傷ついた，けがをした」
・transmit「…を伝える」
・in millisecond「ミリ秒で」
・instead「そうではなく，そうしないで」
・travel「伝わる」
・a third of A「Aの3分の1」
・inch「インチ」
・per minute「毎分，一分につき」
・accordingly「したがって，それゆえに」
・defensive「防御用の，防御的な」
・compound「化合物」
・spoil「…を台無しにする」
・pest「害虫」
・slow lane「低速車線」
・be in danger「危険な状態にある」
・mean that S V ...「…ということを意味する」
・on top of A「Aを完全に支配して」
・structure「構造」
・root「根」
・find *oneself* in trouble「厄介な状況に陥っている（のに気づく）」
・broadcast「…を伝える，…を伝わる」
・trigger O to *do*「Oが…する引き金となる，Oが…するきっかけとなる」
・release「…を放つ」

・*not just A but (also) B*「単に A だけでなく B も」
・*specifically*「特に，とりわけ」
・*formulate*「…を考案する」

第6パラグラフ

・*feature*「特徴」
・*help O (to) do*「O が…するのに役立つ」
・*avoid attack*「攻撃から逃れる」
・*for a while*「しばらくの間」
・*when it comes to A*「A ということになると」
・*insect*「昆虫」
・*accurately*「正確に」
・*identify*「…を特定する，…を識別する」
・*bad guy*「悪いやつ，悪玉」
・*up against A*「A と対立して，A に直面して」
・*match A to B*「A を B とつり合わせる，A を B と照合して一致させる」
・*match*「つり合うもの，適合（すること），照合（すること）」
・*precise*「正確な，的確な」
・*pheromone*「フェロモン」
・*summon*「…を招集する，…を呼び出す」
・*specific*「特定の，はっきりした」
・*beneficial*「有益な，利益をもたらす」
・*predator*「捕食植物」
・*eagerly*「熱心に」
・*eat up A*「A を食べ尽くす」
・*bother*「…を悩ませる」
・*call on A*「A を招集する」
・*parasitic*「寄生性の，寄生的な」
・*lay one's egg*「卵を産む」
・*bit by bit*「少しずつ」
・*from the inside out*「内側から外に向かって」
・*die*「死ぬ」
・*The result is that S V ....*「その結果…ということになる」
・*save A from B*「A を B から救う」
・*bothersome*「厄介な」
・*keep doing*「…し続ける」
・*the fact (that) S V ...*「…という事実」
・*recognize*「…を認識する，…を識別する」
・*incidentally*「付随的に，偶然に」
・*evidence for A*「A を裏づける証拠」
・*a sense of taste*「味覚」

第12問の【語句】リスト

第1パラグラフ

・company「会社」
・employee「従業員」
・vacation「(旅行などのための) 休暇」
・require「…を必要とする」
・booking「予約」
・tourism「観光産業，観光旅行」
・increasing「ますます増加する」
・complaint「不満」
・be overwhelmed with A「Aに圧倒されている」
・tourist「観光客，旅行者」
・furthermore「その上，さらに」
・fragile「もろい，壊れやすい」
・natural site「自然の景勝地」
・coral reef「サンゴ礁」
・rainforest「熱帯雨林」
・place restrictions upon[on] A「Aに制限を加える」

第2パラグラフ

・restrain「…を規制［制限］する」
・first and foremost「何よりもまず，いの一番に」
・duty「義務」
・the global environment「地球環境」
・illustration「実例，例」
・remote「遠く隔たった，遠い」
・location「場所，位置」
・help O (to) do「Oが…するのに役立つ」
・develop「…を展開する，…を進展させる」
・evolution「進化論，進化」
・tens of thousands of A「何万ものA」
・cannot help but do「…せざるを得ない」
・bring about A「Aをもたらす，Aを引き起こす」
・pollution「汚染，公害」
・human waste「人間の排泄物」
・food waste「食品廃棄物」
・non-native species「外来生物」
・distant「遠い」
・shore「陸（地）」
・extreme example「極端な例」
・put a strain on A「Aに負担をかける」
・create「…を引き起こす」
・excess traffic「交通過多，交通渋滞」
・overcrowding「大混雑，過密状態」

第3パラグラフ

・historical site「史跡」
・immune「影響を受けない，免疫のある」
・experience「…を経験する」
・via A「Aの媒介で，Aを通じて」
・appreciation「鑑賞」
・heritage「文化的［歴史的］遺産」
・fail to do「(意志に反して) …しない」
・promote「…を促進する」
・meaningful cultural exchange「有意義な文化交流」
・attract「…を引きつける」
・endure「…に耐える」
・queue「列」
・only to do「だが結局…する」
・brief explanation「簡単な説明」
・limited「限られた，有限の」
・in line「一列に並んで」
・worthwhile「価値がある，やり甲斐のある」

・*magnet*「人を引きつける場所」
・*promise*「…を約束する」
・*authentic*「本物の，真正の」
・*be obliged to do*「…せざるをえない，…することを余儀なくされる」
・*ultimately*「結局，最終的に」
・*fake*「偽物」
・*mass*「たくさんの，多数の」
・*false*「誤った，間違った」
・*accurately*「正確に」
・*instead*「そうではなく」
・*offer a fantasy*「ファンタジー[空想]を提供する」
・*no better than A*「Aと同じレベルに過ぎない，A同然の」

第4パラグラフ

・*promoter*「促進者，奨励者」
・*cite*「…を引き合いに出す，…を引用する」
・*economic advantage*「経済的利点」
・*benefit*「利益」
・*exaggerate*「…を誇張する」
・*housekeeping*「客室清掃」
・*retail*「小売り」
・*transport*「輸送」
・*hold little attraction for A*「Aにとってほとんど魅力がない」
・*youth*「若い人たち」
・*turn to A to do*「Aに…することを頼る」
・*immigrant labor*「移民労働者」
・*moreover*「さらに，その上」
・*seasonal*「ある季節だけに限った，季節的な」
・*suffer*「…を受ける，…に耐える［苦しむ］」
・*off-season*「閑散期，オフシーズン」
・*due to A*「Aが原因で」
・*the slowdown in income*「収入の減少」
・*worse still*「さらに悪いことに」
・*increase in A*「Aの増加」
・*crime*「犯罪」
・*cater for A*「Aの要求を満たす，Aに応じる」
・*bar*「酒場，バー」
・*unsurprisingly*「驚くことではないが，当然のことながら」
・*the locals*「地元の人々」
・*economic boom*「経済の盛況[急成長]」
・*hope for A*「Aを望む」
・*disturbance*「不安，心配，混乱」
・*affect*「…に影響する」

第5パラグラフ

・*desire for profit*「利潤の追求，利益の欲求」
・*drive*「…を促進する」
・*rapid growth*「急成長」
・*fastest-growing*「最も急速に成長する」
・*industry*「産業」
・*according to A*「Aによれば」
・*close to A*「A近く，ほとんどA」
・*billion*「10億」
・*generate*「…を生み出す，…を発生させる」
・*trillion*「1兆」
・*export earnings*「輸出収入」
・*forecast*「…を予想する，…を予測する」

第6パラグラフ

・*nevertheless*「それにもかかわらず」

・*illusion*「幻想，錯覚」
・*less than half of A*「Aの半分未満」
・*income*「収入」
・*mainly because of A*「主としてAという理由［原因］で」
・*arrange*「…を取り決める，…を企画［計画］する」
・*rely on A*「Aに依存する，Aに頼る」
・*foreign-owned*「外国人［外国企業］所有の，外資系の」
・*airline*「航空会社」
・*pay for A*「Aの代金を支払う」
・*access*「…を利用できる，…を入手できる」
・*added*「追加された，付け加えられた」
・*excessive*「過度の，度を越した」
・*existing*「既存の」
・*water supply*「水道設備」
・*ambulance*「救急車」
・*taxpayer*「納税者」
・*housing price*「住宅価格」
・*the supply of accommodation*「住居の供給」

第7パラグラフ

・*eco-tourism*「エコツーリズム，環境を意識した観光旅行」
・*emphasis on A*「Aの強調，Aの重視」
・*sustainability*「持続可能性」
・*small-scale*「小規模の」
・*operation*「運営，運行」
・*portray O as C*「OをCであると描写する」
・*issue*「問題（点），争点」
・*the problem of scale*「規模の問題」
・*negative*「否定的な」
・*environmental*「環境上の」
・*venture*「ベンチャー事業」
・*an abundance of A*「豊富なA，Aの豊富さ」
・*necessarily*「必然的に」
・*contradiction*「矛盾，矛盾する言動」
・*term*「言語，用語」
・*weaken*「…を弱める」
・*tourist demand*「観光需要」
・*address*「…に取り組む，…に立ち向かう」
・*external*「外的な」
・*employ*「…を使用する，…を利用する」
・*some version of A*「何らかの形のA」
・*tourism tax*「観光税」
・*worldwide*「世界中で［に］」
・*funds*「資金」

第8パラグラフ

・*doubt*「…を疑う」
・*evidence*「証拠」
・*suggest (that) S V ...*「…だと示唆［暗示］する」
・*as S put it*「Sが述べたように，Sの言葉を借りれば」
・*explore*「…を探検する，…を探究する」
・*corner*「隅，隅の部分」
・*the globe*「地球」
・*living room*「居間」
・*explorer*「探検家」
・*a form of A*「Aの一形態」
・*entertainment*「娯楽」
・*leisure*「余暇（活動）」
・*moderation*「節度」

第13問の【語句】リスト

第1パラグラフ

・experiment「実験」
・hand over A「Aを手渡す」
・in exchange for A「Aと交換に」
・cucumber「キュウリ」
・deal「取引」

第2パラグラフ

・randomly「無作為に，でたらめに」
・within sight of A「Aの見えるところで」
・fellow「仲間，（一対のものの）片方」
・thrilled「ぞくぞくして，興奮して」

第3パラグラフ

・present「…を進呈する，…を贈呈する」
・pebble「小石」
・insulting「侮辱的な，無礼な」
・throw A back at B「AをBめがけて投げ返す」
・in anger and disgust「怒りと反感で」

第4パラグラフ

・in other words「言い換えれば」
・care about A「Aを気にする，Aに関心がある」
・fairness「公平（性），公正」
・matter「重要である」
・not just A but also B「単にAだけでなくBも」

第5パラグラフ

・offend「…に不快感を与える」
・inequality「不平等」
・scholar「学者」
・examine「…を調べる，…を検査する」
・identify「…を特定する」
・factor「要素，要因」
・result in A「Aに終わる，Aの結果となる」
・incident「事件，出来事」
・passenger「乗客」

第6パラグラフ

・be four times as likely「起こる可能性が4倍ある」
・the risk of A「Aの危険性［リスク］」
・disturbance「騒動，混乱」
・delay「遅延，延期」
・typically「概して，一般的に」
・walk through A「（歩いて）Aを通り抜ける」
・get on「乗る」
・in the middle of A「Aの中央部で，Aの真ん中で」
・scenario「（考えられる）状況，一連の事柄」
・compared with A「Aと比較すると」
・bypass「…を回避する，…を迂回する」

第7パラグラフ

・psychology「心理学」
・brilliant「すばらしい，見事な，異彩を放つ」
・destabilize「…を不安定にする」
・fascinating「魅力的な」
・work「著作，作品」
・argue that S V ...「…だと主張する」
・public-health crisis「公衆衛生上の危機」

第8パラグラフ

・reveal「…を明らかにする」

・annual「年１回の，毎年の」
・bonus「ボーナス，賞与」
・pool「(配当金などの）総額」
・year-round「年間を通じて（の)」
・earnings「所得」
・minimum「最小限の」
・wage「賃金」
・an hour「１時間につき」
・according to A「A によれば」
・weaken「…を弱める」
・tie「絆」
・hold A together「A を団結させる」

第９パラグラフ

・challenge「…に異議を唱える」
・common「共通の，共有の」
・perception that S V ...「…という認識」
・not A but B「A ではなく B」
・poverty「貧困」
・be persuasive that S V ...「…ということに説得力がある」
・shape「…を形作る」
・disadvantage「不利（な状況)」
・spectrum「領域，範囲」
・address「…に取り組む，…に立ち向かう」
・priority「優先事項」
・social creature「社会的な生き物」

第10パラグラフ

・breakdown「崩壊」
・affect「…に影響する」
・those at the bottom「底辺層の人々」
・pay O_1 O_2「O_1 に O_2 を支払う」
・a much wider range of A「はるかに広範囲に及ぶ A」
・salary「給料，給与」
・incentive「動機」

第11パラグラフ

・analyze「…を分析する」
・opposite「正反対なこと［もの］」
・bond「絆」

第12パラグラフ

・what is more「さらには」
・It turns out that S V ...「…であることがわかる」
・flat「平らな，均一の，一律の」
・pay「報酬，給料」
・have a negative effect on A「A にマイナスの影響を与える」
・be meant to do「…することになっている，…するために意図されている」
・expect「…を予想する」
・reduce「…を弱める」
・cooperation「協調性，協力」
・team unity「チームの団結［結束］」

第13パラグラフ

・similar「類似した，よく似た」
・emerge「現れる，出現する」
・statistics「統計」
・gap「格差，隔たり」
・including A「A を含めて」
・killing「殺害，殺すこと」

第14パラグラフ

・instinctively「本能的に」
・liberal「リベラル派の人」
・company president「会社の社長」
・average「平均的な」
・conservative「保守派の人」

・public company「株式公開会社」

第15パラグラフ

・be presented with A「Aを示される，Aを提示される」
・unlabeled「ラベルのついていない，分類されていない」
・chart「グラフ，図表」
・depict「…を描く，…を描写する」
・income distribution「所得の分布」
・prefer to do「…する方を好む」
・modest「控えめな」
・Republican「共和党員」
・Democrat「民主党員」
・A and B alike「AもBも同様に」
・by similar margins「同じような差で」

第16パラグラフ

・ignore「…を無視する」
・act strange「奇妙な行動を取る」
・in the same fashion「同じやり方で」
・systematic「体系的な」
・predictable「予測可能な」
・again and again「何度も何度も」

第17パラグラフ

・make O do「Oに…させる」
・odd thing「奇妙なこと」
・superstitiously「迷信的に」
・cling to A「Aに執着する，Aにしがみつく」
・B rather than A「AというよりむしろB」
・the way S is「ありのままのS」
・divide「…を分ける，…を引き離す」
・split A into B「AをBに分割する」
・camp「同志，仲間，グループ」
・ideology「イデオロギー，観念形態」
・race「人種」
・eat away at A「Aを浸食する，Aをむしばむ」
・trust「信頼」
・one another「お互い」
・generate「…を生み出す，…を発生させる」

第18パラグラフ

・in the context of A「Aの背景の中で，Aの文脈の中で」
・politics「政治」
・term「言葉，用語」
・division「分断」
・sound familiar「聞き覚えがある」

第19パラグラフ

・the national conversation「国について話されること」
・get focused on A「Aに集中する」
・individual「個人」
・B such as A「AのようなB」
・understandable「理解できる」
・suspect that S V ...「…ではないかと思う」
・cause「原因」
・uncover「…を明らかにする，…を暴く」
・root「根，根源」
・go deeper「より深くまで進む，より奥まで行く」
・confront「…と向かい合う，…と対峙する」

第14問の【語句】リスト

第1パラグラフ

- recent「最近の」
- the Netherlands「オランダ」
- apparently「見たところでは(…らしい)」
- protest「抗議」
- cost「費用」
- payment「支払い」
- grit one's teeth「歯ぎしりをする，歯をくいしばる」
- in preparation for A「Aに備えて」
- a year「一年につき」

第3パラグラフ

- university「大学」
- in the end「結局は，最終的に」
- cost O_1 O_2「O_1にO_2（お金）がかかる」
- less than A「A未満」
- compare A to B「AをBと比較する」
- higher education「高等教育」
- private school「私立学校」
- out-of-state resident「州外居住者」
- attend「…に通う」

第4パラグラフ

- key data point「重要なデータ上のポイント」
- hold A in one's mind「Aを心に抱く」
- address「…に講演をする，…に演説する」
- talk「講演，講話」
- title O C「OにCと名称を与える」
- define A to B「AをBと定義する」
- include「(全体の一部として)…を含む」
- term「用語，言葉」
- be used to do「…するために用いられる」
- contrast A with B「AをBと対比させる」
- focus on A「Aに集中する」
- philosophy「哲学」
- technical subject「技術系科目」
- B such as A「AのようなB」
- engineering「工学」

第5パラグラフ

- in spite of A「Aにもかかわらず」
- fail to do「(意志に反して)…しない」
- place a heavy emphasis on A「Aをとても重視する」
- missed opportunity「機会の逸失」
- without A「Aがなければ」
- base「基礎，基盤」
- democratic society「民主社会」
- informed citizen「知識人，知識のある市民」
- deny O_1 O_2「O_1にO_2を与えない」
- a full view of the heritage「遺産の全景，遺産の全体像をとらえること」
- critical habits of mind「批判的な思考習慣」

第6パラグラフ

- value「価値，重要性」
- question whether S V ...「…であるかどうかを問う」
- see A as B「AをBだと見なす」
- higher vocational training「高等職業訓練」
- specific「特有の，特定的な」

・certification「資格」

第7パラグラフ

・push back「反対する，抵抗する」

第8パラグラフ

・sole「唯一の，ただひとつの」
・chance「機会」
・deeply「深く」
・broadly「広く」
・turn A into B「AをBに変える」
・nothing more than A「Aにすぎない，まさにA」
・emphasize「…を強調する，…を重視する」
・pay well「給料が良い，十分割に合う」
・represent「…を表す，…を表現する」

第9パラグラフ

・traditional「伝統的な，従来の」
・vs.「…に対して，…対」
・standpoint「観点，見地」
・scholar「学者」
・stand by A「Aを支持する」
・defend「…を擁護する」
・to the last breath「最後まで，死ぬまで」

第10パラグラフ

・no longer「もはや（…）ない」

第11パラグラフ

・alter「…を変える，…を改める」
・equation「均衡，平衡」
・vast change「巨大な変化」
・sweep through A「Aに急速に広まる」
・with the advent of A「Aの到来とともに」
・run「…を動かす」
・information「情報」
・i.e.「すなわち，言い換えれば」
・with O in mind「Oを考えて，Oを念頭に置くと」
・updated「更新した，最新の」
・response to A「Aに対する返答」

第12パラグラフ

・during the course of one's life「人生を生きていく中で」
・expect to do「…するつもりである，…すると思っている」
・multiple「多数の，複数の」
・career「経歴」
・phase「段階，時期」
・a wide range of A「広範囲に及ぶ[さまざまな] A」
・screenplay「（映画の）シナリオ」
・movie-related「映画に関連した」
・effort「取り組み，試み」
・get one's hands dirty「汚れ仕事［過酷な仕事］をする」
・system architecture「システム構築」
・likewise「同様に」
・start up「立ち上がる」
・put a high value on A「Aに重きを置く」
・storytelling「物語を書くこと[話すこと]」
・require O to do「Oに…することを要求する」
・the relationship between A and B「AとBの関係」
・realm「領域，分野，界」

第13パラグラフ

・combined with A「Aと相まって」

- ever-spiraling「絶えず急上昇する」
- mean that S V ...「…ということを意味する」
- strive for A「Aを目指して努力する」
- clarity「明快さ，明確さ」
- choice「選択」
- fall into A「A（罠など）に落ちる」
- trap「罠，策略」
- educational consumerism「教育消費主義」
- status「高い立場，ステータス」
- opportunity「機会」
- hope for A「Aを望む」
- excellent「非常にすぐれた，優秀な」
- out there「世の中には，外には」
- get into debt「借金を負う」
- expected「想定された，予期された」
- outcome「結果」
- long to do「…することを切望する」
- poet「詩人」
- by all means「何としてでも，ぜひとも」
- pursue「…を追求する」
- passion「情熱」
- realistic「現実的な，実際的な」
- graduate「卒業する」
- be prepared「備える，準備する」
- issue「問題（点）」
- wisely「賢明に」

第14パラグラフ

- the real pressure to do「…せよという現実のプレッシャー［圧力］」
- the understanding that S V ...「…という理解」
- intellectually「知的に」
- morally「道徳的に」
- spiritually「精神的に」
- deal with A「Aに対処する，Aに対応する」
- dilemma「ジレンマ，板ばさみ」
- argue that S V ...「…だと主張する」
- path「たどる道，方針，方向」
- viable「実現可能な，実行可能な」
- alternative plan「代替プラン，代わりの計画」
- double major「2つの専攻科目」
- span「…に橋をかける」
- divide「隔たり」
- culture「文化」

第15問の【語句】リスト

第1パラグラフ

- long-established「長い歴史を持つ」
- government organization「政府機関」
- fund「…に資金を提供する」
- nation「国，国家」
- support「…を支援する，…を援助する」
- not only A but also B「A だけでなく B も」
- a variety of A「さまざまな A」
- including A「A を含めて」
- painting「絵画」
- sculpture「彫刻」
- folk art「民芸（品）」
- cultural institution「文化施設」
- B such as A「A のような B」
- library「図書館」
- theater「劇場」
- museum「博物館」
- in addition「その上，さらに」
- an array of A「ずらりと並んだ A，一連の A」
- encourage O to *do*「O に…するように励ます［勧める］」
- critical「重大な，決定的に重要な」
- especially「とりわけ，特に」
- during economic recessions「経済的な景気後退の時期に」
- far from *doing*「…するどころか」
- withdraw「…を取り消す，…を撤回する」
- state money「国からの資金」
- protect「…を守る」
- increase「…を増やす」
- government funding「政府の資金提供」

第2パラグラフ

- to begin with「まず第一に」
- enrich「…を豊かにする」
- former「以前の」
- director「館長」
- necessity「必要不可欠なもの，必需品」
- individual「個人」
- community「共同体，地域社会」
- choir「合唱団，聖歌隊」
- extraordinary「並はずれた，普通でない」
- poetry「詩」
- share in A「A を分かち合う，A を共有する」
- excitement「興奮」
- worthwhile「価値がある」
- furthermore「さらに，その上」
- in an age of A「A の時代に」
- migration「移住，移動」
- serve an important role in A「A において重要な役割を果たす」
- bring A together「A をまとめる」
- citizen「国民」
- common experience「共通の経験」
- accommodate「…を調整する」
- difference「相違，違い」

第3パラグラフ

- represent「…を象徴する，…を表す」
- heritage「遺産」
- identity「独自性」
- firmly「しっかりと，堅く」
- root「…を根付かせる」
- preserve「…を保存する」
- various「さまざまな」

- according to A「Aによれば」
- novelist「小説家」
- wonder「驚異，驚嘆」
- archive「公文書館，公文書保管所」
- relate A with B「AをBと関連づける」
- stretch back A「Aをさかのぼる」
- shape「形，姿」
- humanity「人類」
- fit into A「Aにはまる，Aに合う」
- indeed「実際は」
- at the very heart of A「まさにAの中心部に」
- heritage-related「遺産に関連した」
- therefore「それゆえに，したがって」
- duty「義務」

第4パラグラフ

- nevertheless「それにもかかわらず」
- field「分野」
- sustain「…を維持する」
- independently「独立して」
- require「…を要求する」
- constant「絶えず続く，不変の」
- continue「継続する」
- in contrast to A「Aとは対照的に，Aとは違って」
- commercially「商業的に」
- grand「堂々たる，立派な」
- lack stability「安定性を欠く」
- limit「…を制限する」
- non-profit「非営利の」
- organization「機関，団体，組織体」
- maintain「…を維持する」
- facility「施設，設備」
- offer「…を提供する」
- support「援助，支援」
- grant「補助金，助成金」
- moreover「さらに，その上」
- artistic innovation「芸術の革新」
- enable O to do「Oが…するのを可能にする」
- take a risk「リスクを冒す」
- experiment「実験する」
- for the sake of art itself「芸術そのもののために」

第5パラグラフ

- argue that S V ...「…だと主張する」
- wherever possible「可能な場合はどこでも」
- private donation「民間からの寄付金」
- replace「…に取って代わる」
- relatively「比較的」
- secure「確実な，確保された」
- take A for granted「Aを当然のことだと見なす」
- extremely「極度に，きわめて」
- wealthy「裕福な」
- corporation「（民間）企業」
- dominate「…を支配している」
- the global economy「世界経済」
- ask A of B「BにAをくれと頼む」
- charitable「慈善的な」
- sector「部門」
- only go so far「そこまでしか行けない，限界がある」
- unwise「賢明でない」
- make A dependent on B「AをBに依存させる」
- overly「過度に，あまりにも」
- political「政治的な，政治に関する」
- economic「経済（上）の」

・demand「需要」
・private enterprise「民間企業」
・difficulty「困難」
・be at risk「危険にさらされている」

第6パラグラフ

・by contrast「対照的に」
・stable「安定した」
・as many (A) as possible「できるだけ多くのA」
・ensure「…を確実にする，…を保証する」
・affordable「手頃な，手の届く範囲の」
・access to A「Aを利用［入手］する機会，Aに触れる機会」
・an integral part of daily life「日常生活の欠かせない一部」
・allow O to do「Oが…するのを可能にする」
・common ground「共通の立場」
・despite A「Aにもかかわらず」
・income inequality「所得の不平等」
・well-to-do「裕福な」
・gain an understanding of A「Aを理解する」

第7パラグラフ

・benefit「利益」
・attract「…を引きつける」
・in turn「今度は，次に」
・promote「…を促進する」
・redevelopment「再開発」
・suburb「郊外」
・tourism-related「観光関連の」
・recognize A as B「AをBだと認める」
・valuable「貴重な，価値のある」
・resources「資源」
・play a part in A「Aにおいて役割を果たす，Aに役立つ」
・renewal「再生，再開発」
・post-industrial「脱工業化の，脱工業化時代の」
・take up the idea of A as B「AがBだという考えを取り上げる」
・creative「創造的な」
・subsequently「その後に，それに続いて」
・develop「…を練り上げる，…を進展させる」
・widen「…を拡大する」
・help (to) do「…するのに役立つ，…するのを助ける」
・drive「…を推し進める，…を推進する」
・urban rebirth「都会の再生」
・fight「…と戦う」
・social exclusion「社会的排除，社会的疎外」
・estimate that S V ...「…だと推定［概算］する」
・benefit「利益を得る」
・investment「投資」

第8パラグラフ

・vital「きわめて重要な，不可欠な」
・make this point「この点を強調する」
・declare that S V ...「…だと断言する，…だと宣言する」
・inspire「…を鼓舞する，…を激励する」
・contribute「貢献する」
・provide B for A「AにBを供給する」
・responsibility「責任」
・continued「継続的な」

第16問の【語句】リスト

第1パラグラフ

・*remain C*「C のままである」
・*hopelessly*「絶望的に」
・*optimistic*「楽観的な」
・*accomplish*「…を成し遂げる」
・*frame*「枠組，枠」
・*matter*「重要である」
・*prediction*「予測，予想」
・*academic term*「(学校の) 学期」
・*be known to do*「…することが知られている」
・*bring home A*「A を家に持ち帰る」
・*ridiculous amount of work*「とんでもない量の仕事，ばかばかしいほど多くの仕事」
・*for weekends*「週末用に，週末に向けて」
・*essay*「エッセイ，小論文，作文」
・*reasonable*「妥当な，無理のない」
・*estimate*「見積もり，概算」
・*project*「計画，企画」
・*wildly*「とても，極めて」
・*It takes O_1 O_2 to do.*「O_1 が…するのに O_2 (時間) がかかる」

第2パラグラフ

・*advice*「忠告」
・*receive*「…を受け取る」
・*appropriate*「適切な，ふさわしい」
・*the amount of A*「A の総計［総数／総量］」
・*require*「…を要求する」
・*double*「…を2倍にする」
・*increase*「…を大きくする，…を上げる」
・*unit*「単位」
・*measurement*「測定，計量」
・*be poor at doing*「…するのが下手である」

第3パラグラフ

・*failure*「失敗」
・*be well known*「よく知られている」
・*fallacy*「誤り，間違い」
・*sort*「種類」
・*incredibly*「信じられないほど」
・*troublesome*「厄介な，面倒な」
・*expensive*「高価な，費用のかかる」
・*cool*「すてきな，すばらしい」
・*wrong*「間違って，誤って」
・*in the past*「過去に」
・*nonetheless*「それにもかかわらず」
・*article*「論文，記事」
・*turn out to be C*「C だとわかる，結局 C になる」
・*silly*「愚かな，ばかな」
・*future writing time*「今後の執筆にかかる時間」
・*be doomed to do*「…する運命にある」
・*repeat*「…を繰り返す」

第4パラグラフ

・*favorite*「お気に入りの，大好きな」
・*research*「研究，調査」
・*a set of A*「一連の A」
・*task*「課題，仕事」
・*pessimistic*「悲観的な」
・*assume that S V ...*「…だと想定する」
・*go wrong*「うまくいかない」
・*on average*「平均して」
・*average*「…を平均する，平均が…となる」
・*in reality*「実際は，実は」
・*guess (that) S V ...*「…だと推測する」
・*as well*「同様に」

第５パラグラフ

・*replicate*「…を再現する，…をやり直す」
・*estimate*「…を見積もる」
・*assignment*「宿題」
・*fix a bike*「自転車を修理する」
・*choose*「…を選ぶ」
・*call back*「再び戻る」
・*end up doing*「結局…することになる」

第６パラグラフ

・*submit*「…を提出する」
・*regarding A*「Aに関して（の）」
・*tax*「税金」
・*anticipate doing*「…することを予想する」
・*refund*「払い戻し（金）」
・*those expecting refunds*「払い戻しが期待できる人々」
・*not (...) any sooner*「少しも早く（…）ない」
・*sit on the table*「テーブルの上においてある」

第７パラグラフ

・*depend on A*「Aによって決まる，Aにかかっている」
・*information*「情報」
・*judgement*「判断」
・*typically*「一般的に，概して」
・*focus on A*「Aに焦点を当てる，Aに集中する」
・*various*「さまざまな」
・*failure to do*「（意志に反して）…しないこと」
・*meet a deadline*「締め切りに間に合う」
・*frequently*「頻繁に，しばしば」
・*on time*「時間通りに」

第８パラグラフ

・*dismiss*「…を退ける，…を捨てる」
・*previous*「以前の」
・*meet a goal*「目標をかなえる」
・*last time*「前回」
・*college student*「大学生」
・*come to mind*「心［頭］に浮かぶ」
・*manuscript*「原稿」
・*disrupt*「…を中断させる，…の継続を断つ」
・*demand*「要求（されること），用件，用事」
・*one-time*「１回限りの」
・*be bound to do*「必ず…する」
・*occur*「生じる，起こる」
・*realize*「…をはっきり理解する，…を悟る」
・*see A as B*「AをBだと見なす」
・*unrelated to A*「Aに無関係な」
・*current*「今の，現在の」
・*to some extent*「ある程度」
・*be unlikely to do*「…する可能性は低い」

第９パラグラフ

・*opportunity to do*「…する機会」
・*apologize to A*「Aに謝る」
・*co-author*「共著者」
・*completely*「すっかり，十分に」